THEY FOUGHT
FOR THE SKY

**Albert Ball · 'Billy' Bishop · Oswald Boelcke
René Fonck · Hermann Goering · Georges Guynemer
L. G. Hawker · Max Immelmann · 'Taffy' Jones
Gervais Lufbery · Frank Luke · James McCudden
'Mick' Mannock · Charles Nungesser
Manfred von Richthofen · Eddie Rickenbacker
William Thaw · Ernst Udet · Werner Voss**

'There won't be any after the war for a fighter pilot.'

During the fiercer periods of World War I the average
life of a pilot was three weeks.

A race apart, these gallant young men of many nations
fought a very personal war with a chivalry long dead.
Here is the breathtaking story of the age of flying aces,
of the famous aircraft and the men who flew them –
what thoughts they had, their likes and dislikes, and
how they spent their all too brief spare time.

Never, in any other war, did so many individuals
become household names.

'Remarkably readable'   *Daily Telegraph*

The late Quentin Reynolds was a well-known journalist, film and radio commentator. Born in New York in 1902, he was educated at St Lawrence University where he took the degree of Doctor of Law. He entered journalism in 1926 on the New York *World Telegram* and was subsequently foreign correspondent of the International News Service and Assistant Editor of *Colliers Weekly*.

During the Blitz he was living and working in London and he made many broadcasts to the United States, mainly with the object of illustrating to the Americans the fighting spirit of the British people and raising enthusiasm for the British cause. He supplied the commentary for the famous documentary on the Blitz, *London Can Take It*.

THEY FOUGHT
FOR THE SKY

*The Story of the First War
in the Air*

QUENTIN REYNOLDS

UNABRIDGED

PAN BOOKS LTD
LONDON AND SYDNEY

First published 1958 by Cassell & Co. Ltd.
This edition published 1960 by Pan Books Ltd.,
Cavaye Place, London SW10 9PG

ISBN 0 330 24011 0

2nd Printing 1974

To
Albert Ball, V.C.

PRINTED AND BOUND IN ENGLAND BY
HAZELL WATSON AND VINEY LTD
AYLESBURY, BUCKS

CONTENTS

The author and publishers acknowledge with gratitude their debt to Mr Gerald Pollinger for valuable information and to the undermentioned works, which have been of the greatest assistance in the preparation of this book.

Aircraft of the 1914–1918 War, by O. G. Thetford and E. J. Riding; Harleyford Publications, Marlow, Bucks.

King of the Air Fighters, by Wing-Commander Ira Jones; Nicholson & Watson, London.

Tiger Squadron, by Wing-Commander Ira Jones; W. H. Allen, London.

ILLUSTRATIONS
IN PHOTOGRAVURE

(between pages 128 and 129)

*The aerial photograph reproduced on the back cover
was supplied by the Imperial War Museum.*

CONFESSIONS OF
A THIEF

IN 1697, Father Francesco Lana of Rome, wrote a scientific treatise on the possibility of building an 'aerial ship'. He was positive that such a craft could be built, and he was the first man in history to foresee its potential as a weapon of war. 'There is one great difficulty that cannot be solved,' the Jesuit wrote sadly. 'God will never allow man to construct such a machine, since it would create many disturbances in the civil and political governments of mankind. Where is the man who can fail to see that no city would be proof against surprise, when the ship could at any time be steered over its squares, or even over the courtyards of dwelling-houses, and brought to earth for the landing of its crew? ... Iron weights could be hurled to wreck ships at sea, or they could be set on fire by fireballs, and bombs; nor ships alone, but houses, fortresses, and cities could be thus destroyed, with the certainty that the airship could come to no harm as the missiles could be hurled from a vast height.'

And although the Almighty did allow two bicycle manufacturers of Dayton, Ohio, to build and fly a machine, everything else that the seventeenth-century cleric prophesied came to pass in World War I. In 1913, flying machines were little more than toys and the men who built them and who flew them were regarded, at best, as amiable eccentrics. For centuries wars had been fought on land and on sea, and no military man of any stature saw the possibility that the sky, too, would become a battlefield. By 1918, however, the lightly regarded aeroplane had become a potent war machine, and the men who flew were international heroes.

This is the story of those gallant young men of a luckless generation, most of whom flew to glorious martyrdom; during the fiercer periods of the war the average life of a pilot at the front was three weeks. They fought a very personal war, but few of them were animated by hatred. There were exceptions.

9

Mick Mannock of the Royal Flying Corps, perhaps the greatest ace who ever lived (he brought down seventy-three Germans before he was killed), was an implacable fighter. Warm, unselfish, free from any greedy obsession with glory, Mannock loved England intensely and he believed that Germany was trying to enslave her; he hated Germany in the way the militant saints hated sin, and when he killed, he felt that he was helping to exterminate evil. Ira Jones, who flew with him, wrote a rather wonderful book about Mannock. "When he died every man in the squadron wept," Jones said, which isn't a bad epitaph for a man.

There were two other great fliers who seemed sustained by hatred of their enemies. René Dorme, one of France's leading aces, hated the Germans who had destroyed his village and imprisoned his aged parents; he fought with fanatical but calculated fury, never counting the odds, and he lasted two years —a long life in the clouds. Manfred von Richthofen, greatest of German fighters, was a killer by nature. His arrogant Prussian nature seemed only satisfied by killing; he gloried in blood, and each night he revealed this side of his nature to his diary, which survived him. He shot down eighty Allied aircraft and exulted every time he slew.

But these were exceptions. Oswald Boelcke, one of the finest German pilots, was a gentle, kind man who visited the graves of his victims and prayed for them; Werner Voss was a gay spirit who fought the greatest air battle ever seen; alone he engaged seven of England's finest pilots (including the great James McCudden), and it took them half an hour to finish him off. Albert Ball, intensely religious, was a fierce fighter, but he hated killing and when he sent a German down in flames, he would try to forget by playing his violin. Eddie Rickenbacker was incapable of hatred; he felt that he was fighting machines, not men. Like René Fonck, he fought a cerebral, not an emotional war.

Elliott Springs, one of the best American pilots, looked upon the war as a joke; plagued by stomach trouble, he always carried a bottle of liquid magnesia and a bottle of gin in his aircraft—if one didn't work the other did. Raoul Lufbery was a boulevardier who knew Paris better than most Frenchmen, but he knew with calm certainty that he owed the Almighty one life and that he would have to pay this debt before the war was over—he eventually paid it the hard way, in flames. The German ace, Franz Zeumer, who taught Richthofen to fly, was in constant agony from the consumption which tortured his lungs—he prayed for death, but it didn't come until he had fought three long years. Guynemer, whom the French called the Ace of Aces, was frail, sickly, possessed of almost feminine beauty, and his only confidante was his sister Yvonne. After killing fifty-three Germans he disappeared one day, and a generation of French school-children believed that he 'flew so high he just couldn't come down'. His body was never found, and a French cardinal, speaking at a memorial service, said, "He belonged to the skies and the skies have taken him." There was the Arizona cowboy, Frank Luke, who spent every Saturday night shooting craps and who religiously deposited his winnings on the collection plate in a small church every Sunday morning, hoping—in vain, it turned out—that this would bring him luck.

They were a race apart—these knights of the air. They fought without parachutes, without safety devices of any kind, and they flew in frail tinder boxes that a wayward spark might ignite. They were individualists. So, incidentally, were the air-craft they flew. Each had different characteristics; you had to woo them gently before you could take liberties with them; if you were clumsy or harsh, they would kill you. I've described these little machines and the way they developed from the 'bird cages' they were called in 1914, to the fine trim, fast machines of 1918 each had a personality of its own. The first story I ever wrote I called *What About Paul Revere's Horse?* I was ten at the time. I felt that anyone could have ridden the twenty miles as quickly as Revere made the Charlestown-to-Lexington trip in April, 1775. The horse deserved most of the credit, but history doesn't even record the name of the noble animal. To most people the aircraft of World War I are almost as anonymous as Paul Revere's horse. I have tried to bring these machines alive, as I have tried to bring the young-sters who flew them alive. Both, I think, are well worth knowing.

This book, I suppose, has been some twenty-five years in the making. In the 1930s I worked in Berlin as a correspondent and knew Ernst Udet, one of the great natural fliers of all time. A gay and convivial soul, he had shot down sixty-two British, French and American aircraft during World War I without rancour, and he would often talk of those days and about his admiration for Mannock and Fonck and Albert Ball and of Rickenbacker, whom he called 'Reek' and of whom he said fondly: *"Reek war ein grosser Kämpfer welcher mit einem Schlag töten konnte."* Rick was indeed a great fighter who could kill you with one punch; he could thread the eye of a needle with his machine gun.

Shortly after that I met and became friendly with the one who was called 'The Man Without Fear'—Billy Bishop, the Canadian who once shot down twenty-five Germans in twelve days. I spent many happy days with Bishop in Montreal, and sometimes would get him to talk about his incredible career which brought him the Victoria Cross and seventy-two aerial victories.

During World War II, I spent a great deal of time at Biggin Hill in England with No74 Squadron, and became a friend of Adolph 'Sailor' Malan, acknowledged by all airmen to be the best air fighter that war produced. It was the Sailor who told me that Wing-Commander Douglas Bader, the great leg-less fighter pilot, had advised his men to read the diaries of World War I pilots; the fighting techniques they developed were still valid, and a man would live longer if he studied them. Malan and Bader survived because they used the diaries of Mannock, of McCudden, of Richthofen and Rickenbacker as textbooks. This led me to Foyle's, the London bookshop, and I found some of those diaries still in print. Years after the war ended I did a book about Jimmy Doolittle, and I learned a great deal about the planes and the men of World War I from him. Then one day I found myself in O'Malley's book store on Fourth Avenue in New York. O'Malley's proud boast is that he can get you any book that has ever been printed, and his boast has never been successfully challenged. He specializes in out-of-print books, and while looking for a book on police procedure as exemplified by Scotland Yard, I came across a whole shelf of books headed *World War I Flying*. I started to thumb through the books and was lost. I was lost for two years. I found that there had never been a book written which embraced the activites of all air forces during the first World War. And I knew I had to write this book, and if it doesn't sell a single copy I already feel well rewarded—for two years I have lived vicariously with the valiant few who fought for the sky from 1914 to 1918, and I have learned to know them and to love them and to admire them.

It is of course impossible to paint on so small a canvas as one book the complete picture of the air forces of the warring nations; this is at best a sketch, not a definitive mural. My search to learn more about the boys (very few were grown men) who fought during those dreadful but exciting years led me to bookshops in Berlin, Paris and London. It led me to such reservoirs of information as the Institute of Aeronautical Sciences on Fifth Avenue in New York, where Elizabeth Brown, the librarian, became an enthusiastic and helpful co-worker. It led me to the Mercantile Library and to the New York Society Library and to the Bedford Village Library, and all yielded rare, or for the most part long-forgotten diaries or books written by the air fighters or about the air fighting of more than forty years ago. It led me to the yellowed back issues of *The Aeroplane*, which in 1914 was edited by Charles G. Grey, one of the few men who believed that the flying machine could be a vital weapon of war, and who was vilified and criticized by Members of Parliament and Government figures who thought he was a crackbrained visionary. Actually he was a great man, and had his advice been followed, Britain might have been prepared for a war that found her hopelessly unready. My search led me to Albert Lewis and Alexis Dawydoff, who for so many years have run the Street & Smith magazines about flying, and Russian-born Dawydoff, an early flier, opened up the immense store of his memories to me. I found two men who had made a hobby of World War I flying, and I shamelessly begged their knowledge. Robert Loomis, brilliant young editor for Rinehart Publishers, was one. The other was Gerald Pollinger, of London, who writes of flying with authority and who somehow managed to beg, borrow (or perhaps steal) scores of photographs of, and dozens of books written by or about, World War I pilots. It was through these books and the letters from the pilots to their families and friends that I learned to know the men who lived so fiercely and who died so gloriously. My search led me to the Lafayette Corps history written by, of all people, James Norman Hall and Charles Nordhoff. By now it had become an obsession with me; this was not to be just another book by a man whose profession it is to write books. In Berlin I found a huge tome, *Die Deutschen Luftstreitkrafte im Weltkriege* and the author-itative history of the German Air Force by its leader, General von Hoeppner, translated them laboriously and stole from them copiously. My search led me to Paris, where I found lives of Fonck and Guynemer and René Dorme, and a book about gay, laughing, indestructible Charles Nungesser, and I borrowed (to use the polite term) much from these.

Once I went to law school, but about all I retain from those three years is a law degree and a line that Judge Brandeis wrote about plagiarism. 'If a man steals from one book it is plagiarism,' he wrote. 'If he steals from hundreds of books it is research.' The bibliography listed at the end of this ex-periment (every book is an experiment) lists nearly seventy books, but does not list the hundreds of magazine and news-paper articles I lived with for so long. If this be stealing, I hope my critics will at least pay me the compliment of accusing me of grand larceny, not petty theft.

Bob Loomis and Gerald Pollinger told me that no one could write about World War I flying without having absorbed the seven-volume *The War in the Air*, begun by Walter Raleigh (a direct descendant of the original) and finished after Raleigh's death by H. A. Jones. This is an official history of the Royal Flying Corps (which became the Royal Air Force only eight months before hostilities came to an end), and it is based on official British documents to which the authors were given access. The 1,500,000 words in these seven volumes became my bible—I learned about World War I aircraft from those words. I learned, too, from surviving French, British and American fighter pilots.

The critical reader may be puzzled by the conversations

between pilots I recorded in this book. Not one of these is fictitious. They came out of diaries or out of letters written by the men involved. This is in no way a definitive history of air fighting during the first war; it is in the main a story of the aircraft and the men who flew them. But I was more interested in what the young pilots ate and drank, what songs they sang and what thoughts they had, and what they did in their spare time, than I was in the horsepower of the engines which powered the aircraft they flew. I make no pretence to being a serious student of war.

Now that the book is finished I am disturbed by the thought that I didn't really write it—I merely typed it out. I picked the brains of hundreds of men, dead and living, and this is the result. A preface to a book often strikes me as an apology. This definitely is not an apology: it is an explanation and a confession. The material in this book was for the most part written by those who figure in it, and I, the predatory professional writer, have stolen their thoughts, their emotions and in some cases their very words. I make no apology—I think they bear repeating.

QUENTIN REYNOLDS

'There won't be any after
the war for a fighter pilot'
—RAOUL LUFBERY

Chapter One

A WEAPON IS BORN

ONE BRIGHT afternoon in February, 1915, four German two-seater observation aircraft were flying lazily over the front lines at about 10,000 feet. Far below, a million men were trying desperately to kill one another, but from this height bursting shells were unheard and seen only as tiny puffs of white cotton. The muddy trenches were only dark lines irregularly crawling across the land; the war was clean and not a bit dangerous here at ten thousand feet. Occasionally some crazy Englishman would empty a rifle or a revolver at you as you flew by him, and you might return to your aerodrome with three or four bulletholes in the cloth fabric of your fuselage, but that was merely something to joke about in the mess hall that night. A few British two-seater aircraft carried machine guns for the use of the observer. He could shoot to either side and he could shoot to the rear, but the guns were heavy and few of the machines which carried them could climb to ten thousand feet. And the guns, in addition to being inaccurate, were constantly jamming, so most British pilots had abandoned them in disgust. The aeroplane was a flying machine, not a fighting machine, and its job was observation—nothing else.

The observers in the four German aircraft had seen all they wanted to see, and the leader was about to give the signal to return when a tiny speck appeared in the distance. It grew, and now the Germans could see that it was a little single-seater French aircraft. It headed directly for them but they ignored it. Its propeller was spinning like a solid disc; it didn't manœuvre to get above or below the German machines. They watched its approach curiously but without any apprehension, and then suddenly—impossibly—a small burst of golden flame blossomed from the end of a machine-gun mounted directly behind the propeller, and a stream of lead began to spurt from it. This burst of fire killed one German pilot, and his machine, out of control, began to spin crazily towards the ground. Then the French aircraft swerved a bit and again the hail of lead came to hemstitch the fuselage of a second German machine. Bullets cut through the fuel line and petrol spattered over the hot engine, ignited, and the machine roared down in flames.

The remaining two German machines turned quickly and headed for home, the pilots white and shaken, for today they had seen something no airman had ever seen before: they had seen a gun which apparently shot its bullets directly through the whirling blades of the propeller. Back at the field their reports were received with scepticism and ridicule. The two-bladed propeller revolved 1200 times a minute, which meant that it passed a given point 2400 times every sixty seconds. The conventional machine gun shot 600 bullets a minute—if this stream of bullets was aimed at the propeller, perhaps the first twenty by some miracle might miss the blades, but certainly the next few would smash the prop to splinters, and the aircraft and its pilot would very likely be destroyed. But it happened again the next day and the following day. The news spread all over the German air front, and the pilots were now in a state of panic. They had to revise quickly all of the established theories and practices of aerial observation. For the first time they were on the defensive. If a French fighter flew directly towards them, they now fled.

During the weeks that followed it seemed probable that the revolutionary tactic was being launched by just one French aircraft. The pilot's method of firing from the nose of his machine, through the whirring blades of his propeller, was not a technique that as yet had been adopted by the whole Allied air force; it seemed to be the brain-child of one French flier, for most reports mentioned the same distinctive markings on the fighter that was doing so much damage. But suppose the entire French and British air forces adopted this fantastic technique? It would be only a matter of days before the whole German Air Force was cleared from the skies, and if this happened, Allied troops and artillery could move to new positions unseen and unreported by German air reconnaissance and thus gain an overwhelming tactical ground advantage.

Then one day a French single-seater aircraft developed engine trouble over the front and glided to safety behind the German lines. It was routine then for all pilots landing in enemy territory to burn their machines immediately, but before the French pilot could set fire to his aircraft he was grabbed by alert German infantrymen. The aircraft and pilot were immediately dispatched to the nearest German air base, the pilot to be wined and dined by the Air Force mess, according to the custom of the day, and the aircraft to be examined thoroughly by experts. Some of the German pilots recognized the machine; it was the one they had been fleeing from for weeks. It had a free-firing automatic rifle mounted directly on the cockpit, pointing dead ahead towards the propeller. Closer examination showed the way it operated. The near side of each propeller blade had been fitted with a triangular steel wedge which would deflect most of the bullets that hit the blade. It was a dangerous, almost suicidal device, for a bullet striking the blade cleanly would, of course, smash it, and even if it deflected the bullet, it might well ricochet back to smash either a vital part of the engine or a vital human part of the pilot. Nevertheless, crude and dangerous as it was, it had been so successful that the pilot had shot down six German aircraft in three weeks, and spread near-panic through the German Air Force.

When the pilot ruefully gave his name, the commanding officer ordered more champagne, and the toasts to the intrepid French airman lasted far into the night. This was no ordinary pilot; this was Roland Garros, known even before the war as France's greatest stunting airman. Pilots of both sides in 1915 looked upon their air war much as the knights of King Arthur's court looked upon jousting. There were, of course, occasional and regrettable casualties, but there was nothing (except in isolated cases) personal about the killing. Fighting in the air was a gentleman's game; it could almost be compared with the tennis matches at Wimbledon or the international polo matches on Long Island. When it was over, victor and vanquished filled their glasses, toasted each other in extravagant superlatives, and then the victor and his squadron would escort the vanquished to a very superior prison camp, where he could live the life of a retired and respected hero until the war was over. Roland Garros, now that the secret had been discovered and now that the war (for him) was over, relaxed, and over the champagne discussed aerial tactics with these affable Germans, who until an hour ago had been his enemies. The Germans respected a brave man, and this Garros was indeed a brave man; every time he pulled the trigger of his gun he was gambling that the bullets from it would not destroy him and his machine. It was the 1915 version of Russian roulette.

Were there other aircraft using the device? Garros smiled and said reproachfully, "You know you shouldn't ask such questions of a prisoner of war." The German colonel in charge angrily reproached the pilot who had shown such discourtesy to a guest and apologized to Garros.

But it appeared obvious to the German colonel that it was merely a matter of time before the whole Allied air force would adopt the device, a sobering thought. He immediately phoned Berlin to break the news to higher officers of the General Staff. They gave quick, terse orders.

Garros had made his unfortunate landing at eight o'clock on a Tuesday morning. At five that afternoon the clogged fuel line that had forced him down had been cleaned and the little Morane was flown to Berlin to be inspected by members of the General Staff and by a lean, rather short-tempered young Dutchman who had been urgently summoned from his aircraft factory at Schwerin, some 220 miles north of Berlin. They examined the revolutionary device thoroughly, and Colonel von Hoeppner of the Signal Corps turned to an aide and told him curtly to produce a Parabellum machine gun immediately. This was the standard infantry air-cooled gun which shot a continuous band of one hundred bullets. While the aide ran to a nearby hanger to get the gun, Hoeppner gave the Dutchman some orders.

"Within a few days or within a week," he said, "the French and British may have a hundred aircraft in the air using this gun. Hurry back to Schwerin, copy this method of shooting through a propeller and equip as many fighters as you have with it. I want this within forty-eight hours."

The aide was now on hand with the machine gun. He handed it to the Dutchman, who held the unfamiliar object in his hand almost helplessly. He was twenty-five now, and although he was recognized as one of the greatest of all aircraft designers, he had never fired a machine gun in his life.

Heavy weather descended over the airport as darkness came, and the little Dutchman was hurried to the Friedrichstrasse Bahnhoff to catch a train to Schwerin. With him was the machine gun and the propeller from Garros' aircraft. He was given a compartment to himself, and as the train hurtled through the night, following the River Elbe, he considered the assignment—a strange one to be given a noncombatant who didn't much care who won the war, but a provocative and flattering challenge to a practical engineer.

He took the gun apart to familiarize himself with its most intimate secrets. He opened his briefcase, took out a pad and pencil and began to make some calculations.

An unsummoned and incongruous childhood memory welled out of the deep recesses of his subconscious mind. Walking home from school, he and his schoolmates always passed the huge, creaking windmills that dotted the countryside outside his native Haarlem. Invariably they would stop, pick up stones from the road and throw them at the turning wooden blades. Strangely enough, it wasn't easy to hit the broad blades even though they moved slowly. As often as not the stones went right between the blades without touching them. The train roared by Rossov, passed Ludwigslust, stopped briefly at Hamburg and then went on towards Mecklenburg. When it reached Schwerin, the Dutchman thought that possibly, just possibly, he might have found the answer.

He had been born Anthony Herman Gerard Fokker, the son of a Dutch tea planter who had made a fortune in Java and had then returned with his family to spend a life of slippered ease in Haarlem, a small city on the north coast between Amsterdam and the dunes bordering the North Sea. When he was sixteen, he built his first aeroplane in the kitchen of his

Dutch home. When he was twenty, he constructed what he felt to be the fastest, most stable little monoplane in the world. Proudly he exhibited it to the military authorities of his own country, but Holland was buying aircraft from experienced British firms, not from young visionaries with no engineering education and with no experience. He tried unsuccessfully to peddle it in Russia, in France, and in England. Finally he made an exhibition tour in Germany, and when he became the first man in the country ever to loop the loop he was hailed as The Flying Dutchman, and Germany made a national hero out of the young pilot-designer. And in 1913 the German Signal Corps ordered him to manufacture a dozen aircraft to be used for scouting and observation.

His eyes were so concentrated upon his drawing-board in the German-built factory at Schwerin that they never saw the war clouds overhead. His ears were so attuned to the roar of the eighty-horsepower Argus engine which powered his little machine that they heard neither the rumble of destiny nor the gun caissons rolling towards the French border. If the major powers were getting themselves involved in a war, he felt that as a neutral Dutchman it was no affair of his. But the day that war broke out, high military officials rushed to Schwerin to tell Fokker to build as many aeroplanes as he could. To begin with, the Signal Corps wanted twenty-four single-seater sporting aircraft which could be used for observation purposes.

"You must hurry with these," the men from Berlin said. "The war will be over in three months, and we want a chance to demonstrate how much better aircraft can do the job of observation than the balloons we use now."

The war wasn't over in three months, but within that short space of time the politically naïve but mechanically mature Dutchman had made a reputation as the finest aircraft designer in Germany. Pilots respected him not only because he gave them machines which during most of the war were infinitely superior to those flown by the enemy, but because he, too, was a pilot and a better one than most of them. Tony Fokker met every challenge the German High Command threw at him. And then in 1915, within the short space of forty-eight hours, this Hollander, who resisted every attempt on the part of the Germans to make him a naturalized citizen of their country, almost changed the tide of war for them.

It was midnight when the train pulled into Schwerin. Reinold Platz, an imaginative welder, had made Fokker's first steel tube fuselage in 1912 and was now in charge of his experimental department. Heinrich Luebbe had been a barnstorming pilot with Tony Fokker, but he was always experimenting with machine-guns and now he was in charge of production at the Schwerin plant. Bernard de Waal, a boyhood friend, was his chief test pilot. They were waiting for him at the station, alerted by a message he had sent before boarding the train at Berlin.

As their car rushed them to the Fokker Flugzeugwerke, a combined factory and airfield outside the city, he told them of what had transpired. Not one of these men had ever gone to an engineering school, but each was a brilliant mechanic and to them this was a mechanical rather than an engineering problem. They made thoughtful suggestions; Fokker listened or shook his head sharply. When they reached the plant, they knew what they had to do.

First they anchored the gun and shot several hundred rounds to judge its rate of fire accurately. They attached the Garros propeller to an engine and checked its revolutions. Dawn crept over the field and into the hangar, but beyond giving curt orders to bring coffee, neither Fokker nor his assistants took notice of the time. Within two hours Fokker had completely rejected Garros' desperately brave but unpredictable method of avoiding the propeller blades: the vibration alone, caused by the deflection of the bullets, would in time shake the engine loose from its moorings.

Fokker immediately saw that the only practical method of firing without smashing the blades was to have the propeller itself fire the gun. He hurried to his drawing-board to work out this simple principle in practical terms. Within two hours he had the basic answer. It looked very well in the spidery white lines that crawled across the blue paper, but would it work? He hurriedly attached a small knob to the propeller which struck a cam when it revolved. The cam was attached by strong wire to the hammer of the machine-gun. He loaded the gun and slowly revolved the propeller by hand. The gun actually shot bullets between the blades. He had the basic problem solved, but now he had to establish some sort of liaison between pilot and propeller. The pilot after all had to control the shooting. He worked on it for another few hours, and then he felt ready to demonstrate it. Exactly forty-eight hours had passed since the challenge had been tossed to him; now that it was over he was too excited to seek any sleep. He phoned Berlin and asked that representatives of the General Staff be on hand the next morning.

It was only long after the war that Fokker learned that the solution to the problem of firing through a propeller had in theory been solved in 1910 by August Euler, but although Euler had patented his device, he never quite developed it to the point where it was practical. Besides, no one then was interested in aerial warfare; aircraft, if they were to be of any military use at all, would be restricted to scouting and observation. Just before the war began, Georges Constantinesco of Roumania had the problem almost solved, but again he hadn't perfected a way to use it in a practical sense. Sopwith in England and Browning in the United States had been working on an electrical synchronizing system, but none of these engineers was able to do what the young Dutch mechanic accomplished in a mere forty-eight hours. Fokker was never anything but an inspired mechanic, but his inspiration amounted to sheer genius.

That night he installed the device in one of his Fokker E-Is. This was the machine used so extensively during the early period of the war. Its eighty-horsepower Oberursel rotary engine gave it a maximum speed of eighty miles an hour at 6000 feet. When he was satisfied that the gun and propeller were working perfectly, he locked the little monoplane in a hangar and took a nap.

A dozen high-ranking Air Force and General Staff officers were on hand the next day. They looked with disappointment at the propeller blades: there were no steel wedges protecting the thin wooden props as there had been on Garros' machine.

Fokker first demonstrated the machine gun from the

ground, starting the engine and firing through the propeller toward the rifle butts at the end of the field. He fired three burst of ten shots each before stopping the engine. The officials looked interested but puzzled; certainly none of them realized that what they were watching meant that a completely revolutionary era of aerial warfare was about to dawn. They examined the blades and found them undamaged. One of them, apparently suspecting a trick by the young wizard, suggested that although the Fokker scheme seemed all right if you shot a burst of ten bullets, how would it work if the pilot fired the whole band of a hundred bullets? Fokker shrugged his shoulders and proceeded to fire bursts of one hundred, and now the observers were satisfied that his scheme worked—while the plane was on the ground. But would it work in the air?

Impatient at the conservative and sceptical attitude of the group and a little annoyed that not one of the observers had congratulated him on performing an engineering miracle in so little time, Fokker decided to give them a bit of a scare. He directed his workmen to place some old wings on the ground near the end of the field and told the observers to watch closely to see if he could really hit the target from the air. As he took off, he saw that they had gathered close to the wings. He went up to 1000 feet, nosed over, pointed the aircraft at the ground target and began to fire. He knew that the ground beneath the wings was hard rock. The bullets streamed through the frail cloth texture of the wings and, hitting the rock beneath, ricocheted in every direction. The dignified observers scattered wildly, some running for the safety of the nearby hangar. Fokker landed, and the observers, recovering from their panic, walked timidly toward the wings, which were completely riddled. They examined the propeller blades, which had not even been nicked. Then they consulted among themselves and gave their verdict.

"There is only one sure way to test this gun," their spokesman told Fokker. "Take it to the front, teach a pilot how to use it and then let him go up and shoot down an enemy aircraft. This will prove that the gun works in combat."

Fokker's protests fell on deaf ears, and within twenty-four

hours he found himself at the front, at the headquarters of General von Heeringen, near Laon, not far from Verdun. The general, who had been warned of the arrival of Fokker, said that the Crown Prince had been informed of Fokker's experiment and he would like to see it in action. The next day the Crown Prince, clad in the smart white blouse, breeches and highly polished boots of the Hussars, arrived to be introduced to Fokker. He towered over the small Dutchman, who as usual was dressed in the nondescript clothes of the civilian pilot— unpressed, chequered black and white breeches, wrap puttees, worn tweed coat with a pair of goggles hanging from a pocket, and a tight-fitting woollen flying helmet.

"*Kaiserliche Hoheit,*" General von Heeringen said stiffly. "This is Herr Fokker, inventor of our fighting aeroplane."

The Crown Prince blinked in amazement at the strangely dressed, beardless youth in front of him. "Surely it was your father who invented the fighting aeroplane, not you?"

"My father is growing tulips in Holland," Fokker said dryly.

He showed the amiable son of the Kaiser his simple mechanism and then demonstrated it for him. When he landed, the Crown Prince congratulated him but said ruefully that he still couldn't understand how the bullets could stream through the whirling blades without ever hitting the propeller.

"Try to explain in simple layman's language," he asked.

"First of all," Fokker said, groping for an easily understood analogy, "The gun can fire through the space between the revolving blades safely only because the speed of the bullets is so much greater than the speed of the blades. As children in Holland we used to throw stones between the big blades of the windmills. They revolved quite slowly—about ten times a minute. We threw our stones swiftly and it was easy to throw them between the blades."

A few days later incredible orders came from Berlin to the effect that Fokker should take up his machine and himself prove the capabilities of the synchronized gun by shooting down a French or British aircraft. In vain Fokker protested that he was a 'neutral'. His argument fell upon deaf ears. A German uniform was put on him and an identification card stuck in his grey field-tunic pocket, stating that he was Lieutenant Anthony Fokker of the German Air Force. Now, if forced to land behind Allied lines, he would not be shot as a spy but treated as a prisoner of war.

Before he could protest further he was in the air, a reluctant fighter looking for enemy prey. At about 6000 feet he saw a Farman two-seater observation aircraft ambling out of a cloud. Now he could prove the worth of his gun. He nosed over and dived at the enemy. Fokker wrote afterwards:

This aircraft had no reason to fear me. I was going straight for it, my nose aimed at it, and they couldn't possibly have any reason to fear bullets fired through my propeller.

While approaching, I thought of what a deadly accurate stream of lead I could send into the aircraft. It would be just like shooting a sitting rabbit because the pilot couldn't shoot back through his propeller at me.

As the distance between us narrowed the aeroplane grew larger in my sights. My imagination could visualize my shots puncturing the petrol tanks in front of the engine. The tank would catch fire. Even if my bullets failed to kill the pilot and observer, the machine would fall down in flames. I had my finger on the trigger. . . . I had no personal animosity towards the French. I was flying merely to prove that a certain mechanism I had invented would work. By this time I was near enough to open fire, and the French pilots were watching me curiously. . . . In another instant, it would be all over for them.

Suddenly, I decided that the whole job could go to hell. It was too much like 'cold meat' to suit me. I had no stomach for the whole business, nor any wish to kill Frenchmen for Germans. Let them do their own killing.

Returning quickly to the Douai flying field, I informed the commander of the field that I would do no more flying over the Front. After a brief argument, it was agreed that a regular German pilot would take up the machine. Lieutenant Oswald Boelcke, later to be the first German ace, was assigned the job. The next morning I showed him how to manipulate the machine gun while flying the aircraft, watched him take off for the Front, and left for Berlin.

Fokker arrived in Berlin to receive a message that Boelcke had brought down an Allied machine using the synchronized gun. A day later Lieutenant Max Immelmann, who was also on his way to becoming one of the early aces of the German Air Force, duplicated the feat, and now every flight leader at the front was calling for the synchronized gun. Fokker hurried to Schwerin to turn them out as quickly as possible. During the following weeks the French and British fliers were helpless. Their losses were enormous, and there was nothing they could do about it. They tried to adopt Garros' scheme, but soon discovered what Fokker had suspected on his first inspection of the steel-edged propellers—when the bullets were deflected a terrific vibration invariably followed, often making the machine unmanageable. And constant pounding by the bullets weakened and then smashed propeller blades, sending the aircraft plummeting down to destruction.

For a time the air was almost cleared of Allied aircraft. Now the German infantry could move huge masses of troops without fear of detection by Allied observers, and of course the German fliers could spot any significant movement of Allied troops and artillery. A surge of confidence swept not only over the German Air Force but over the ground troops and public as well. If the skies could—as it appeared—belong to Germany and Germany alone, it might mean the decisive turning-point in the war. When General Staff officers congratulated Fokker and enthusiastically (if prematurely) gave him credit for winning the war, he merely shrugged his shoulders. He wasn't interested in winning the war for the Germans; he was only interested in turning out faster, safer, more manœuvrable and more durable aircraft. His dreams were never troubled by the fact that Allied airmen were dying because of the superiority of his planes and his synchronized gun.

Fokker's gun was considered to be so important that pilots using it were forbidden to fly over Allied territory lest the secret fall into enemy hands. But four months after Boelcke had used the gun with such telling effect, a German pilot, lost in a fog, landed behind the French lines. Before he could set fire to his machine he was captured and the aircraft hurriedly flown to Paris, where experts analysed and quickly mastered the secret of the havoc-wreaking gun. British and French engineers combined the Fokker device with a gun-gear invented by Constantinesco. This latter did no rely entirely upon mechanical gear but on hydraulic oil-pressure, operating on the principle of the motor-car brake. A few weeks of feverish work and it was ready, and the war in the air, which Tony Fokker, a neutral, had almost won for the Germans, now once more resolved itself into a bitter, fairly even struggle.

But all this happened in 1915.

Chapter Two

MACHINES TO FRIGHTEN HORSES

DURING THE night of August 4th, 1914, the Germany Army crossed the frontier into Belgium and the 980th war to plague mankind since the dawn of civilization had begun. Within six hours, 1,500,000 Germans were marching in accordance with a plan drafted in 1905 by General Alfred von Schlieffen. Meanwhile the French, following a plan devised in 1913 by General Joseph Joffre, had hurled their five armies towards Metz. The war came to the continent in the roar of artillery, the staccato bark of machine guns, the shrill whine of rifle bullets and the interminable sound of marching feet.

The war announced itself to the people of Dover on the English Channel in a more bizarre but equally memorable way. Four days after hostilities started a huge covered van bearing on its red sides the one word BOVRIL roared through the streets of the old town and headed for the plain at the edge of the white cliffs above the ancient castle. The van was not laden with that excellent beef extract which almost rivalled tea as a defence against the chill of late autumn and winter afternoons. Hurriedly requisitioned by the fledgling known as the Royal Flying Corps, it was filled with such miscellaneous objects as canned bully beef, water bottles, tools of all kinds, chocolate bars and red flags. While the puzzled citizens of Dover looked on, the red flags were planted along the edges of the ditches which bordered the field. Unfortunately, they ran out of flags before all the ditches had been marked, but the following day three additional vans arrived. Three less warlike vehicles could hardly be imagined. One bore on its sides the proud label:

LAZENBY'S SAUCE
(The World's Appetizer)

The second carried the familiar sign: 'Peek Frean's Biscuits', while the third told the world that it was in the proud business of conveying 'Stephens' Blue-black Ink'. In addition to red flags, they brought to the improvised aerodrome such articles as field-glasses, small stoves, goggles, jars of jam, spare aircraft struts, soup cubes, carburettors, sparking plugs and revolvers. These four vans, plucked from the streets of London, were the nucleus of the transport and supply service intended to care for the men and aircraft which were heading for Dover, from where they would take off for France. Then the aeroplanes began to arrive, and the fascinated citizens of Dover, who hadn't seen so much excitement since the year 1217, when Hubert de Burgh destroyed the French fleet under Eustace the Monk in the same harbour, lined the cliffs to watch the strange-looking creatures of the air make their landings on the morning of August 13th. Some came to grief in the ditches, for a strong wind had come up during the night to blow many of the warning red flags away. Others landed nicely and then, for no discernible reason, turned lazily on their sides or buried their noses in the muddy ground with their tails high in the air, looking like plucked birds seeking worms in the rabbit holes.

By now mechanics had arrived and with piano wire, spare struts of silver spruce, cloth fabric and a gluepot they managed to patch up the damaged machines. Finally there were thirty-seven of them ready to go to war. They comprised Nos 2, 3, 4 and 5 Squadrons, and it had taken a miracle of organization by Brigadier-General Sir David Henderson, commanding Britain's Royal Flying Corps, to concentrate so many service-able machines in one spot. This was England's striking air armada in August, 1914; although there were an additional

116 aircraft scattered among training schools and in repair shops, only half of them were fit for duty.

The people of Dover looked with great interest at the flimsy-looking aircraft. Most of them had seen at least one aeroplane before; all but the youngest remembered that never-to-be-forgotten July 25th, 1909, when Louis Blériot had made the first hazardous flight across the Channel to land his little monoplane in a meadow not far from the spot where the thirty-seven aircraft now rested. A great many of these looked much like the machine that had rested in the meadow, guarded by a single Dover policeman, just five years before, for most of the British aircraft were direct descendants of that original Blériot model. In 1912, Geoffrey de Havilland, one of the country's first pilots and certainly its foremost aircraft designer, had produced a two-seater called the BE which, although a biplane, had many features of the original Blériot. It had been built at the Royal Aircraft Factory which had been established for the sole purpose of experimentation, and aircraft produced by this aerial laboratory were frankly labelled as such. The BE designation stood for Blériot Experimental (although most newspapers referred to it as British Experimental). De Havilland had improved on his original model and now it was the BE2, Britain's finest aircraft. The designer himself had set a speed record of seventy miles an hour in it, and he had climbed to the incredible height of 10,560 feet. The BE26 was a frail-looking machine which appeared top-heavy, and it is true that a brisk gust of wind would topple it, but its seventy-horsepower Renault engine and the soundness of its design gave it both speed and what pilots call 'inherent stability'.

In addition to the BE2s, the people of Dover had a chance to view a few single-seater Avros, several Henri Farmans and some BE8s. The Avro 504 had been designed by Alliot Verdon Roe, one of the first men actually to fly a plane in England. Called 'A.V.' by his associates, it seemed logical to call his brain-child the Avro. The Henri Farmans bought from the French the year before were slow biplanes which had only one redeeming feature: they could stay aloft several hours. This aircraft aroused much curiosity among the Dover spectators.

Its top wing had a spread of forty-four feet, while the lower wing was considerably shorter. Its top speed was only sixty miles an hour, but Britain was so lamentably short of aircraft that she was grateful for even the small blessings of a handful of Henri Farmans. There were five BE8s among the heterogeneous collection assembled on the field outside Dover. This one differed from other aircraft in that it had a double cockpit where pilot and observer must huddle together and, without even trying to, get nicely in each other's way. It was never intended to be anything but a training machine, but so desperate was the shortage that even trainers had to go to war.

If the spectators derived a great deal of excitement and amusement out of watching the strange machines sway perilously every time the wind swept across the Dover plain, the thirty-seven pilots had quite different reactions. The less-experienced men looked forward with sober apprehension to the trip across the Channel. Each aircraft was carrying spare parts, emergency supplies, rations and extra cans of fuel. Thus overloaded, the armada would have to fly over the Channel from Dover to Gris Nez. If anything went wrong, the choppy surface of the Channel promised a quick watery grave for pilot and aircraft. Their final destination was Amiens, and their job would be to observe movements of enemy troops. These aircraft had not been designed for war, and the more knowledgeable pilots knew that their chances of survival were slim. But little of this apprehension was apparent on that last night in England when they were cheered and fêted by the citizens of Dover, who mistakenly thought that these thirty-seven machines were merely the first of a huge air fleet which would soon be headed for France. And so the usual closing hour was suspended in the pubs, and pilots, mechanics, drivers of vans and observers enjoyed the hospitality which for the past few hundred years Dover had usually reserved for naval heroes. And none among those who urged the airmen to have just 'one more for the road' had the slightest idea that within a year most of these friendly, smiling young men would be dead.

It was not the German military machine which had passed the sentence of death upon these young pioneers of the Royal

Flying Corps; it was the criminal negligence of military and government officials who had given Britain nothing except a token air force as unsuited for war as the commercial vans from the meat extract, biscuit and ink concerns were for battle-field duty. Many of the pilots, tossing restlessly in sleep, trying to forget the hazards of the next day's flight to France, might have had bitter dreams. They knew how woefully unprepared their country was and they knew, too, how desperately a small nucleus of civilian airmen, aircraft designers and officers had fought to convince the sacred organization of conservative traditionalists known as Whitehall that the aeroplane in time of war would be a vital and necessary adjunct to army and navy. But the fight had been lost and now most of them and hundreds like them were to pay the price.

British, French and German military leaders all used the same or similar textbooks, and from them they had all learned one basic lesson of warfare—everything else being equal, it is the commander with the most complete knowledge of his enemy who wins the battle. For the past half-century or so the general term 'intelligence' had been applied to this knowledge. In a full-scale war 'intelligence' is made up of a vast amount of information amassed in varying ways. Every major power in the world had made use of paid espionage agents as well as its own secret operatives. But though this kind of information might well reveal the long-term strategic aims of an enemy, it will not tell an Army commander in the field 'what lies over the hill'. This is the kind of information that wins battles—and the lack of it loses battles.

Yet, as late as 1911, neither the British War Office, the Royal Navy nor the Government itself showed any interest in the aeroplane as the inevitable answer to observation and the gathering of intelligence in war. By then the German Kaiser was publicly rattling his sabre, raising a huge army, building a navy, and every military expert in the world knew that he was preparing for a war of conquest—but the British ignored these portents. They have never been very good at preparing for a possible war; they seem to regard such preparation as a contradiction of their democratic and religious principles, and their honest conviction has always been that differences between nations can always be resolved around a conference table.

In keeping with its traditional policy, Britain refused to do anything but give token recognition to the fact that a potential weapon of war, sired by two bicycle manufacturers of Dayton, Ohio, had been born on the sand dunes of Kitty Hawk in 1903. When the Wright brothers offered to sell all of their patents to the British Government for $200,000, the offers were politely refused. In 1911, the Committee of Imperial Defence did recommend the creation of a British Aeronautical Service, but it was several months before its recommendation was acted upon and then, in answer to the traditionalists, who thought spending money on aircraft was absurd when there was hardly enough to spend on the more vital item of cavalry horses, there was an official report which indicated that the Government regarded this merely a benevolent experiment that should be encouraged. 'However,' the official report read, 'the policy of the Government with regard to all branches of aerial navigation is based on a desire to keep in touch with the movement rather than hasten its development.'

Tradition has always been the credo by which Colonel Blimp lived, and the Colonel Blimps in the cavalry divisions were especially articulate in their opposition to developing the aeroplane as a war machine and establishing a separate service to train the idiots who wanted to fly these machines. Because it had already been suggested in the report by the Committee of Imperial Defence that the task of the aeroplane would be 'to keep the Army commanders in the field as fully informed as possible of the movements of the enemy', the cavalry was outraged. Reconnaissance had always been entrusted to the horse, and there was no reason to believe that these absurd flying bird cages could do the job which the cavalry had been doing successfully for the past few centuries. 'Besides,' wrote one cavalry officer in an impassioned official protest, 'the noise these damn things make will frighten our horses.'

But somehow Britain always manages to move in the right direction, and in 1912 the infant Royal Flying Corps was born and the Central Flying School established on Salisbury Plain to train men for both army and naval air service. At long last the seed had been planted and it would eventually bring forth a mighty crop. During the first weeks of its existence the Central Flying School which was headed by Captain Godfrey Paine, RN, had only four aircraft at its disposal and nineteen student pilots enrolled. Then came a tragic accident which in retrospect assumes a tremendous significance. On the morning of July 5th, 1912, Captain Eustace Broke Lawrence, an experienced and skilled pilot, and his observer Staff Sergeant R. H. V. Wilson, were killed when the two-seater monoplane Lawrence was flying crashed near Stonehenge. Captain Paine not only paid the supreme honour to his dead friend Lawrence, he created a tradition that for ever remained a part of Britain's Air Force. He called all of the student fliers then at Salisbury together and announced calmly that there would be no interruption in the afternoon's flying activities. If he was grieving for his friend, he grieved inside where none could see. The student pilots may have been shaken by the order, but generations of airmen have followed the tradition; no man, least of all an airman, can live with ghosts, not even the ghosts of friends. Within the following weeks there were accidents that took the lives of four more men, and then the authorities put a ban on using monoplanes for training purposes.

Six months after the Royal Flying Corps had come into existence a Member of Parliament, prodded by an article which that week had appeared in *The Aeroplane*, edited by Charles G. Grey (who at that moment probably knew more about aircraft and their potentials than any man alive), made the startling statement that the Royal Flying Corps possessed only twenty-five machines. The House of Commons greeted this statement with a collective yawn, and did nothing about it. Which meant that the War Office was under no pressure to make additional appropriations. Charles Grey sat in the gallery feeling sick at heart. He trudged back to his office and continued to scream in the columns of his weekly publication for an air force which would at least be equal to those which he knew France and Germany were building. Happily, the young men of England (especially the young officers) read his magazine assiduously and many of them were impressed to the extent that they enrolled at Hendon and other civilian flying schools where they learned to master the strange contraption which Charles Grey said would one day be useful in time of war.

A survey late in 1912 disclosed the fantastic fact that only eight officers of the Royal Navy and eleven of the Army were actually able to fly an aeroplane, and no official encouragement was given to young officers who might want to make a career in the air arm. Most of those pilots gathered on the Dover airfield in August, 1914, had learned to fly at their own expense at private flying schools.

There were perhaps only two men of military stature in the world who actually had the prophetic vision to foresee the war potential that lay in the flimsy, awkward, unreliable contraption called the aeroplane, and although their views were published for all to read, no one in the British Government, Army or intelligence service became converted. Had Britain believed implicitly in the views as expressed by General Giulio Douhet of Italy and Captain Ferdinand Ferber of France, and acted upon their theories, the country would have begun the war with a tremendous initial advantage, and the thirty-seven pilots waiting to fly across the Channel would not have been facing almost certain death—either by accident or enemy action.

As early as 1909, Giulio Douhet saw the true vision of air power as it would be used thirty years later in World War II. At a time when the aeroplane had scarcely demonstrated its capacity to stay aloft, he had already grasped the full significance of the new machine. In 1911, he was commanding Italy's Aeronautical Battalion (which consisted chiefly of balloons) and writing *Rules for the Use of Aeroplanes in War*. He was one of the first to state that henceforth war would be a clash between nations, not merely the traditional series of battles between armies. General staffs the world over, the zealous Italian said, tended to look backwards exclusively, trying to solve the problem of the next war only on the basis of how the last war was resolved without taking into account the new realities. The aeroplane was a new reality.

The conventional experience of war taught by all military experts, from West Point, St Cyr and Sandhurst to the German War College, was that the way to secure victory in combat was to concentrate force at decisive defence points. One of the most important objects of an air force, Douhet declared, was to weaken this decisive point by the use of bombing. But the strong point should not itself be the only target: rear bases, lines of communication, railways, sources of production and the civilian population behind this point should be attacked. The air force, he argued strongly, should never be merely an 'arm' of either army or navy but must be a separate striking force.

Douhet was a complete realist who believed that there was no such thing as a gentleman's war—chivalry had no place in armed conflict. Douhet was an intellectually honest man; he felt that war was a dirty business and that the sooner it could be ended by any means at all, the better for all concerned. He laughed at those who said that he was a barbarian for suggesting that cities be bombed, and he reminded them that in every European country virtually all factories producing guns, shells and other weapons were located in the midst of cities.

Italian generals and admirals seemed to take his view as personal affronts, for their attacks on him were vicious. They said that no air force could ever hold ground, and that since time immemorial victory had resulted only when enemy territory was physically occupied. You win a war, Douhet answered, when you compel the enemy to submit to your will. In 1812, he reminded them, Napoleon occupied Russia all the way to Moscow yet failed to subject the apparently conquered and occupied country to his will. If the aerial arm can create intolerable conditions (panic, hunger, fear, immobility, loss of production), the enemy must admit defeat no matter what the status of its ground forces. Once defeat is conceded, land forces can take care of occupational details without further combat.

This was called by his critics 'The Douhet Theory of Frightfulness'. Douhet was a man ahead of his time. His unpalatable but realistic and militarily sound theories and his insistence upon bitterly and tactlessly criticizing decisions of his superior officers led to his court martial (a fate which General Billy Mitchell was to share for much the same reason in 1925). He was found guilty and sentenced to a year's imprisonment, but even the walls could not still his voice. Now he could devote all of his time to writing and to corresponding with some of the few converts he had made.

Douhet's ideas were not military secrets: they were published in Italian newspapers and aviation magazines, and of course his *Rules for the Use of Aeroplanes in War* was not a classified document. It is still a mystery why no major power took his views seriously. And so the voice of the Italian, Giulio Douhet, went unheard; it was not until 1933, after his death, that his books were translated into French and finally English.

There was one man in France who had the vision to foresee the future of the aeroplane as a weapon, but no one paid much attention to him either. He was Captain Ferdinand Ferber, one of the earliest disciples of Blériot, Santos-Dumont and the Wright brothers. In 1911, he was interviewed by a writer for a French aviation magazine. The writer, after hearing his theories of the potential importance of the aeroplane in warfare, asked in honest bewilderment, "But how could a fight actually take place between two aircraft?"

The great flying pioneer said prophetically, "In the same way as all fights between birds have ever taken place. When a falcon, for instance, wants to attack a raven, it first pursues it; and, as soon as the raven finds itself overhauled, it ascends slowly, in spirals, and the falcon starts to rise in a parallel line. If the raven can rise higher than the falcon, it is saved; if it cannot, its resource is to drop to earth, although during the descent it is liable to be hemmed in by the falcon. Every time the falcon darts upon the raven the latter will try, by means of a clever sideslip, to avoid the impact. If the falcon has been dodged, there is a respite, for, carried beyond its aim, the falcon loses an elevation which it must painfully regain. The race for altitude may recommence, but now the flight is no longer doubtful; the raven will finally come to the ground, and will be vanquished. In a like manner will aerial craft struggle."

The magazine, to its everlasting credit, did not dismiss Captain Ferber's ideas as absurdities, but the editorial comment was in the same reserved vein as magazines and editorial writers today treat the possibility of eventual travel to neighbouring planets. 'Until exceptionally large and fast aeroplanes are built, capable of throwing explosives, Captain Ferber's theories must remain more or less theoretical,' the magazine commented, 'but great nations should beware of the grim potentialities he warns us against.'

The great nations did not become aware of the grim potentialities mentioned by brilliant Captain Ferber (who died a few months after the article appeared).

Because there was no one in any position of military authority who believed in the aeroplane as a vital weapon, the little craft had to make its own way, almost by evolution. That it was able to do this within the brief span of a year or so was due more to the courage, spirit and ingenuity of the early pilots themselves than to the completely inadequate aircraft most of them flew.

For some time after the war began they themselves were the only ones who had any confidence at all in the usefulness of their machines. But even the more mature of them never realized that eventually they and their aircraft would play, if not a decisive, a vital role in resolving the world conflict. Meanwhile they were embarked on a thrilling adventure, and the letters the thirty-seven pilots at Dover wrote home the day before they left and the thoughts they confided to their diaries indicate that even the more stable of them felt a great pride in being part of a revolutionary and exciting new part of warfare. These thirty-seven young men were an extraordinary group. Were they alive today (the best evidence is that only two survive), they would undoubtedly be making plans to be on the first space ship to travel to the moon.

These thirty-seven were good men, Britain's finest pilots. Lieutenant H. D. Harvey-Kelly, gay, lighthearted, high-spirited, would make brilliant air history until claimed by death; Lieutenant Louis Strange, who had learned to fly because of a bet, would have some amazing and bizarre aerial adventures during the next four years and surprisingly enough, would live to look back upon them with wonder; Lieutenant G. W. Mapplebeck, one of the first to be shot down and hidden by the people of Lille (they showed him the printed circulars offering a reward for his capture), would escape to fly again and to die as did most; Major Charles James Burke of the Royal Irish Regiment, famous for the number of his crashes, was too strict to earn popularity from the men of No 2 Squadron which he commanded, but without exception they admired the utterly brave and determined man who would die in 1916 on the first day of the Arras offensive. Major Salmond had No 3 Squadron, while Major Raleigh commanded No 4, and No 5 was led by Major Higgins. These were some of the young men of the luckless generation which would earn glory, fame and for the most part an early death. But they would establish a tradition that would save England twenty-six years later.

Their attitude can perhaps best be reflected by a cartoon which appeared in *Punch* some years before. It depicted a young subaltern in a crack cavalry regiment being put through his paces by an examiner.

"And can you tell me, just what is the use of cavalry in wartime?" the examiner asked.

"To give tone to what would otherwise be merely a vulgar brawl," the youngster answered disdainfully.

Those gathered on the plain above Dover Castle felt much the same way about their branch of the service. It wasn't important, but damn it all—it was *chic*. They freely acknowledged that the vulgar, brawling infantrymen would eventually win or lose the war, but meanwhile they were part of a glorious unprecedented venture. Most of them were products of England's fine public schools; some of them liked to quote the prophetic verse of Tennyson:

'For I dipt into the future, far as human eye could see,
Saw the Vision of the world, and all the wonder that would be;
Saw the heavens fill with commerce, argosies of magic sails,
Pilots of the purple twilight, dropping down with costly bales;
Heard the heavens fill with shouting, and there rain'd a ghastly dew
From the nations' airy navies grappling in the central blue;

They didn't really believe in Tennyson's vision for a moment, but it gave them a spiritual lift to realize that a Poet Laureate of England had once thought in more realistic terms than did their own War Office. The thirty-seven men waiting for the signal to take off from Dover plain were quite ready for the great adventure.

The French and British were now allies in a war for which both were lamentably unprepared and for which both would substitute desperation and sheer doggedness of purpose for the weapons they long since should have perfected. France at least had anticipated the war, and its army was ready to defend the 170-mile-long Franco-German frontier, but both Foch and Joffre, the architects of France's defence, had ignored the danger of a great German thrust through neutral Belgium. Neither, incidentally, had the slightest faith in the aeroplane as an important aid to observation, although a small group of French aviation enthusiasts had been clamouring for years that this new device should be considered seriously by the Government as a potential war weapon. France, aeronautically, was as good as any other country in the world, but the progress had been made by her civilians—not by the military, for France too had her Colonel Blimps.

It was a French-born American citizen, Octave Chanute, who really inspired the French to experiment and advance in the new medium. This bridge builder, engineer and pioneer in the field of aeronautics had been publicly given credit by the Wrights for the important and unselfish help they had received from him. Chanute, known as the father of American aviation, delivered one address to the Aero Club of Paris, and the reaction of his listeners was such that he might well be called the godfather of French aviation. Some of the men who heard the elderly and witty French-speaking American that night were Louis Blériot; Albert Santos-Dumont; Ernest Archdeacon, president of the Aero Club and a wealthy sportsman; Robert Gastambide, another wealthy air enthusiast; Leon Levavasseur, designer of automotive engines; and Gabriel and Charles Voisin, two young aircraft designers. Captain Ferber was the only important military figure present.

After listening to Chanute discussing his advanced aeronautical theories that evening, Captain Ferber, then an artillery officer, a student of science and a teacher in the military school at Fontainebleau, became a strong devotee to the aeroplane as a part of war equipment. He was a thorough believer in the Wright philosophy of trial and error. 'To design a flying machine is nothing: to build one is nothing much; to try it in the air is everything,' he wrote and cried out in lectures to his military students. He did his best to persuade his military superiors to purchase the patents which the Wright brothers were peddling, but they were as shortsighted as their neighbours across the Channel, and the development of the French aeroplane was left to civilians of faith and vision.

Levavasseur designed an eighty horsepower engine weighing less than five pounds per horsepower and Robert Gastambide put up the money to transfer it from the blueprint to the hangar. His only stipulation was the graceful Gallic one that it be named the *Antoinette*, after his lovely daughter. It was used by Blériot, Santos-Dumont, Farman and virtually all of the early French aviators. Charles and Gabriel Voisin began to manufacture aeroplanes, as did Blériot, and Henri and Maurice Farman. But although the great French flying pioneers held just about every flying record, the military pinned its hopes on Foch and Joffre; and when war came, France was only slightly better prepared in the air than was England. She had a great many more aircraft, but they were of a bewildering variety, and few were suited for military purposes. She did, however, have plenty of pilots and plenty of young men who wanted to be pilots.

In August, 1914, the French pilots fell into three quite distinct classes. The first class was made up of 'gentlemen sportsmen'. They were men who in pre-war days had the means to buy sporting aircraft and the inclination to fly them. They chose the Air Force because it stimulated their imagination; it was more exciting and adventurous than fighting in the trenches. They included the young sons of the oldest families in France.

The second class was comprised of professional pilots and

aviation mechanics. In peacetime these had been the French equivalent of the barnstormers, stunt fliers or test pilots.

The third class consisted of men who in civilian life had been chauffeurs and motor-car mechanics. In some ways the French were a bit more discriminating in their acceptance of candidates for the brevet of the pilot than either the British or the Germans. The British, whose choice was dictated by desperate necessity, were accepting youngsters who seemed to be the 'pilot type'; they didn't have to know what went on behind the cowling that enclosed the engine if they showed an aptitude for flying the machine. Mechanics would do the worrying about the engine itself. The French insisted that a prospective pilot either know or learn something about the engine that powered his machine. The civilian chauffeurs and mechanics who knew engines were presumably men whose specialized knowledge would ultimately help them to become good pilots. The future was to vindicate the French view.

The aerodrome eight miles outside Pau was France's main training school. There were four separate camps and a large repair station at Pau. Each of the four camps was named after a great hero of aviation, and a small wooden building where repairs were made to damaged aircraft and faulty engines was called Wright Barn; it was here that the Wright brothers, ridiculed and virtually repudiated in their own country, developed their ideas and eventually made flights over Paris that convinced even the United States that they were not merely two visionary bicycle makers. It was to Pau that most *'élèves pilotes'* came for training before they received their brevet.

"At the Front," every pilot was told by the chief instructor, "each pilot has two *mécaniciens* to take care of his engine. But if you have a breakdown and have to land in hostile territory, you will have no mechanics to help you. If you have to land behind enemy lines, the engine failure may be caused by some minor fault of carburettor fuel line or magneto. If you know what is wrong, you may be able to fix it quickly and take off before German patrols capture you."

When the novice had finished his apprenticeship and had demonstrated in flight that he at least seemed 'air-minded', he was sent to the advanced school at Chartres. To tourists before the war this old city was known as the birthplace of Pasteur and the home of a beautiful eleventh-century Gothic cathedral. In the summer of 1914, Pasteur and the cathedral were forgotten; Chartres was the place where most French pilots flew solo for the first time, although there were four similar and only slightly smaller installations where finishing touches were put on the neophyte fliers. Most of the advanced training was done on the Caudron G-2, too slow for use at the Front, but the four wheels attached to its sturdy undercarriage saved many young pilots whose poor landings might otherwise have resulted in disaster. The Maurice Farman Longhorn was another used at Chartres. Dual controls were still in the far future, and a pupil learning to fly a Longhorn was seated high behind the pilot in front of the nacelle. When the instructor thought that his pupil had observed enough, he allowed him to lean over his shoulder and reach for the controls. Two hours of this and the neophyte was considered ready to solo. Many crashed on their first attempt due to the tricky habits of the front elevator, which was the bane of all novices.

In appearance it looked like two box kites strung together with wire, with an old-fashioned bathtub—the kind in which Marat was murdered—perched on the lower wing of the forward kite. Sixteen thin wooden struts joined the upper and lower wings. French records describing the aircraft in technical language add with commendable understatement, 'wire-braced'. It was almost encased in wires, but somehow it flew, a tribute to its fine little seventy-five-horsepower Renault pusher engine.

A modified version, the Shorthorn Type S-II, sometimes had a Lewis machine gun mounted on its front cockpit, but although the gunner in the front seat had unlimited vision and field of fire, there is no record that any German aircraft was hit by it in the autumn of 1914 when it was very active. When the Shorthorn headed into a strong or even a moderate wind it had a tendency to remain almost stationary, and its sluggishness in adverse weather made it an easy target for ground defences, primitive as they were. Then, too, the Lewis had a persistent habit of jamming almost every time it fired a burst.

Before a pilot was given a single-seater to fly, he had to

44

become proficient in handling the slower, relatively safer machines. Once he had graduated from Chartres, he was declared to be a *pilote aviateur*, a fully-fledged member of the aerial light cavalry of France and a recipient of one of the highest rates of pay in the French armed forces.

There were very few really first-class aeroplanes available in France (or anywhere else) in 1914. The reason was obvious enough; because the aeroplane had not been considered to be a machine of war, most research and development had to be done by private companies whose capital was restricted. The only real commercial market available to these companies outside the limited military market was that of sportsmen and barnstormers. The average age of a pilot was twenty; very few of the aircraft were more than three or four years off the drawing board, which meant they hadn't as yet discarded the careless, infantile habits of babyhood. To survive they had to grow to maturity together.

Every British and French aircraft available for flying duty in August, 1914, would be completely obsolete within a year, but neither the British nor the French knew this during the early weeks of the war. France thought that in the Blériot XI, produced both as a single-seater and as a two-seater reconnaissance aircraft, it had the best flying machine ever built. This was an improved version of the machine designed, built and flown by Louis Blériot across the Channel only five years before. By the standards of the day it was a good aeroplane.

In general, this little monoplane foreshadowed future design in aircraft. Its amazingly sound construction had enabled the best pilots before the war to perform what were then considered to be advanced, almost suicidal acrobatics. Pegoud had performed the first loop ever demonstrated in his country in 1913 in a Blériot, and Marcus Manton, Gustav Hamel, Henri Salmet, Roland Garros, Graham D. Gilmore and others had made remarkable speed, endurance and altitude records in this machine. Because of its accomplishments and the magic which surrounded the name of Blériot, this was perhaps the best-known aircraft in the world on August 4th, 1914.

Each model had an eighty-horsepower Gnome rotary motor

capable of propelling it at sixty-six miles an hour at sea level and a few additional miles at higher altitudes. It used wing warping instead of loose ailerons. Its wings were fortified by the wooden spars and wire-braced fabric covering, and it had an openwork fuselage behind the cockpit. Thus it had a naked, plucked appearance. There were a great many wires on this Blériot, which gave rise to what may (or may not) be an apocryphal story told of a British pilot taking his first look at this machine.

"So many wires!" He shook his head doubtfully and then asked a mechanic, "How do you keep track of them all?"

"That's easy," the mechanic said with a straight face. "Every morning we release a bird inside that part of the aeroplane enclosed by wires. If the bird escapes, well, then we know there is a wire missing."

Thereafter it was known as The Bird Cage.

The Morane Bullet was another single-seater France liked. It was a development of the Morane Saulnier and the Morane Borel racing machines of 1912. In flight it bore a striking resemblance to the German Fokker E-1 monoplane, and during the first year of the war many of them fell victims to French anti-aircraft fire.

France also had a few Voisin pusher biplanes and a number of Henri Farman biplanes with eighty-horsepower pusher motors. Although many other designs were in the process of being brought into the world by French engineers, these were the only ones actually available in August, 1914. It was hardly an impressive array, but it was all that France could offer.

France, which had the best aeronautical brains and best pilots in the world and which should have been far out in front of the other warring nations, could only muster 136 serviceable aircraft on August 4th, 1914. These, plus the forty-eight British aircraft ready for service, gave the two great powers a discouraging total of 184 aeroplanes, and it is understandable that they went unnoticed as huge armies and gigantic artillery units unleashed their tremendous power.

None of the great military leaders guiding the destinies of the Allied armies took much notice of the 184 aeroplanes placed at their disposal. Not one of them had ever been even

46

a passenger in an aircraft, and they tolerated them as they would have tolerated any frankly experimental project. It was hard for a Haig, a Kitchener, a Joffre or a Foch to take a bird-cage seriously.

Every aircraft carried within its frail body and unpredictable engine the seeds of its own destruction. Put it into the wind and it would lose all forward momentum, stall and crash. Land it on uneven ground and as likely as not it would smash a wheel, turn over and disintegrate in a mass of snapped wooden struts, broken piano wire and torn wing-fabric. If a temperamental engine broke down while you were in the air, you seldom glided down safely; usually the wind took you, shook you the way a terrier shakes a rat and then hurled you to the ground.

In 1783, Benjamin Franklin saw his first balloon ascent in Paris. The public looked upon a balloon flight as entertainment and nothing else, but the scientific mind of Franklin grasped the great potential that could eventually grow out of this silk-encased gas-bag. That night he talked about it with fierce excitement and enthusiasm to several French military men, who remained unimpressed.

"It's an amusing toy," one said, "but of what use is it?"

"Of what use is a new-born baby?" Franklin snapped.

In August, 1914, the aeroplane was a new-born baby. Except for a relatively few fond stepfathers, no one cared much for the noisy child. And the cavalry officer was right. The damn thing did frighten the horses.

Chapter Three

THE FLEDGLING FEW

ON AUGUST 14th, 1914, England's brave little air fleet of thirty-seven machines took off from Dover bound for the war. It was the first mass flight in history.

Each pilot and observer had been given a revolver, field glasses, a spare pair of goggles, a small stove, a tin of biscuits, some cold meat, a piece of chocolate, soup cubes, and orders that nothing else be carried in their aircraft. The transport, made up of a collection of ninety-five army lorries, private motor-cars and commercial vans (plus a quantity of office furniture), had left by boat a day before. This comprised the air power of the British Expeditionary Force.

The advent of the Royal Flying Corps was received with the greatest enthusiasm by the French. The fliers were showered with fruit, wine and cheese by the local populace. In obedience to their orders they arrived only with the scanty kit that could be carried in their aircraft—nothing else. Pyjamas had not been included, and the pilots spent the first few days shopping for these and other staple articles of clothing. The French for some centuries had been committed to nightgowns as a sleeping garment, and the members of the four squadrons had to become accustomed to the flowing raiment which came in odd sizes and odd colours.

Thousands of deliriously happy French spectators surrounded the field and gathered outside the Hôtel du Rhin in Amiens, where the flying officers were quartered. They greeted the British as white knights dropping from the skies to save them from the terrible bombing attacks they expected any moment from Germany's huge fleet of Zeppelins. They had been conditioned to this attitude by the French Press, which for some years had been picturing most luridly and describing most graphically (if inaccurately) the devastation that could be caused by dirigibles if war came. Until now the nervous people of Amiens had seen no French aircraft at all, but from their frightened hearts poured fantastic stories.

Already a Zeppelin had attacked Nancy, they told the British pilots. Yes, indeed, this huge airship carrying tons of explosives reached the outskirts of the city early on the morning of August 4th, and if it had not been for the incredible bravery of Roland Garros, who sacrificed his life by ramming the dirigible with his machine, Nancy would now be in ruins. Such stories, born at the tables of Paris pavement cafés, swept the country, and official denials seldom caught up with the original and more interesting rumours. Each morning they scanned the skies looking for the Zeppelins which never came

48

—no one in the area would see a Zeppelin during the whole course of the war. But they would soon see German aircraft, and they would continue to see them until November 11th, 1918.

The people of Amiens were not the only ones who were apprehensive about German air power; the British War Office and French Government were vitally concerned, not only about the Zeppelins, but about what they felt to be Germany's huge aeroplane force. How this could be used they weren't sure, but they were positive that the brilliant German Staff had dire plans for it. It was some months before they came to realize that actually Germany wasn't much better prepared in the air than they were. The day that war broke out Germany had some thirteen dirigibles ready for service—not the 'several hundred' mentioned so often in the London and Paris Press— and 180 aeroplanes available for front-line observation work. (She had also about 300 training aircraft.)

Germany should by that time have been a first-rate air power; she had been preparing for this war for years, and she had the aeronautical brains, the engines and the productive power to turn out an effective air armada; but in Germany as in France and England tradition was overpowering, and the Air Force was relegated to an unimportant position in the Signal Corps. Flying was even more popular in this country than it was in France, but for the most part it was confined to sportsmen. Otto Lilienthal had been one of the truly imaginative pioneers of aviation during the 1890's and it was his experiments in the new art of gliding which had great influence on the Wright brothers. He was experimenting with a biplane that would be driven by a two-and-a-half-horsepower engine when he met his death in 1896; if he had not died, it is conceivable that he might have beaten the two Americans to the goal of keeping a power-driven glider in the sky.

His many experiments (he had made more than 2000 glides) and his willingness to share his knowledge with anyone who was interested gave aviation a great impetus in Germany. By 1911 there were fourteen flying schools going strong, and two factories, the Albatros and the Aviatik, were producing and selling aeroplanes. They had the Daimler and Mercedes engines available, and at that time these were the two finest water-cooled motors in the world. Army officers watched demonstrations of these aircraft with apparent interest but with no appreciation as to their potential military worth. There is an old German axiom that army officers look wiser than they are, and naval officers are wiser than they look. Because the Army was committed to the dirigible, it spent relatively little on the heavier-than-air machines.

It is almost incomprehensible that the German High Command, so thorough in studying military treatises by experts of all nations, should have completely ignored Douhet's theories of total warfare which seem to be so well suited to the pattern of Prussian war tactics. The truth was, of course, that although Germany was military-minded, her leaders were intellectual prisoners of the past and their god was a man who died in 1831 of cholera, and his military theories were gospel to them (and for that matter to Foch and other French generals.) His name was Karl von Clausewitz, and after seeing service in the Rhine campaigns of 1792–94 he became an instructor in the War College and military adviser to the Crown Prince. He became a general of artillery and later chief of staff to Marshal Gneisenau. When he died, he left a mountain of writing which his widow turned over to military friends for editing. They were published in ten volumes, and one of these, *Vom Kriege* (On War) was the masterpiece which perpetuated his memory and influenced military thinking in Europe until 1945. His philosophy of strategy in war so took hold of the Prussian mind that it became the basis of all military teaching and in a practical sense brought Prussian arms to victory in 1866 and 1870. Clausewitz believed that 'the immutable principle of war is the annihilation of hostile armies in battle'. Ludendorff, who was often called 'Hindenburg's Brain', was a devout disciple of Clausewitz. So too were Moltke and most other Prussian officers. They could recite with delight the axioms of the long-dead strategist. 'We have only one means in war—battle. . . . The bloody solution of the crisis, the effort for the destruction of the enemy's forces, is the first-born son of war. . . . Only great and general battles can produce great results. . . . The complete disarming or destruction of the enemy must always be the aim of warfare. . . . To introduce into the philosophy of war a principle of moderation would be an absurdity. . . . War is an act of violence pushed to its utmost bounds. . . .'

The German General Staff in 1914 believed that mass slaughter of the enemy army was the only really vital concern; once the enemy army was destroyed you could dictate your own terms. The Germans could not have taken exception to the Douhet Theory of Frightfulness; they just dismissed the whole concept of an aeroplane being anything but an observation outpost, and a rather unreliable one, at that. Even Ludendorff, perhaps the most imaginative of the German generals, had nothing but contempt for the mass of wires, struts, frail wings covered with cloth, and unreliable engine called the aeroplane.

Nevertheless, the German aircraft which went to war on August 4th, 1914, were on the whole better than those available for duty with the French and British, and if they were not taken seriously by the High Command, they wasted no time in calling themselves to the attention of the Allies. Young Max Immelmann, who within a year would gain fame as the first German ace, flew a Rumpler Taube over Paris. It dropped nothing more lethal than a note, but the unmolested visit by the German machine instilled considerable consternation among the civilian population. The note said that the German Army was at the gates of Paris and it exhorted the people of the capital to surrender. A week later another Taube dropped the first bombs to land on French soil; they were small four-pounder missiles and they exploded harmlessly on the outskirts of Paris, but they aroused the people to the potential danger of air attack and both French and British authorities to the excellence of the German two-seater. The German High Command took little notice of either incident as the German Army continued its smashing path towards Paris. Everything was going according to plan.

The misconceptions as to the potential worth of the aeroplane, and the haphazard manner in which observers were selected for service in the Air Force, is almost unbelievable in view of the pride of Germany's pre-war army in its military efficiency. Reconnaissance, as in England, had been traditionally a job of the cavalry; the air observer was considered to be merely the flying counterpart of the cavalry scout. In theory this sounded fine, but even the astute German High Command overlooked the difference between the horizontal observation of the cavalryman and vertical view of the airman. No one understood that an air observer needed special and extensive training for what was a brand-new science. The cavalry observer had absolutely no idea what a supply establishment, a munitions dump, a moving column of men and vehicles, or artillery defences looked like from the air.

The observers for the most part were volunteers from the cavalry and artillery. They were invariably officers, while the pilots were not. The observer was in command of the aircraft at all times. In most of the German aeroplanes available in 1914, the observer sat in the front cockpit. If it was a biplane, his downward view was cut off by the lower wing; and the engine, exhaust pipe and radiator ahead of him blocked his forward view. His view was further restricted by the mass of wires and struts that held the wings together. If he were in the front seat of the Rumpler monoplane, his view was cut off by the curve of the wing. It is hardly to be wondered that, during the opening phase of the war, the infantry and artillery commanders paid little attention to reports from air observers. Their lack of faith was certainly justified, for during the first months of battle German reconnaissance reports were misleading, inaccurate and completely worthless. One example: the British Expeditionary Force landed in France during the week of August 7th. Hiding an army of five divisions is a little bit like smuggling a bass drum into a crowded tube train, but the German General Staff did not know of the presence of the British until August 22nd, when General von Kluck's army ran into some British outposts. Not one air observer (flying unmolested over the territory occupied by the British) had reported their presence.

On August 4th, 1914, when Germany assigned her 180 first-line aircraft to duty with the seven armies which made the initial assault, sixty per cent of these were of the Taube type.

The name Taube (dove) was not that given to a particular make of aircraft—the word was applied to a general type manufactured by some twenty German aeroplane builders, including the Albatros, Goodekker, DFW, Gotha, Halbertadt, Jeannin and Rumpler concerns. All of these were monoplanes which, because of a common characteristic—they resembled birds in flight—were called *Tauben*. This was the result of the peculiar shape of their ailerons, which were of the warp control type, and their curved wings. In the beginning the most successful of the Taube type was the Rumpler, with a one-hundred-horsepower Daimler motor which gave it a speed of seventy-five miles per hour. The Rumpler people had bought the design for this machine from Josef Etrich, an Austrian engineer. After twenty had been built and had proved their worth, the design was standardized, even though different engines were used and minor modifications were made. The Rumpler was especially noted for its high-flying qualities. It held the world's altitude record at just under 20,000 feet.

The French nicknamed the Rumpler Taube 'The Invisible Aeroplane'. The fabric which covered the fuselage and wings seemed transparent if the aircraft was up about 1600 feet—it was almost impossible to see on a really bright day.

Tony Fokker had hardly swung into top-gear production in August, 1914, but some twenty-four of his monoplanes were ready. This was the Fokker Eindekker (one-wing) Scout whose military appellation was the E-1. Some designers believed in all-wood aircraft; others risked their reputations, and the lives of the fliers, on all metal machines. Fokker was a man with a flexible mind—he would combine wood, steel tubing for the undercarriage, and use aluminium to cowl the engine. No conservative traditionalist, he was one of the few aircraft builders who kept in touch with front-line pilots and who took suggestions from them. His first FE-1 was not an extraordinary aircraft compared with his later masterpieces, but it was his basic aeroplane and most of his others were its very attractive offspring. Fokker's first machine carried an eighty-horsepower rotary, an engine which he never liked. He felt that it was tricky, unreliable, difficult to operate and that it consumed an enormous amount of petrol and oil for the small power it supplied. A great deal of its power exhausted itself in the mere rotation of its parts. If the ignition was shut off without throttling down, petrol flooded the engine. Occasionally, instead of picking up when the ignition was turned on again, it caught fire. Each rotary engine seemed to have individual characteristics. The Fokker E-1 was structurally too weak to permit of any prolonged power dives. If it dived too fast, it left its wings behind. Yet with all its faults, this was Germany's fastest and best observation aircraft. It was no sooner in the air than Fokker went to work to improve it.

On August 12th a German Taube passed a French Morane at 5000 feet. The two pilots waved cheerfully to each other and then each went his separate way. There was nothing else that either pilot could do or was expected to do. Neither aircraft carried a gun, and if the pilots had revolvers strapped to their belts, it was just an affectation; revolvers were issued to them as part of their equipment. They carried them because it gave them a feeling of kinship with the real fighting men of the war, the trudging, suffering infantry.

The life of a pilot was rather a pleasant one in 1914. To begin with, he was always quartered twenty or thirty miles behind the Front. Each pilot had his own special mechanic and his own batman, who was his personal servant. The German airmen lived especially well, for until the end of the war they were bivouacked in French territory; they merely had to requisition the most comfortable château or inn near their airfield.

Moreover, the duties of a pilot during the early months were not arduous or particularly dangerous. If he flew low enough, there was the remote possibility that he might be hit by small-arms fire, but during the first months of the conflict very few aircraft became the victims of bullets. Casualties were caused by engine failure, by wings inconveniently dropping off, and by bad landings by pilots who were at the Front with only a few hours of solo flying behind them. There was another not exactly dangerous but annoying and debilitating experience

54

suffered by nearly all pilots. Because ordinary crude oil congealed in the cold of high altitude, castor oil was used to lubricate the engines. The fumes, of course, travelled directly from the engine to the pilot in his open cockpit, and a one-hour inhalation of such fumes had the same effect upon the human system as would a direct dosage of three or four spoonfuls of the stuff. This was one of the perils of 1914 wartime flying avoided in the memoirs of the pilots and left tactfully unmentioned in all known histories of aerial fighting. Eventually most pilots developed an immunity to the embarrassing effects of castor oil fumes; those who didn't drank huge quantities of blackberry brandy before, during and after flying, and so far as is known not a single casualty resulted from the castor oil or its rugged antidote.

The British squadrons were put to work two days after they arrived in Amiens. The infantry (four divisions) and one cavalry division had already arrived in France, led by Sir John Moore and Sir John French. They took their places in the Mons–Le Cateau area, really the left flank of the defensive alignment. Seventy-two French divisions occupied the right and centre. Almost immediately the British Army had to follow the unhappy precedent, set in 1808 in the Peninsula, of retreating at the beginning of any war in which it was engaged. It is quite literally true that Britain always lost the first few battles and then ended up winning the war, for England, always thinking in terms of defence, relied primarily on its Navy to protect it and never imposed conscription upon its citizens except under pressure of overwhelming events.

The Belgian Army fought heroically during those early weeks, but only demonstrated the truth of the old prize-ring adage, that a good big man can always beat a good small man —and the British, of course, had to retreat or be annihilated. First they retreated from Mons and then fell back to the River Marne. It was partly due to reports from RFC observers that the retreat was not a rout.

One important omission in the gear each pilot had brought to France now manifested itself. They had no maps of this part of France. The French couldn't help—the infantry, artillery and intelligence services had all military maps. Someone conceived the idea of asking André Michelin, the tyre manufacturer, for some of the maps he distributed to motorists who used his products. The helpful industrialist sent one map to the British (the military had requisitioned his whole supply). It was an excellent map for the motorist but hardly the type needed to pinpoint accurately positions thousands of feet below an aeroplane. They did help pilots returning from missions to find the general Amiens area, but it was the bright-red Bovril van which had been shipped across the Channel that became the beacon for which pilots aimed on their way home. It stood in the centre of the field, a friendly and useful touch of home. Despite primitive aircraft, absurd maps, the inexperience of observers and bad weather, these dedicated pioneers did useful work, much to the surprise of the British High Command. The Germans took no notice of British observation aircraft beyond the casual pot shots taken at them by infantry; they didn't bother to mask their troop movements at all.

During the final days of August, General von Kluck tried desperately to outflank the British Army. He had moved west to a point only a few miles north-east of Amiens; now if he could strike sharply to the south he could encircle the British Army. The men of No 5 Squadron, acting as the eyes of the British commanders, saw the concentration of troops and the lines of supply vehicles moving up. Lieutenant A. E. Borton and Captain E. W. Furse reported the movement of troops leaving Noyon and Ribecourt; Captain de G. Pitcher and Lieutenant A. H. L. Soames of No 4 Squadron reported a German column stretching from Roye to Chevrincourt, and a few hours later Lieutenants C. G. Hooking and K. Atkinson reported a column on the move. This information was immediately sent to General Sir John French and he, gambling that the intelligence was accurate, ordered a retreat across the Marne. Until then Headquarters had been reluctant to accept reports from air observers. Could they tell an artillery battalion from a machine gun detachment from the air? Could they tell combatant troops from service or labour troops?

On August 4th, 1914, not one experienced British military leader in a hundred would have accepted the aeroplane as even a potential help to ground forces. Now, three weeks later, Sir

John French wrote in an official dispatch, 'I wish particularly to bring to your notice the admirable work done by the Royal Flying Corps. Their skill, energy and perseverance have been beyond all praise. They have furnished me with the most complete and accurate information which has been of incalculable value in the conduct of operations.' General Joffre this same week sent a similar message to the leader of his own French Air Force.

It appeared during that tragic first week of September, 1914, that the Germans would cross the Marne and walk into Paris, a situation which might conceivably put them in a position to dictate the peace terms. Around midnight on September 4th, General French received independent reports from three squadrons that von Kluck's over-eager army had marched into a pocket between the French Fifth Army on his left flank and French Sixth Army on his right. The British stood at the bottom of the pocket. Joffre had received similar reports from his pilots. He realized that the decisive moment had come. Inactivity and defensive tactics, no matter how tenacious, could only slow the German advance, not stop it. He ordered an all-out attack at dawn, September 6th. The Battle of the Marne, which began then, lasted for three horribly bitter days, but the assault saved Paris and in the opinion of many military experts made possible the eventual victory four years later.

The line was more or less fixed now at the River Aisne. Only a few British aircraft were equipped with sending sets, but their Morse Code reports on the accuracy of artillery fire —transmitted within seconds after the shells had burst—were immensely valuable. Lieutenant D. S. Lewis and B. T. James of No 4 Squadron (both subsequently killed) were the two pioneers in flying over enemy installations in a wireless-equipped aircraft. One afternoon late in September, three well-hidden German artillery batteries were causing tremendous casualties among the British. Lewis and James, flying almost at treetop level, finally located the artillery. They wirelessed back and waited for the British artillery to open up. It did— and a record of the messages from Lewis to the artillery commander has survived the years. They read tersely but eloquently:

4.02 p.m.	A very little short. Fire. Fire.
4.04 p.m.	Fire again. Fire again.
4.12 p.m.	A little short; line O.K.
4.15 p.m.	Short. Over, over and a little left.
4.20 p.m.	You were just between two batteries. Search two hundred yards each side of your last shot. Range O.K.
4.22 p.m.	You have them.
4.26 p.m.	Hit. Hit. Hit.
4.32 p.m.	About fifty yards short and to the right.
4.37 p.m.	Your last shot in the middle of three batteries in action; search all round within three hundred yards of your last shot and you have them.
4.42 p.m.	I am coming home now.

This marked the first successful co-operation between artillery and air, something which of course in time became routine tactics.

Another if less successful method of signalling the position of attractive targets on the ground was the use of Verey lights by pilots. This was resorted to only because of the shortage of wireless-equipped aircraft, whose sending range in any case was only about three miles.

To obtain accurate information about ground targets the aircraft usually had to fly very low. Whenever an aeroplane flew over troops, of course, it was greeted by all kinds of small-arms fire; and although an aircraft is a target that moves in three dimensions, making firing at it woefully inaccurate unless done by prediction, 500 Germans emptying their rifles at a low-flying machine had a good chance of scoring a few hits. On August 22nd, Sergeant-Major Jillings of No 2 Squadron, flying as observer with Lieutenant Albert Noel, spotted a regiment of Uhlans to the east of Mons-Ath-Lessines. He motioned to his pilot to fly lower so he could get a better estimate of the size of the cavalry detachment. Noel obligingly flew over the Uhlans at 200 feet, and they promptly discharged their carbines at the aircraft. A bullet hit Jillings in the fleshy part of his rear end; he was the first of 16,623 casualties the RFC would suffer during the war.

The Germans also began to use a crude method of anti-aircraft fire. They mounted elevated three-inch guns on trucks, but these were successful only when they had a concentration of them. A pilot from No 4 Squadron (whose name unhappily is lost to history) seemed to attract anti-aircraft fire every time he flew. He would laugh uproariously at bursting shells and start singing a popular and slightly ribald song of the day, 'Archibald, Certainly Not!' His squadron mates would greet him when he returned from a flight with 'Archibald give you any trouble today?' Eventually the long name was shortened to 'Archie' and to the end of the war German anti-aircraft fire was known as such.

Two of the first victims of Archie were Lieutenants L. Dawes and W. R. Freeman of No 2 Squadron. Both were pilots, but on a certain day Freeman went along as observer. A German shell silenced their engine and they glided to the relative safety of a piece of flat ground near Soissons, just 200 yards from a German troop column. The two men leaped from their aircraft and ran to the shelter of a nearby wood. German cavalry searched the forest, but the aviators remained hidden among the undergrowth. That night they walked through territory held by 50,000 Germans to swim the Aisne and report back to the squadron. Their mates, who had given them up for dead, congratulated them happily on their escape; but their tight-lipped commanding officer, Major Charles Burke, reprimanded them severely for violating an order that no two pilots should fly together in the same machine.

During World War II, Air Marshal Sir Sholto Douglas was in command of the RAF fighters; in 1914 he was a young observer in No 2 Squadron. After the war, in recalling the early days, he emphasized the fact that pilots had not as yet begun to think of their aircraft as weapons at all—merely as 'eyes' to help see what the enemy was doing:

The first time I ever encountered a German machine in the air both the pilot, Harvey-Kelly, and myself were completely unarmed. Our machine had not been climbing well, and as I was considered somewhat heavy for an observer, Harvey-Kelly told me to leave behind my carbine and ammunition. We were taking photographs of the trench system to the north

59

of Neuve Chapelle when I suddenly espied a German two-seater about a hundred yards away and just below us. The German observer did not appear to be shooting at us. There was nothing to be done. We waved a hand to the enemy and proceeded with our task. The enemy did likewise. At the time this did not appear to me in any way ridiculous—there is a bond of sympathy between all who fly, even between enemies. But afterwards just for safety's sake I always carried a carbine with me in the air. In the ensuing two or three months I had an occasional shot at a German machine. But these encounters can hardly be dignified with the name of 'fights'. If we saw an enemy machine nearby, we would fly over towards it, and fire at it some half a dozen rounds. We scarcely expected to shoot the enemy down; but it was a pleasant break in the monotony of reconnaissance and artillery observation.

The RFC bagged its first German aircraft on August 26th. Lieutenant H. D. Harvey-Kelly, commander of No 2 Squadron, started the war right by being the first British pilot to land at Amiens on the historic August 14th. Some pilots always played it by the book, using only tactics which had been tried and proved successful. Harvey-Kelly was an innovator. On August 26th, he and two of his squadron—flying BEs—were fairly high when they spied a German aircraft far below. Harvey-Kelly dived on it, closely followed by his two mates. The German, apprehensive perhaps that the mad pilot of this machine would hit him, also dived earthward. Harvey-Kelly kept on his tail and when the German straightened out the British pilot was just above him. By now the other two pilots had caught on; each flew close to the German, one to his right, another to his left, hemming him in. The three British machines shepherded him down to earth much as a police car forces a speeding motorist to the kerb. He landed safely, hopped out of his Taube and made off to a nearby wood. Harvey-Kelly landed and chased after the German; bringing back a live Boche pilot would be something to laugh about in the mess. But the German had disappeared and the British squadron leader returned, set fire to the aircraft, took off and returned to his base.

The report of what Harvey-Kelly had done spread to other

squadrons, Lieutenant Norman Spratt of No 5 and Lieutenant John Mendlicott of No 2 Squadron both jockeyed German aircraft to the ground.

These were just a few of the men who were beginning to give birth to a tradition. The other two services had long and honourable histories, but this new venture—operating in an element largely unknown and flying aircraft whose worth was so little established that many were frankly labelled 'experimental'—did not possess the advantage that tradition confers upon a ship's company or upon an old regiment. They and their machines were new and untried, and it was this perhaps that made for a strong feeling of comradeship among them; the relationship between officers and men, between pilots and mechanics, was far closer and warmer than that which existed in the two older services. These youngsters were to create, not to inherit, a tradition which a later generation would embellish with matchless gallantry. Almost everything they did during the early months of the war was a 'first'.

Only one British aircraft carried a machine gun during August. This was the two-seater Farman Shorthorn, flown by Lieutenant Louis Strange. Strange became a flier because the stimulating effect of a party one night prompted him to make a rash wager. His father was a successful farmer in Dorset, and when his son came down from Oxford, it was a settled thing that he would join the Dorsetshire Yeomanry, become a farmer and settle down to the rustic life of a country gentleman. But the youngster's imagination had become stirred by reading the articles written by Charles Grey in *The Aeroplane*.

At the annual dinner of the officers of the Dorsetshire Yeomanry, nineteen-year-old Louis Strange threw a conversational bombshell into the animated and convivial gathering by declaring that not only they, but the Navy and all cavalry regiments, would eventually become obsolete. Quoting the theories of Charles Grey, he said emphatically that Britain had ceased to be an island the day that Blériot had flown the English Channel. His friends—reared in the tradition of the Army like Strange himself—laughed at his enthusiasm, insisting that aeroplanes were death-traps, absurd contraptions no matter how you looked at them. Strange defended his point of view emphatically if illogically by offering to bet anyone present that he would learn to handle an aeroplane and would fly over the Yeomanry camp at its next manœuvres. His fellow officers were quick to take him up.

So young Louis Strange went off to Hendon to take flying lessons. From there it was only a step to entering the Central Flying School, and when August, 1914, came around, Lieutenant Strange was one of that small band assembled at Dover, ready for war. Charles Grey, like Douhet in Italy and Ferber in France, anticipated the time when observation aircraft would be doing such valuable work that a means of destroying their effectiveness would have to be found. You could, he felt, destroy an aeroplane only with another aeroplane. Louis Strange agreed with Grey. When his squadron established itself at Amiens, he decided to mount a Lewis machine gun in his cockpit for the use of his observer, Lieutenant Penn Gaskell. Strange was positive that eventually all aircraft would carry machine-guns, though no one else in his squadron (except Gaskell) had any faith in his theory. But Strange went ahead and devised and attached a crude mounting for the Lewis gun to the top of the nacelle in front of the observer. Since the Shorthorn was a pusher machine, the firing of the gun would not interfere with the propeller. This was the first Allied aircraft to carry a mounted gun. Strange and Gaskell were very proud of it, and on August 22nd it appeared as though they would have a chance to use it. On this momentous day a Taube flew leisurely over the British aerodrome and the squadron was told to get into the air and chase him away with a few rifle shots. The aircraft took off quickly, with Gaskell's eager hand ready to press the trigger as soon as he was able to get the Taube in his sights. But there was one thing Strange hadn't counted on—the weight of the Lewis gun. The Taube was at 5000 feet. The Henri Farman rose to 3500 feet, but Strange, fine pilot though he was, couldn't coax another foot of altitude out of her. He had to watch sadly while the Taube turned away slowly, disdainfully to head for its home base.

The commanding officer of the squadron had been watching

closely. When Strange landed, he told him curtly to get rid of his Lewis gun and its heavy mounting. "Machine guns are for use on the ground," he said icily. "If your observer wishes, he may carry a rifle with him, but nothing heavier than that."

And so the pilot who might have gained immortality sadly stripped the aircraft that might have made history of its machine gun. But eventually Louis Strange would be vindicated and there would come a day when he would use a machine-gun mounted on his aeroplane with telling effect.

Bombing, too, was in a primitive state. Some pilots carried bombs of various types with them. They were eight- and ten-pounder affairs and a pilot tied them to his belt. On September 1st an unnamed RFC flier dropped two of these on a column of German cavalry near Villiers-Cotterets, causing a stampede among the frightened steeds. Pilots also carried hand-grenades in their pockets. Once the pin was pulled they had about eight seconds to get rid of the grenade before it exploded. But by far the most primitive and least successful of all 'bombs' was a French device used by some RFC pilots. This was a tin container holding a great number of *fléchettes*, small steel arrows about the length and thickness of a pencil. There is no record of any German casualties resulting from their use, but they did come in handy for the odd game of darts; and long after their uselessness as a weapon had been established, British fliers requisitioned them for sport in their own messes.

While the fledgling members of the RFC were beginning to learn their way about the air and to spot German artillery positions, the Royal Naval Air Service had been far from idle. On August 4th the service under the command of Captain Murray Sueter and Captain G. M. Paine boasted forty-three flying officers and ninety-one Flight Sub-Lieutenants and Warrant Officers, some few of whom could pilot aeroplanes. Petty Officers and enlisted men numbered some 700 and the service had at its disposal fifty-two seaplanes and a few landplanes, about half of which were available for flying duty. Sixteen of the seaplanes had been fitted with wireless-telegraphy apparatus with which to keep in touch with seaplane bases when on patrol. The Navy also had seven airships, including the *Willows IV*, the *Delta*, the *Gamma* and the *Eta*.

The main job of the RNAS was to defend the east coast from air attack and to safeguard shipping in the Channel. Only one ship, the *Hermes*, had been refitted to carry three seaplanes, but she was torpedoed during the early weeks of the war, and three cross-Channel steamers, the *Empress*, the *Engadine* and the *Riviera*, were converted to serve as seaplane carriers. The scouting flights made by seaplanes over the Channel and the North Sea were by no means safe. Bad weather and rough water were the chief enemies of the RNAS, and both took a toll in aircraft and lives. Commander J. W. Seddon and his observer, Leading Mechanic R. L. Hartley, lost in fog, became the first men to ditch a plane in World War I. They drifted for eight hours clinging to the wings of their water-soaked but miraculously floating aircraft before being picked up by the small steamer *Orme*.

It now appeared obvious that the Germans were not planning any immediate invasion of England across the Channel, so Mr Winston Churchill, then First Lord of the Admiralty, irritatingly but intelligently suggested to Sir David Henderson of the RFC that perhaps a few naval aircraft could be released from Channel patrol duties and be of some use on the Continent. Henderson, conceding graciously that the Royal Naval Air Service was an ally of sorts, agreed that they could be useful and the Eastchurch Squadron was immediately transferred to French soil, based at Dunkirk and given orders 'to deny all territory within a hundred miles of the city to German Zeppelins and aeroplanes'.

This made Commander Rumney Samson, one of England's most experienced and imaginative pilots, perhaps the happiest man in the Royal Navy, for he commanded the Eastchurch Squadron and he was a man who loved action. His men not only liked the affable, friendly officer, they respected him enormously because he could do anything they could do—better. Three years before, Samson had made the first flight ever from a British warship, *HMS Africa*. He had landed in the water but had been rescued. When designer Horace Short produced England's first seaplane, it was Samson who took off from the water on its initial flight. Samson left for Dunkirk with a group of only four aircraft; the rest would arrive within a week or so, he was told. His other pilots, his fifty mechanics, his few more-or-less armoured cars and a group of marines were ferried across the Channel to Dunkirk to establish a base.

Four aircraft couldn't cover the whole territory, and bad weather was keeping them grounded most of the time, so Samson decided to do a little ground reconnaissance on his own. He was frustrated by the fact that he had no adequate maps of the Dunkirk region, but fate in the person of sixty-nine-year-old Captain Pierre de Moduit of the French Army gave him a helping hand. The elderly captain arrived to welcome Samson in a limousine, accompanied by twelve bottles of champagne, his blonde young wife, eight cans of *pâté de foie gras* and a long-barrelled pistol. He had been born in the district and when he boasted that he knew every road within a hundred miles, Samson smiled and invited him to go on a little scouting expedition. They would take one of the armoured cars on which Samson had already mounted a Maxim machine gun and go looking for Boches. The old gentleman was delighted; he kissed his wife a fond goodbye and he and Samson went looking for trouble. They found it.

Twenty miles from Dunkirk they encountered a German staff car carrying six officers. The doughty Samson opened up with his Maxim, wounding two of the Germans. Meanwhile, de Moduit was banging away with his old-fashioned pistol. But the German car escaped. It was an insignificant engagement but it had a significant result. The German officers indicated that a large German force had occupied the Dunkirk-Cassel district. Two days later a report of German cars in the Lille region sent Samson to that city. He didn't find the German cars, but he found an excited populace which became wildly enthusiastic on seeing a British car for the first time. One delirious character showed his love for his brave ally by exuberantly tossing an empty wine-bottle at the car. It smashed the windscreen and landed squarely on the jaw of the lieutenant.

Samson's urgent pleas for aircraft and armoured cars were heard by Churchill, and the First Lord, with his typical ability to cut through red tape, somehow managed to send some well-armoured cars, several aeroplanes and 250 marines to Dunkirk. Samson worked out a satisfactory form of reconnaissance. He sent his wireless-equipped aircraft out, and when they reported the presence of German detachments, he'd lead his small fleet of cars to the spot. A fairly large German force was reported moving toward Douai, south of Lille. Samson rushed his cars to a bridge over the canal on the eastern outskirts of the city. He held up the German advance just long enough for the entire French garrison of Douai to escape. When the German shellfire became too hot, Samson retired with his cars to the rear. Eight of his men were wounded, a small price to pay for the rescue of a large group of French infantry.

Now Samson, acting on orders from the Admiralty, put himself and his command under the orders of the French general in charge of the district. One of the best airmen alive, he continued to lead his motor cars in what we would now call guerrilla operations. His reasoning was simple: there was no danger in air scouting, there was considerable danger in fighting from poorly armoured cars equipped only with machine guns—and as commander of the squadron he felt that his job was to be in the danger spot. He harried advance German groups, striking quickly and then darting away before the enemy heavy artillery could be brought up to destroy him. These raids put great heart into the desperate, reeling French of the region at a most critical moment.

Meanwhile Samson, impatient of the three or four hours a day for which nature demanded that he should sleep, was directing not only reconnaissance but bombing raids as well. He established an advance base at Antwerp (soon to fall into German hands) and from there sent four aircraft to drop bombs on the dirigible sheds at Düsseldorf and two more to attack Cologne. The weather was bad, with fog and low visibility, and none of the machines reached its target, but significantly all four returned safely. "Looking for the sheds at Düsseldorf," Lieutenant L. H. Collett, one of the pilots, said in disgust, "was like going into a dark room to look for a black cat who wasn't there."

A few days later while Antwerp was actually being evacuated, Samson sent Flight-Lieutenant R. L. G. Marix and Squadron Commander Spenser Grey to try again. Each flew a Sopwith Tabloid to which was attached two twenty-pounder bombs. Grey actually managed to hit the main railway station in Cologne, and Marix, finding clear weather at Düsseldorf, went down to about 600 feet to drop his two eggs squarely on the airship sheds. The sheds immediately burst into flame, destroying a newly-completed Zeppelin (the Z-19). Small-arms fire had pierced his Tabloid in fifty spots but he managed to coax it to within twenty miles of Antwerp before it gave out. He borrowed a bicycle and pedalled to his base. This was the first successful bombing attack on German soil. Twenty-seven years later almost to the day Air Vice-Marshal R. L. G. Marix was to bomb and sink a German vessel in the Norwegian harbour of Aalsund.

Samson had a magnificent group of pilots under his command. In an official report on the activities of the Eastchurch Squadron he was able to make a proud boast. 'Never once,' he wrote, 'did I have to deal with a single disciplinary offence.' The part which airmen of Britain's senior service played during the war has for some obscure reason never fully been publicized, but Samson, Collett, Grey and Marix were typical of the men who flew—or fought in armoured cars—under the insignia of the Royal Navy.

The Naval Air Service was technically a defence force whose job it was to protect England itself from invasion. Churchill, always a belligerently-minded character, believed as did everyone else that the only danger of England being hurt would come from the Zeppelins, but he believed too that the best way to minimize this danger was to destroy the dirigibles in their own lairs. So he passed the word along that the bombing of any Zeppelin shed anywhere at all would be part of the defence tactics of the Royal Naval Air Service. The delighted naval pilots took the hint.

Zeppelins, unlike aeroplanes, could not be hidden. British intelligence knew that at least two of them were in sheds at Friedrichshafen on Lake Constance. Lieutenant Pemberton Billings planned and Commander E. F. Briggs led an aerial foray against the sheds which was in every way a model of preparation and execution. Four Avros with eighty-horse-power engines were utilized for the operation. Four pilots—Briggs, Flight-Commander John T. Babington, Sub-Lieutenant R. P. Cannon and Flight-Lieutenant S. V. Sippe—together with eleven mechanics moved to an airship shed near the frontier town of Belfort, the closest French point to Lake Constance. Because spies were prevalent in this border area they made the move at night. The raid would be a dangerous one and Pemberton Billings, whose brain child it was, decided to be sure that the Zeppelins were still nesting at Friedrichshafen. Disguising himself in peasant clothes he crossed Lake Constance in a small boat, thoroughly explored the potential target and returned with the information that the Zeps were resting comfortably. Had he been caught, he would, of course, have been shot.

Each aircraft carried four twenty-pounder bombs. On take-off the Avro, piloted by Cannon, found the extra eighty-pound bomb load too much for it; it failed to rise from the ground, smashed its tail skid, and a rueful Cannon had to nurse his bruises and discouragement while his three squadron mates took off safely. The flight was complicated by the fact that they had to fly an erratic course in order to avoid violating Swiss neutrality. The course, as planned so meticulously by Billings, was from Belfort to Mulhausen, across the Black Forest to a point north of Schaffhausen and then south to Lake Constance—a distance of 125 miles and a long, long trip for a heavily laden little Avro. All three aircraft arrived at Lake Constance on schedule. They went down to within ten feet of the water to avoid detection and then, when they were five miles from the target, climbed to a height of 1200 feet. Flight-Lieutenant Sippe's log tells the story graphically but tersely:

When half a mile from sheds, put machine into dive and came down to 700 feet. Observed men lined up to right of shed, number estimated 300 to 500. Dropped one bomb in enclosure to put gunners off aim and when in correct position put two into shed. The fourth bomb failed to release. Made several unsuccessful attempts to get it away, turned, went down to just above surface of lake and made off.

Babington and Briggs delivered equally successful attacks and had the satisfaction of seeing the sheds and adjacent gas-works in flames. They heard a frightful explosion which threw flames several hundred feet into the air. Babington returned safely, but machine-gun fire from the ground pierced a fuel line in Briggs' aircraft and he was forced to land not far from the burning sheds. The civilians who grabbed him treated him badly, but he was rescued by German troops who took him to hospital. When he recovered, he was wined and fêted by German air officers, for these men had an admiration for bravery and they recognized that this was one of the most courageous feats of the war. And at this early stage Briggs was not an enemy to them—he was a comrade of the air who happened to be wearing a British uniform.

But the raid gave rise to two charges by the Germans: first they claimed that the bombs were dropped in a 'barbaric' manner upon civilians at Friedrichshafen, and secondly that the British aircraft had violated Swiss neutrality. The first charge was dismissed as absurd by the British Foreign Office (those who were killed were German Air Force mechanics and crewmen of the Zeppelins), but the second charge was considered carefully. The meticulous plan of Pemberton Billings was studied, as were the log books of the two pilots who had returned. Then the Foreign Office delivered a very temperate diplomatic note to Swisss authorities, stating that if there had been any violation of neutrality it was entirely unauthorized and unintentional.

The Swiss Government and the Swiss Press accepted the gracious explanation. Strangely enough, the *Berliner Tageblatt* printed the whole story, complete with British explanation and the Swiss acceptance of it. 'The incident,' the influential newspaper said, 'is now regarded as closed.'

The war had lasted only two months and both the RFC and the RNAS had seen some action and had proven their worth. Of course, they hadn't really been hurt as yet, but severe tests were waiting for them.

Meanwhile, the French had done little in the air except provide interesting targets for their own infantrymen.

The first French air casualty was the dirigible *Montgolfier*.

It had been sent aloft to see what direction the German First Army was taking. As it flew over the lines, thousands of French *poilus*, mistaking it for a Zeppelin, opened up enthusiastically with rifles and machine guns, and the *Montgolfier* died a lingering death.

The aeroplanes had only slightly better luck. The heaviest concentration of machines was in the Verdun-Toul-Nancy area. Three dirigibles and three escadrilles (six aircraft each) were stationed here, for the French expected that the principal German attack would be hurled at this region. Actually the main attack was launched through Maubeuge and Mezières and westwards into Belgium. The French had two escadrilles at Mezières, but mists and low clouds were constant visitors to this vicinity, and though the bad weather didn't bother the German ground troops, it grounded the aircraft during five important days in August while the pattern of attack was being developed by the Germans. When the weather improved, the handful of machines was told to find out where the Germans were concentrating, but the area assigned was far too large to be covered adequately. In all fifteen flights went out from Mezières: seven were ordered over Belgian Luxembourg, five into Luxembourg itself and only three to reconnoitre the railroads north of Luxembourg, where German troops were actually massing. It was the French plan that all reports of aerial observation be immediately forwarded to the Deuxième Bureau (Intelligence Section) to be interpreted, summarized and then sent to GHQ.

This was done, and the Intelligence Section, after due deliberation, gave its estimate of German strength to GHQ, and it was this estimate on which General Joffre relied. The estimate made by Intelligence was that the Germans had eight army corps and four cavalry divisions between Holland and a point north of Luxembourg. Actually, at that moment there were sixteen army corps and five cavalry divisions ready for the attack. The first French attempt at strategic aerial reconnaissance was completely ineffective, although some of the blame must go to poor interpretation of information gathered by the pilots. Just as pilots were inexperienced in judging numbers

of troops and installations on the ground, so were the intelligence officers inexperienced in interpreting correctly the
information received.

Both would soon improve tremendously.

Chapter Four

MAD DAYS OF TRIAL AND ERROR

DURING THE first months of the war the majestic scale of
the fighting by infantry and artillery and the huge scale
of the casualties caused the spotlight of world attention to be
centred on the ground fighting to the exclusion of everything
else. By November, the Allies had suffered a 1,000,000 casualties, a fantastic figure never to be eclipsed in any three-month
period throughout the war. The aeroplane had been responsible for for virtually none of these dead or wounded. As yet,
the public—and this was true of every belligerent country as
well as the United States—hadn't awakened to the fact that a
young and potentially terrible weapon was being forged in the
crucible of war.

An interesting commentary on the ignorance of the German public as to the part being played by the aeroplane was
reflected in the German Press. Careful examination of every
article, news story and official report in eight leading German
newspapers—*Norddeutsche Allgemeine Zeitung, Berliner
Lokal-Anzeiger, Vossiche Zeitung, Berliner Tageblatt, Vor-
wärts, Frankfurter Zeitung, Kölnische Zeitung* and *Ham-
burger Nachtrichten*—reveals only one story which mentions
air activity during the whole month of December, 1914. On
December 22nd the *Kölnische Zeitung* (Cologne Press) carried a story on one of its back pages. Its single headline ran,
A GERMAN NAVAL AIRMAN OVER DOVER, and it was written by
Dr George Wagener. It read:

I was at noon today in a place on the Belgian seacoast, a
witness of the safe return of naval airman First Lieutenant

von Prondzynsk who ascended at 9.30 am in the direction of Dover. He had reached Dover and there thrown several bombs, one of which might have hit the harbour railway station. He observed between Dover and Calais two rows of torpedo-boat destroyers drawn up in line from the English to the French coast, apparently to protect traffic, also several ships in Dover harbour, among them one of the *Majestic* class; likewise ships not far from Dunkirk. . . . Clear weather prevailed there, while we had fog and rain. With the wind he flew back in an hour from Dover to our positions. The bold airman was heartily congratulated for this first excursion of a German seaplane to the English coast.

In the same month Chancellor Dr von Bethmann Hollweg, wearing the field-grey uniform of the General Staff, addressed the Reichstag. He reviewed the whole conduct of the war up to that time in a two-hour speech which was fully reported on the front pages of the newspapers mentioned. He went into detail concerning the activities on the Western Front, and he praised the *Landwehr* (infantry) which had captured the 'impregnable fortresses' of Liège, Namur, Antwerp and Maubeuge, and he paid fulsome tribute to the heroic efforts of the cavalry and artillery. He told of the naval victory at Coronel and eulogized the cruisers *Goben* and *Breslau*, and then paid eloquent—and deserved—tribute to the *Emden*, "the little ship which has made every sea unsafe for the enemy and before which fleets of our enemies tremble. I call your attention," he continued, "to the glorious deeds of our submarines which are today the terror of the whole British Navy and the whole British nation." But he never mentioned the Fokkers, the Taubes or any of the aircraft that had been doing earnest if unspectacular work during the first months of the war.

Occasionally bombs dropped upon cavalry induced temporary panic, and once in a great while a bombing operation like the one at Friedrichshafen really produced results, but on the whole, bombing was nearly worthless as a deterrent to the movement of ground troops. A close survey made by RFC experts revealed the disquieting fact that only three out of 141 attempts to hinder movements of ground troops by bombing railway stations and like objectives had been successful.

The British and French co-operated efficiently, and when both had studied the bombing reports, they made a joint decision to restrict bombing operations to enemy headquarters, telephone exchanges, ammunition and poison-gas dumps, and railway crossings or goods yards. To send a single aircraft or even four or five to find and hit such relatively small targets would be too much of a haphazard affair.

If the effect of bombing was disappointing, the results of air reconnaissance were at least promising, and in the retreat from Mons, and in the battles of the Marne and the Aisne, better than that. But observation was limited to the eyesight and judgment of the observer, and the eye is a notoriously fallible organ. Deficiencies of the eyesight and of human memory kept observation from being really accurate. The answer, of course, was the camera. The French were far in advance of the British in experimenting with cameras, and Major W. G. H. Salmond of the RFC was ordered to make a thorough study of their equipment and methods. As a result of his report, a separate photographic unit—consisting of Lieutenant J. T. C. Moore-Brabazon (later Lord Brabazon of Tara) and Lieutenant C. D. M. Campbell, working in co-operation with the Thornton-Pickard Manufacturing Company—was organized and told to design a camera that would take pictures from a height and whose plates could be quickly developed. They came up with the basic answer in two months. The observer held the camera by two straps, leaned over the side of the aircraft and took his pictures. In the first weeks of 1915 this camera proved its worth. An attack had been ordered across the La Bassée Canal. Photographs were taken of the German-held territory south of the canal, and a new German trench, bristling with infantry and machine guns, the existence of which had been unsuspected, emerged clearly from the prints. The attack was modified accordingly and was completely successful. Now additional cameras were ordered and men were trained to use them and to interpet the pictures.

The role of the observer and his camera was becoming increasingly important, and both sides realized that new and improved two-seater aircraft would be needed. The mortality among aeroplanes was high, although very few were caused by enemy action. Engine failure, poor maintenance and the fact that most airfields were merely hastily converted pastures or meadows all combined to destroy a great many aircraft and their pilots. After three months of war the official German records show that already fifty-two German pilots had been killed and one hundred machines destroyed. French and British anti-aircraft fire was almost non-existent, however, and most of these casualties were caused by accidents. As yet no air force recognized the importance of frequent checking and overhauling of machines; they were flown until sheer exhaustion of wings and engines resulted in crashes that proper maintenance would have prevented.

Towards the end of 1914, both sides began to realize that the best way to prevent observation aircraft from returning to their bases with useful information about troop movements was to destroy the machines. No one was quite clear about how this would be done, although the Germans did improve their anti-aircraft guns and gave their production a higher priority than they had enjoyed before. Later in the year an order from the German General Staff said:

> Aviators on reconnaissance should be provided with pistols and hand-grenades. Though these latter produce no appreciable result for the most part, nevertheless they have an important effect in creating alarm among the enemy and should therefore be employed.

The idea that you might destroy an enemy aircraft by hurling a hand grenade at it is a bit fantastic, but nothing was too bizarre to be tried in the dying months of 1914. The German public was beginning to get rather impatient about the inactivity of the Zeppelins. Berlin newspapers still fed them stories of what the dirigibles were going to do: there was apparently no restriction on what military correspondents were allowed to write. It is possible that the stories were inspired by official sources to keep high the hopes of the people. One story which had wide circulation in the German Press was to the effect that during the last week of 1914 a fleet of fifty Zeppelins would visit London and destroy the capital. Another story, front-paged prominently, revealed that a fleet of flat-bottomed boats would soon be ready to carry an invading army across the Channel and that this fleet would be escorted by thirty Zeppelins. There was absolutely no basis of fact in either of these reports.

There was one thing that was kept from the German public: the initial failure of the reports by German observers in aeroplanes had on the whole been just as bad as those given by the French, and the German Staff felt that this was due to the fact that the aircraft travelled too fast to permit an observer to make accurate observation. The dirigible could glide along at ten miles an hour if necessary and theoretically it could rise far above the range of machine gun and rifle fire from the ground. The High Command decided to try out the Zeppelin as a combination bomber-observer.

Late in August one Zeppelin, the Z-6, made a dramatic but hardly successful appearance. The German First and Second Armies under General von Emmich encountered strong and unexpected opposition from the Belgian forts at Liège. The Z-6 was assigned to bomb these forts. At that time no one in the world knew much about aerial bombing. For three days the efficient German artillery had hammered away at the forts; now some highly imaginative German officer assigned a dirigible to do a job that the finest artillery known had found too difficult. The Z-6 actually carried artillery shells on its strange mission. Badly overloaded, although its bomb load was only 440 pounds, the dirigible couldn't rise above 3000 feet. Its artillery shells fell harmlessly, but the airship was so low that it became vulnerable to machine gun fire from the ground. Riddled with bullets, its gas began to seep away, and instead of reaching its home base it fell into a forest near Bonn, to be completely wrecked.

A few weeks later the Z-7 and Z-8 were sent over Lorraine in an attempt to determine the exact French positions. Each carried a small bomb load. The Z-7 was met with machine gun fire and hastily dropped its absurd 'bombs', more to lighten its load than to inflict damage. It was the custom to carry a General Staff officer on each Zeppelin, and he was in command. Despite the fact that Z-7 was losing a lot of precious gas from the wounds inflicted on her frail body, the staff officer (making his first flight in an airship) insisted that the crew carry on. It could now attain a height of only 2500 feet, and when it flew over another French infantry group, it received its death blow from machine guns. The Z-8 was surprised by gunfire from German troops as it approached the front. They had been warned, but trigger-happy infantrymen had got into the habit of shooting at anything in the air, and they inflicted several bad wounds on the Z-8 which lost altitude as it reached French positions, and a few well-placed machine gun bullets finished it off.

Later the Zeppelin would develop into a pretty formidable psychological weapon, but during the early months of the war it was virtually useless. General Krafft von Dellmensingen, chief of the Sixth Army, who had ordered the aerial reconnaissance by the dirigibles, now decided that such means of locating enemy positions were worthless. He wrote his opinion to the German Staff in no uncertain terms. 'More and more I arrive at the conviction,' he said acidly, 'that we can only create clarity by battle.'

Which is exactly what Karl von Clausewitz had said one hundred years before.

It was obvious that the two-seater observation aircraft, if not the perfect answer, was the only available answer to finding out what the enemy was doing. As the importance of the aeroplane became more evident, it became equally evident that more accurate means than a hurled hand grenade had to be devised to stop it. The Germans began to do a great deal of shooting at French and British machines; in addition to rifles and revolvers they had mounted machine guns on the front of their pusher-type aircraft and on the side of the fuselage. They hadn't as yet done any real damage, but it was becoming obvious that a new weapon of war was being forged.

The British and the French, too, were experimenting with guns.

Some French and British pilots had sockets on either side of and behind the cockpit into which a Lewis could be slipped. When this didn't work out too well, someone conceived the idea of mounting a machine gun on the centre section of the top wing to be fired over the propeller. The gun could be triggered by a cable running from the gun to the side of the pilot. One disadvantage (never really resolved) was the difficulty of changing the empty drum of ammunition on the gun while still retaining control of the single-seater aircraft. The pilot had to grip the control stick with his knees, reach high over his head with both hands, remove the empty drum and attach the new one.

Lieutenant Louis Strange had a harrowing if bizarre experience while trying to change the ammunition drum of a Martinsyde equipped with one of these guns. Strange was still intent upon marrying the aeroplane and machine gun. Transferred to No 6 Squadron, his commanding officer was Major Gordon Shepherd, and Shepherd, who a year later would become the youngest brigadier-general in the Army, was a man who liked imaginative pilots. Pilots, of course, had not yet attained the status of specialists; there were no bomber pilots, fighter pilots or observation pilots as such. A pilot was expected to be—and had to be—a man capable of flying any aircraft on any assigned mission. In one week Strange, for instance, flew an Avro, a Farman Shorthorn, a BE2 and finally a Martinsyde Scout.

One afternoon Strange was on a photographic mission in the BE2 with Lieutenant Awcock handling the camera. A German Aviatik made six passes at the British aircraft, but its observer was apparently a bad shot, for although he had a machine gun, all of his bullets went wild. Finally Strange managed to get his plane between the blazing sun and the German machine. He headed for it, swerved, and Awcock raised his rifle and fired one shot—it killed the pilot and the Aviatik plunged to the ground in a vertical spin. Strange followed it down to watch it crash in Houthulst Forest.

The next day a Martinsyde single-seater biplane arrived at No 6 Squadron. Strange took one look at it and asked Shepherd if he could make the aircraft his own. Strange didn't know anything about the Martinsyde except what he saw— that it was a single-seater with machine gun attached.

He was given the machine and he tried it out. A year later an improved Martinsyde would be welcomed by pilots, but Strange discovered that this early version was an unstable affair with very little aileron control. Even though it was a single-seater, the weight of the machine gun mounted on the top wing hampered its performance to such an extent that it climbed no faster than the Avro, which carried two men. It took nearly half the fuel and all the pilot's energy to get this clumsy aircraft up to 8000 feet, but Strange loved it—it had a machine gun.

One day early in 1915, the Martinsyde gave him the fright of his life. Strange had finally pushed his plane up to 8500 feet when an Aviatik dived at him. Happy to be in single combat at last, Strange emptied his whole ammunition drum at the German without apparent effect. Now he had to change the drum. He stood up in the cockpit and yanked at the empty drum. It stuck, and he gave it another yank. He pulled too hard and lost his balance, inadvertently releasing his control stick, and before he could recover it his aircraft had turned over on its back. The strain snapped his safety belt, and he was tossed completely out of the cockpit. By some miracle of mental and physical co-ordination he maintained his desperate grip on the ammunition drum. He was dangling in space, and then his machine dropped away, spinning crazily toward the earth. By a superhuman effort he was able to swing his legs into the cockpit above him. He scrambled for the stick and somehow managed to right the aircraft, which was only a second or two from crashing. The strain had tossed his pilot's seat out of the aircraft, and his instruments were either whirling dizzily or not indicating anything at all. By superb flying instinct he guided the unresponsive machine back to his base. When it was examined, it was discovered that every instrument had been broken, but Strange wasn't even bruised.

These were the mad days of trial and error. There was no precedent for the kind of flying one had to do. Manœuvres had to be improvised, and many pilots met their death by falling out of aircraft in incidents like the one which Strange experienced. Parachutes? There were plenty of them, but they were reserved for the men in the observation balloons. There was nothing new about the parachute. It had been anticipated by Leonardo da Vinci in the fifteenth century and actually used successfully by S. Lenormand, a French balloonist, in 1783. In 1912, Captain Berry, an American pilot, baled out of an aeroplane and landed safely. One reason why parachutes were not adopted was their size; they were heavy and bulky. There just wasn't room enough in the cockpit of an aircraft for pilot and parachute. Then there were so many naked wires and struts on some machines that it was thought it would not be possible to clear them if a pilot had to jump. A month of research would undoubtedly have resulted in the compact 'seat pack' developed in Germany sometime in 1916 and perfected by the United States late in 1918, but in 1915 the lack of the life-saving canopy of silk caused the deaths of hundreds of airmen who might otherwise have been saved.

Designers on both sides had been working desperately to improve all existing types of aircraft, and in 1915 a few of them made their bows. Some turned out to be so hopeless that they were immediately forgotten, but a few would make aerial history. Early in the year the French produced two relatively useful machines. The first was the two-seater reconnaissance Caudron G-III with an uncowled 100 hp Anzani engine. Its great virtue was the fact that it could stay aloft for four hours, making it the first really effective machine for long-range observation work. It could also rise above the then limited range of the German guns. The second was the first of a long series of Nieuport single-seaters. This was a vee-strutter, a fast little biplane capable of 107 mph. It was not very strong structurally, but it was watched with keen interest by French designers and, as its weaknesses were noted, engineers immediately went to work to eliminate them.

This first Nieuport Scout was the forerunner of the great fighting aircraft which in the months to come would make Captain Albert Ball and Billy Bishop famous, and which would bring world-wide recognition to the 'Stork' group of the French Air Force.

The Bristol also brought out their new Bristol Bullet: it had no armament but it was a delight to fly, and the 178 pounds (not gallons) of petrol and oil it carried in its tanks could keep it aloft for two and a half hours, even at its maximum speed of ninety miles an hour.

Germany produced the Albatros, a two-seater bomber or reconnaissance aircraft. Battle Squadron No 1 (colloquially known as the Ostend Carrier Pigeons), commanded by Baron von Gerstoff, used this biplane with considerable success. On January 28th, 1915, Gerstoff led his squadron in a night bombing expedition over Dunkirk, the war's first such operation. Several dozen fires were lit in the city and all of Gerstoff's aircraft returned safely. Five young German pilots who would later gain immortality were flying the Albatros under the leadership of Baron von Gerstoff—Buckler, Goering, Loerzer, Richthofen and Udet.

The Germans produced only one new single-seater aircraft at this time, but it was the Fokker E-2 and it was responsible for making the names of Wintgens, Immelmann, Leffers, Hohendorf, Boelcke, Parschou and von Althaus household words in Germany. It was with the advent of the E-2 that the period of the Fokker Scourge began.

It started, of course, when Roland Garros made his unlucky forced landing, and the secret of his primitive method of shooting through a propeller became German property. When Tony Fokker devised a scientific version of the same thing, it gave the German Air Force domination in the air. Oswald Boelcke, the first to fly the Fokker E-2 with the synchronized gun, reported that the weight of the gun spoiled the performance of the machine, so Fokker hurriedly supplied a more powerful engine and forwarded one aircraft to Boelcke and another to Lieutenant Max Immelmann.

Immelmann was more imaginative than most pilots. His orders were to lurk high above the German lines and wait for British aircraft on their way to photograph installations. He was one of the first to use the sun as an aid; he often swooped down out of the sun upon the tail of an unsuspecting Allied aircraft, and as often as not the first inkling of danger to the victim would be the rattle of machine gun fire over his head. If his shots went wild, he had another trick up his sleeve that enabled him to initiate a second attack without waste of time.

He would pull his stick up sharply, making the nose of the Fokker rise as though he were beginning a loop; but at the top of the loop he did a half-roll and came out flying in the opposite direction, with the needed height regained. It took the British airmen completely by surprise.

They soon afterwards paid him the compliment of imitating it, and the Immelmann Roll became a standard manœuvre. But in the spring of 1915 it was a frightening, revolutionary way to destroy an opposing enemy aircraft.

Immelmann, the war's first aerial hero, was a short man with piercing eyes and an inquiring mind. Fighting in the air was a serious intellectual pursuit for him. Even the men who flew with him and who admired him never understood him. He was arrogant, unsocial and petulant. War was not a sporting adventure to Immelmann, as it was to be a bit later with Richthofen; it was, for the moment, his profession and he studied it and mastered it as few others ever did. After his fourth victory over Allied aircraft, the German Staff decided to make a national hero out of him. He was the first pilot to be widely publicized, and the German public, weary of the impersonal, formal reports from the Front and anxious to transfer its fanatical nationalistic urge to something more tangible than praise of a crack division, poured out its collective heart in worship of Max Immelmann. Immelmann, with the Prussian's contempt for the masses, would have none of it. He was more interested in the development of new aircraft and techniques.

German aircraft and engine manufacturers were in sharp competition. To a great extent the orders they received depended upon what the pilots themselves thought of their engines and their machines. Each manufacturer rented rooms in Berlin's best hotels, and a pilot on leave could bask in luxury at the expense of those who made the aircraft they flew. There was no word in German for 'lobbyist' then, but the industrialists of 1915 anticipated the manufacturers and pressure-groups of today by providing everything in the way of alcoholic and feminine charms for the customer. And the pilot was the customer.

Young Tony Fokker had a passion for sugar, a dislike for alcohol and an indifference towards the well-equipped and cheerfully acquiescent Berlin girls. But like the other aircraft manufacturers, he had to play the game, and at Berlin's fine

Bristol Hotel he always kept several suites well stocked with the usual alcoholic, caloric and pulchritudinous commodities for the use of pilots. Max Immelmann came back from the front, checked in at the Bristol as Fokker's guest, and then dismissed the usual entertainment with an impatient frown. He wanted to talk aeroplanes with Tony Fokker. The relieved Fokker hurried him to Schwerin and for two days the pilot and designer discussed aircraft, engines and machine guns.

Especially machine guns: Immelmann had become a deadly shot. He had discovered that most machine guns operated erratically: they were constantly jamming and they were inaccurate. Immelmann believed that no pilot could hit a moving target with the existing guns at more than seventy-five or eighty yards. He invariably held his fire until he was close enough (in the inelegant phrase of his fellow pilots) 'to spit into the enemy's cockpit': allowing his opponent to have the first few hundred shots from a distance was a calculated risk he was willing to take. He felt that a good pilot shouldn't need more than twenty or twenty-five shots to hit his man. Once he returned from having shot down a French aircraft with only thirteen bullets gone from his ammunition drum. He seldom needed more than twenty-five.

He and Fokker talked earnestly about how to improve the existing E-2. Out of these conversations came the Fokker E-3 and its twin air-cooled Spandau machine guns.

Like every other World War I aircraft of this phase, its instrumentation was almost non-existent. There was no instrument panel as such. It had no air-speed indicator, for example. In terms of combat specifications that would develop a year later, the E-3 was notoriously weak, but it had little or no opposition. The aircraft itself wasn't designed for air combat; it was a reconnaisance machine to which Fokker had added his synchronized gun. It was highly successful only because German pilots like Immelmann and Boelcke were smart enough to exploit its strength fully and correspondingly exploit the basic weaknesses of Allied aircraft.

Max Immelmann took his new machine to the front and became an even more spectacular success than he had been with the E-2, and after his eighth victory he was awarded the

Empire's highest decoration for military bravery, the *Pour le Mérite*.

Coincident with his rise was that of his friend Oswald Boelcke, a Saxon, and the son of a schoolteacher. Trained as an engineer, Boelcke took to flying almost instinctively; he flew solo after seven hours of instruction, and in 1914 and early 1915 did reconnaissance work. His natural flying ability soon manifested itself and he was transferred to a single-seater aircraft. Boelcke soon earned the love of the whole German people and the ungrudging respect of his foes, not only because of his ability but because of his nature. Generous, warm-hearted, he shrank from killing, and when he shot down a British aircraft without meting out death to the pilot, he invariably visited the defeated pilot in the hospital or prison camp. He would arrive laden with wine, cigarettes and food, and long after the war British pilots wrote warmly of this generous enemy.

Boelcke and Immelmann were at this time the only two pilots known to the German public; neither the French nor the British had as yet realized the morale factor of creating national heroes. But the pilots who would be national, and in some cases international, heroes were learning their trade in 1915, and soon they would emerge not only as the most glamorous, exciting figures ever to stir the imaginations of their countrymen, but as great national assets.

By the summer of 1915, both French and British aircraft had been equipped with the synchronized gun, and the overwhelming advantage which the Fokkers had enjoyed for the past months was lost to them. Now when a French machine shot down a German, the Paris newspapers noted the fact. On July 19th, 1915, Corporal Georges Guynemer destroyed a Taube. During the next week he shot down two more, and then, in what was the most spectacular aerial feat of the war, he shot down three Germans in one morning! Overnight the name Guynemer flashed like a rocket across the eyes of France. It had been a sorry winter, a discouraging spring; and now, at long last, France had something to boast about.

Newspapers sent feature-writers scurrying to gather material on the war's first French air hero. They were delighted to discover that he came from an old and honoured family. Guynemers had helped to mould history from the days of Charlemagne to the time of Napoleon; August Guynemer had courageously opposed Robespierre, and Achille Guynemer had fought with great distinction in Spain in 1812. The young pilot's father had been a distinguished officer and scholar. Georges, his only son, was the last of the line.

The twenty-year-old pilot had been a sickly boy of almost feminine beauty. Too frail to engage in outdoor sports, he threw his energies into studying, and at the Stanislaus College in Paris he received highest honours in mathematics as well as Latin. He wanted to be an engineer and he spent his holidays haunting factories which manufactured engines. Blériot and Santos-Dumont were his idols, and he told his schoolmates with confidence that one day he too would be a pilot and designer of aeroplanes.

The war came and this impetuous son of a long line of military ancestors rushed to enlist. He was shocked when rejected as being physically unfit. Three more times during the following months he was rejected, and then he went to the aviation camp at Pau, bearded a friend of his father's, Captain Bernard-Thierry, in his office and made out such a strong case that he was accepted as a student mechanic. It was about as humble a beginning as the future Ace of Aces could have made, but it wasn't long before the fine technical knowledge he had attained at college, added to the practical knowledge he had picked up in factories, made him outstanding. The *Étude Raisonnée de l'Aéroplane* by Jules Bordeaux had been his bible, and he could discourse with authority to his awestruck fellow mechanics on kinematics and dynamics, and he could explain to them what was meant by the resultant and the equilibrium of forces. At Pau he assisted in repairing smashed aircraft and soon knew every bolt, screw, wire and part of this winged contraption which would soon release him from the voluntary servitude he was undergoing. He asked his father to put in a word for him; many of the men with whom the elder Guynemer had gone through St Cyr were now generals, and the influence of one of them helped to promote the son from mechanic to student pilot. He took to flying in much the same manner as had Oswald Boelcke.

He flew solo in a fifty-horse power Blériot on March 10th, 1915, and killed his first German four months and nine days later. In his approach to flying he was much like Immelmann; above all he was a technician who wanted to make himself almost literally a part of the machine he flew. Each of his senses was receiving an education which, little by little, would make it an instrument capable of registering pertinent facts and effecting security for himself and his aeroplane. His eyes were excellent, and he soon became an outstanding marksman; his ears compensated for the frailness of his body; they could interpret the sound made by the wind on the piano wires, the struts, the tension wires, the canvas of his machine. The determination that had made him insist upon excelling in mathematics and Latin at school now made him determine to be the best pilot in the world, and there are those still alive who say that he reached his goal.

It was during the first week of June that he was assigned to Escadrille MS3 at Vauciennes near Villes-Cotterets in the beautiful Valois country. This would later be the famous Stork Escadrille. He was given a two-seater Morane-Saulnier Parasol monoplane to fly, and each day he went up carrying an observer. This early Parasol was awkward and sensitive to fly and many pilots shied away from it; Guynemer never had any trouble with it. On several occasions while on observation flights he had been fired on by rifles in the hands of German observers; he was lucky enough not to have met any of the Fokkers with their synchronized guns. He decided to fit a machine gun to his Parasol, and although the extra weight was at times a handicap, it was the gun which brought him his first victory on July 19th. His companion on that day was Jean Guerder, an observer-gunner. When they returned Guynemer wrote in his diary:

Started with Guerder after a Boche reported at Couvres and caught up with him over Pierrefonds. Shot one belt, machine gun jammed, then unjammed. The Boche fled and landed in the direction of Laon. At Coucy we turned back and saw an Aviatik going towards Soissons at about 3200 metres up. We followed him, and as soon as he was within our lines we dived and placed ourselves about fifty metres under and behind him at the left. At our first salvo, the Aviatik lurched, and we saw a part of the machine crack. He replied with rifle shots, one bullet hitting a wing, another grazing Guerder's hand and head. At our last shot the pilot sank down on the body frame, the observer raised his arms, and the Aviatik fell straight downwards, in flames, between the trenches....

Their job on that day was to gather information and land with it at Carrière l'Eveque, artillery headquarters for the sector. The brief three-minute battle had been in full view of thousands of troops and of the men at the artillery post. When they landed, the colonel in charge congratulated them and poured champagne.

"How old are you?" he asked Guerder.

"Twenty-two," the observer said.

"And you?" he turned to the pilot.

"Twenty," Guynemer answered.

"My God," the colonel exploded, "Have we only children left to do the fighting?"

But Guynemer was not the only young pilot who was attracting the attention of his countrymen. Lieutenant Charles Nungesser, a crack boxer before the war, began the war as a member of a regiment of Hussars. By the end of August, 1914, he had already won the Military Medal. He transferred to aviation and after a few months was given a Morane to fly. He made an inauspicious beginning: he crashed, breaking both legs and his jaw and acquiring a variety of internal injuries. But although he couldn't walk without canes, he had a savage obstinacy; within a month he was flying again and when he brought down two Germans in one day his name came to the notice of the public. Adjutant René Dorme, called 'The Unbreakable' (he brought down four Germans in eight hours), Lieutenant Navarre and Lieutenant Jean Chaput were others whose names began to make news. Chaput was an engineer in the *École Supérieure d'Electricité* before joining the Air Force, and he was one of those who in early 1915 referred to himself as 'Fokker Fodder'. He was wounded and shot down twice by Fokker E-2s, but somehow survived. He introduced a suicidal manœuvre in aerial combat which few had the temerity to follow. He couldn't outshoot the Fokker, he told his friends in his squadron, but his engineering experience convinced him that if he could make contact with the frail rear end of the Fokker with his propeller, the impact would sheer the fabric and rudder away, leaving the aircraft helpless.

"But won't you crash, too?" he was asked.

"Ah," he laughed, "My engineering training hasn't given me an answer to that question, but I am going to try it."

He did, and lived to tell the story. He sheered off the tail of the Fokker, but his propeller smashed when it made contact. The broken German machine went down and Chaput managed to glide to earth to make a landing just behind his own lines. During the spring of 1915, he also brought down four balloons, a feat in those days ranking with the destruction of four German aircraft; and then he destroyed a Fokker with only four bullets from his machine gun. A fine shot, he invariably aimed not for the enemy aeroplane but for the enemy pilot. A few days later, in a fight two miles above the earth, he was seriously wounded in the thigh. He fainted but recovered consciousness 1000 feet from the ground. By that time he had picked up two more bullets in his right arm. He had lost all sense of direction, but he recognized the French lines. Half conscious, he flew above the lines until he saw an ambulance below. He reasoned that where there was an ambulance there must be a doctor—so he made a hurried descent, pancaking his aircraft on the rough ground but winding up reasonably intact fifty yards from the ambulance. The twenty-two-year-old pilot made a rapid recovery and was in the air again within a month.

There were several Americans serving obscurely in the French forces, quite unconscious of the fact that destiny had a sharp eye on them. Gervais Raoul Lufbery had been born in France and had remained there when his parents went to America. Later he joined them in Wallingford, Connecticut, and became an American citizen. He was a man of insatiable curiosity with the incurable virus of wanderlust in his veins.

After a spell in the United States Army, he wandered around the Far East working at any odd job in any city until his curiosity was satisfied. He finally wound up in Calcutta, where he met Marc Pourpe, an itinerant French pilot, and became his mechanic. Pourpe taught him to fly and the two adventure-some souls gave exhibitions all over India, China and Japan. They transferred their activities to Egypt, where Pourpe made history in a non-stop flight, Cairo to Khartoum and return. In the summer of 1914 they went to Paris to buy a Morane, but August caught up with them. When war was declared, Pourpe went into the Air Force while Lufbery enlisted in the Foreign Legion. After a few weeks he transferred to aviation, and his request to be made Pourpe's mechanic was granted. In December, Pourpe, one of the most experienced pilots in the world, was killed and Lufbery, determined to avenge his friend, immediately applied for pilot training. During the spring and summer of 1915 he was learning the game on Maurice Farmans and Voisins, was breveted as a pilot and assigned to Bombardment Squadron No 1. He was disappointed at not being given a single-seater to fly, but, rather incredibly in view of his experience (and his later record), he had shown no aptitude for handling the smaller, faster machines. His instructors said that he was clumsy, lacking in the sensitivity of control necessary to fly as a *pilote de chasse*.

Bert Hall of Kentucky, who enlisted in the Foreign Legion two days after war broke out, had transferred to the French Air Force and was flying with Escadrille MS38; William Thaw of Pittsburg, who had served as an observer during the first months of the war, was now a pilot with Escadrille C42. James Bach (later to hold the unhappy distinction of being the first American to be taken prisoner of war), Kiffin Rockwell of Asheville, North Carolina, Norman Prince of Boston, Massachusetts, and Elliot Cowdin of New York were also in the Air Force. Victor Chapman of New York had just transferred from the Foreign Legion to aviation and was training at Avord. Prince, Thaw, Cowdin, Hall, Rockwell and Chapman would be six of the original seven members of the *Escadrille Americaine*, later the *Escadrille Lafayette*.

Bert Hall was the prototype of the soldier of fortune. He

learned to fly in France in 1910, and by 1913 was in the service of Abdul Hamid, Sultan of Turkey, who was engaged in a little war with Bulgaria. It is a strange paradox that this Mohammedan was one of the few reigning rulers to have read and absorbed the principles of Giulio Douhet. He decided to have an air force and the rumour reached Paris that the Near-East potentate would pay a hundred gold dollars a day to any experienced pilot. Hall had just scraped up enough money to buy a Blériot, and he and his mechanic, André Pierce, hurried to Turkey to offer their services at the prevailing wage rate. They flew observation for one day and were handed a large paper bag filled with Turkish paper money. The Kentuckian might have taken old bourbon or a well-bred young foal in payment, but not a bag of shabby paper money. He and his mechanic refused to fly until they received gold.

Hall regarded the paper money much as the AEF a few years later would look upon the French paper one-franc notes —as cigar coupons. Finally the gold was forthcoming. It kept on coming every day, for the canny Bert Hall insisted on being paid every twenty-four hours. But as the Turks kept on losing, the hundred dollars a day dwindled to fifty, and then forty. This, and the vital matter of the deficiencies of Turkish coffee to the French palate of mechanic André Pierce, resulted in a separation of Bert Hall and the Turkish Air Force.

So the two young adventurers kissed the Turks goodbye, and after a few detours arrived in France just in time to participate in the larger adventure.

In the summer of 1915, Hall, with typical flamboyance, performed one of the more bizarre feats of the war. He had been assigned one of the newly arrived Nieuports; the pilot sat aft and the observer-mechanic forward. As often as not, pilots flew alone, but occasionally they brought their mechanics with them for the ride. Leon Mourreau was now Hall's mechanic, and one morning Hall asked him to go along. It was good psychology; if you treated a mechanic as a junior partner now and then he'd take much better care of your engine. On this fateful morning Hall's objective was St Etienne-à-Arnes. As they approached the village, held by the

Germans, a German Albatros appeared out of a cloud flying at the same height and almost parallel to them. Mechanic Leon Mourreau had the despised machine gun in his cockpit, and he motioned excitedly to Hall to get closer. Hall did, and the mechanic, who had never fired a gun before, sent a stream of bullets in the direction of the Albatros. By sheer luck one of them hit the enemy observer, who slumped out of sight. Hall now flew closer to the German aircraft. The pilot had no gun, and he was completely defenceless without his observer. Hall motioned to him to descend, and mechanic Mourreau fired a scattered burst at the machine to emphasize Hall's orders. The German reluctantly allowed himself to be herded to earth. He landed on a field south of Siuppes, dragged his wounded observer out of the machine, and then tried to set a match to the Albatros. Hall landed right behind him in time to throw a right-hand punch at the startled German officer. A French ambulance hurried up, took charge of the wounded observer, and a detachment of French infantrymen nabbed the pilot, who that night lodged an official protest at the vulgar method of warfare being practised by French pilots. Had Hall shot him or stuck a knife into him, he would have accepted this as a hazard of war, but to be hit on the chin by a fist was a humiliating way of being subdued.

In any case, Hall was able to present France with a completely intact Albatros and an equally intact, if indignant, German pilot. Hall and other members of the squadron flew the captured aircraft and found it cumbersome and insensitive. The knowledge was useful. But this episode remained anonymous until later when Hall (with the help of ghost writers) discovered that the simple declarative sentence could be a source of income; he wrote two best-sellers on his flying experiences.

These were just a few of the fledgling pilots who were trying out their wings and gradually attaining proficiency. The RFC, too, was of course an incubator in 1915, out of which would emerge fully-fledged fliers, but as yet the British public knew very little of the individual pilots. Fliers who had distinguished themselves were well known in RFC circles, but except for those few who received the Victoria Cross from the hand of the King, they fought in anonymity.

The first Victoria Cross to be won in the air was awarded to Second-Lieutenant W. B. Rhodes-Moorhouse, one of the real pioneers, who took his pilot's certificate in 1911. He began flying regularly after he had come down from Cambridge, and joined the RFC in August, 1914, before which time he had already earned a considerable reputation in the air. One of his feats was to make the first cross-Channel flight with two passengers.

Following the terrible fighting in 1915 at Hill 60, to the south of the Ypres salient, pilots of No 2 Squadron, stationed at Merville, near Hazebrouck, received orders to bomb railway trucks and infantry reserves behind the lines, and among these men was Rhodes-Moorhouse, who, with a hundred-pound bomb in his BE, set off for his objective near Courtrai station.

Heavy machine gun and rifle fire met him as soon as he crossed the lines and he was badly wounded, but in spite of that he flew lower and lower until he was almost on the level of Courtrai belfry, from which the Germans were firing furiously. He dropped his bomb and made for his aerodrome at Merville, where in spite of his severe wounds he managed a landing; but to live only for a day. He insisted on making out a report, and then collapsed. His report was later confirmed as correct, his bomb having made a direct hit on the railway, west of the station.

The achievement of Rhodes-Moorhouse was a remarkably courageous one, for it must be remembered that the slow speeds of the aircraft in those days made them quite vulnerable at low altitudes; and it was Rhodes-Moorhouse's determination not to miss his target. It may be said that his was the first attempt at a low-altitude attack, and there was no mistake about its success. His life, alas, with No 2 Squadron, was short. He joined the squadron in March 1915, twenty-eight years of age and already married, and within about a month his comrades were mourning his loss.

All histories of the Royal Flying Corps treat the year 1915 as merely an interval of flying with crude equipment punctuated by the deadly Fokker era. But actually both the RFC and the French airmen were learning how to handle war's newest weapon; they were constantly if clumsily probing its potential. Perhaps the chief contribution made to the Allied cause by the RFC during 1915 came when British observers photographed the whole German trench system at Neuve-Chapelle. By now, intelligence officers had become more experienced in the interpretation of aerial photographs. A standard system of co-operation between artillery and air service was developed.

Many important lessons were learned that would pay dividends later on. During the first part of the year (even at Neuve-Chapelle and Loos) both the RFC and the French were attempting to accomplish too much with too little. The air forces were being assigned too many objectives, which meant they had to spread their aircraft very thinly. Both learned in 1915 that the only way to hit an important target was to concentrate a great number of aircraft upon it, and hope for the best. Above all, 1915 made air converts of every general staff.

At long last the traditional militarists on both sides had been brought to the revolutionary and reluctant conclusion that the huge, cumbersome beast of war was helpless without eyes. Only an air force could give the gigantic monster the power to see what lay 'on the other side of the hill'.

Chapter Five

THE GAME BECOMES DEADLY

TONY FOKKER'S synchronized gun had made the flying machine into a fighting machine, the first new weapon to emerge during the war. Every major war during the past twenty-five centuries has produced one or more revolutionary weapons which in most cases resolved the conflict in favour of the side which produced the device. Philip of Macedonia equipped his army with twenty-four-foot-long spears called *sarissas*, and this single weapon made everything that had preceded it obsolete and made the Macedonian kingdom the dominant power in Greece. But this weapon was useless when Dionysius, the Tyrant of Syracuse, produced the wooden *ballistae* and catapults.

There have always been the traditionalists in warfare who hated any change in the well-ordered plan of attack. Such a one was Archidamus, the Colonel Blimp of Sparta, who groaned unhappily when he saw the catapult directed at his men, "Oh Hercules, the valour of man is at an end."

The valour of man, of course, did not end with the introduction of ancient artillery. The relatively long-range weapons merely made the task of the foot soldier a little easier.

The crossbow, developed in the thirteenth century, could penetrate a four-inch oak door and slice through the mailed shirts of knights as though the armour was of cloth. A hundred years later, Berthold Schwartz of Freiburg, Germany, devised gunpowder for the propulsion of missiles, although the first military leader of importance to use it on a large scale was the Turkish Sultan, Mohammed II, in the siege of Constantinople. About the same time the Venetians developed incendiary shells (red-hot lead balls) to set fire to wooden defences or cities built primarily of wood.

Then came the inevitable progression to musket and rifled musket. There was the same outcry against these barbaric weapons that was heard after the atomic bomb had been dropped on Hiroshima. The Chevalier Bayard in France was the prototype of the noble, chivalrous knight. He ordered the men whom he led in battle to hang immediately any prisoner whose equipment showed him to be a cannoneer or musketeer. He felt that the use of gunpowder was ungentlemanly, obscene and uncivilized. It was correct and in the Christian tradition to hack at a man with a sword, run him through with a spear or pierce him with an arrow, but it was against all tradition for an anonymous churl, standing a mile away, to light a fuse which would release a slug of lead that could decapitate a noble knight. No one asked the Chevalier who suffered the most pain, the knight who was decapitated by a cannon ball or the knight whose bowels were pierced by the spear.

An important refinement on all existing artillery was the machine gun, invented by Doctor Gatling of Chicago, and developed by another American, Hiram Maxim. The British refused to use the new weapon to any great extent; they still felt that the duty of the infantry was to 'close with the enemy', and even as late as 1913 they didn't realize that this newly perfected weapon would make that virtually impossible. It dictated the shape of the early years of the war and inflicted more casualties than all other weapons combined.

A defence had to be found against the machine gun, and it appeared in September, 1915, to join the fighting aeroplane as one of two new weapons which would emerge from the war. It was called a tank.

The incongruously named 'tank' grew out of a contraption demonstrated at an agricultural exhibition held in Belgium a few months before war broke out. Benjamin Holt of Peoria, Illinois, brought a tractor of his design to the exhibition, and it aroused considerable attention among farmers.

No one knew what prompted Colonel E. D. Swinton of the British Army to drop in to the agricultural exhibition, but he did, and his fertile mind immediately realized the advantages of an armoured tractor, mounting guns, crawling over torn ground. He persuaded reluctant British Army authorities to buy one of Holt's tractors, and it was given to military engineers in the hope that they might design a fairly light defensive armour for it. But no one really encouraged them and nothing was done about it until the frightful carnage produced by German machine guns during the first few months of the war made it imperative that some defence be devised.

The new device was worked on in absolute secrecy, with different factories making different parts. Those in the secret called the new device a 'land cruiser' or a 'land ship', but spies were very active in England, and an order went out forbidding anyone to use either term even in casual conversation. Several of the parts consisted of rolled steel plates which might readily be parts for building vessels to hold either water or petrol, and the men working to fashion the rolled steel plates were so sure that this was what they were constructing that they referred to the products as 'tanks'. It seemed a good and misleading code name for the new device, and henceforth it would be for ever known as the 'tank', a rather absurd name for the significant new weapon of war.

It made its début on September 15th, 1916, waddling across No-Man's-Land, contemptuous of barbed wire and machine gun emplacements, spewing death to German infantrymen from its guns. Within a week German engineers were working desperately to produce a 'tank' of their own, and within a few months they had one just as good if not better than the British version. As is always the case, the defence once more caught up with the offence.

Now aerial observers had a new problem. Tanks could be moved during the night and aircraft were in the air at sunrise trying to keep their ground troops from being surprised and annihilated by the frightening monsters. It was also more important than ever that these observation aircraft be given adequate protection, and pressure was put on the aviation industry in every country to produce better and faster fighting machines.

The battle to gain what could never be more than a short-lived superiority in aerial equipment was a desperate one, and now that all warring nations had awakened to the fact that a new and important weapon had been born, cost did not matter. Men like Fokker and Junkers in Germany; Sopwith, de Havilland and Handley-Page in England; Becherau and the Farman brothers in France; and Ansaldo and Caproni in Italy were bending all of their efforts to improve existing aircraft.

The British allocated huge sums for the fast-growing RFC. The race to develop the aeroplane was no longer a business venture but a matter of national importance—perhaps of survival—to every warring nation. Major Henry H. Arnold, who some twenty-five years later would command the greatest aggregate of air power in history, described the development of 1916 as follows:

> One country would bring out a plane that could climb to a high altitude for fighting, only to see a plane of a hostile country far above it during a patrol. A designer in England would produce a plane having a speed of 115 miles an hour and believe it was the fastest fighter on the battle front, only to hear that a German plane was much faster in the chase.

Fighting in the air caused the production of very manœuvrable, rapid climbing, extra strong planes. . . . The types changed so fast that the best plane on the line one day might very well be called obsolete the next day. The resources of almost the entire world were engaged in producing the best possible aircraft, and the results achieved certainly justified the efforts expended.

Producers of aircraft engines and armament could afford to be (and had to be) daring. No one was more daring or less orthodox than Tony Fokker, who turned out almost sixty distinct aircraft designs from 1914 to 1918. His daring nearly killed his friend, Max Immelmann, early in 1916, when he built a machine especially for the German pilot. This was a monoplane equipped with three machine guns firing 1800 bullets a minute, a terrifying hail of lead spurting through the synchronized propeller. Spies reported that there was a French plan to bomb the vast Krupp munition works at Essen, and Fokker hurried his new machine to the airport outside the city where Boelcke, Immelmann and their colleagues had been stationed to repel the attack. Fokker accompanied his new aircraft, but before he allowed Immelmann to fly it he suggested that he himself should test it. He went aloft, went through his usual repertoire of stunts while the whole Jagdstaffel watched in awe. Then, flying low, he opened up with the three machine guns, which made an unholy racket and quite demolished some old wings Fokker had ordered to be placed at the end of the landing strip as targets. It appeared as though Fokker had created the most deadly air weapon of the war, but the pilots watching were disappointed when he landed not in front of them, but at the far end of the field. He taxied hurriedly to a hangar and smilingly asked pilots and mechanics to leave him alone. He wanted to make one or two minor adjustments before he let the Staffel inspect the aircraft.

It was not innate shyness, but stark fear that prompted his reticence. When he had been shooting, he had suddenly felt a horrible vibration (not discernible to observers on the ground) and he knew that one of the three guns had temporarily jammed; when it had resumed firing, it was no longer synchronized and had nearly shot off his propeller. He released his trigger thumb before the engine was shaken loose from its bed. Alone in the hangar he examined the damage; sixteen bullet holes had riddled the prop and one blade was about ready to fall off. He immediately had a new propeller fitted to the aircraft and tried it out the next day. Satisfied that it would live up to his hopes, as long as none of the three guns jammed, he turned it over to Immelmann. A week later, while Immelmann was flying over the German lines after an enemy machine, the rocker arm of the captured Gnome rotary broke; it flailed through the air like a revolving knife, cutting through the steel supports which attached the engine to the nose of the fuselage. The vibration nearly shook the motor free from its bed. With the engine hanging by only a single, twisted steel tube, the cool-headed pilot with superlative skill somehow managed to land the aircraft. He immediately phoned Fokker to report, not in anger, but in sorrow, that somehow the Gnome engine and three heavy machine guns did not make a happy marriage. The three-gun battery was immediately abandoned to await the time when the machine guns wouldn't jam, and when the rocker arm of a rotary would never break. The E-4, as Fokker called it, was scrapped.

Every country was experimenting and the pilots were the willing guinea pigs. Most of the aircraft arriving on the scene were now in every way superior to the ones flown during the first year and a half of the war. These were not machines adapted for war—they were designed for war. It may have been the fierce cut-throat competition among German designers, engineers and manufacturers that produced machines that were superior to Allied aircraft during 1916, for not since the first appearance of Fokker's synchronized gun had Germany enjoyed the advantage which was hers in the second half of that year. The aircraft produced in 1916, which reached the Front in the summer and autumn, ushered in the most glorious chapter in German air fighting.

Rather surprisingly, Tony Fokker didn't have much to do with this sudden rise in German air strength. Rumours—Fokker always claimed they were begun by jealous competitors—were circulating that he was sending much of his huge profits out of Germany to his native Holland. Because Fokker had never given up Dutch citizenship, the General Staff didn't have the authority they could exercise over a national, and now they again tried to force him into becoming a German citizen. Fokker refused indignantly. About this time German Intelligence also intercepted a message sent to Fokker via Holland by the British, offering him £2,000,000 to come to England and design aircraft for the RFC. Fokker never knew of this offer until after the war, but the German High Command did and they made the erroneous inference that the Dutchman was negotiating with the British.

Early in the year Fokker had produced a revolutionary fighter (the D-1), the first German biplane to be powered by a stationary motor. The finest engines in existence at the time were the high-horsepower Mercedes—but Fokker was refused the use of them for the D-1 and had to be satisfied with the standard, less powerful models.

Ever since he had been making aircraft, Fokker had stressed the quality of 'stability', but strangely enough it was this apparently desirable quality that made the D-1 a failure. Boelcke was asked to try one out in combat. To the Dutchman's dismay, Boelcke complained that the very quality of stability Fokker was so proud of hurt the aircraft's manœuvrability. In vain Fokker protested that his machine needed only the extra forty horsepower of the new 160-horsepower Mercedes to give it both the manœuvrability and the climbing speed essential to the stepped-up requirements of aerial combat. Instead, he was given a contract to build 400 training aircraft and a few thousand machine guns.

Unlike Fokker, the Albatros company had considerable influence with the military authorities, and now it was assigned the greater portion of the new engines. The Albatros designers immediately began work on a single-seater which would use the 160-horsepower motor, and rumours of the progress of this potentially best of all fighters reached the Front. The appetite of front-line airmen was further whetted when a new Albatros two-seater was sent to them. The fuselage was streamlined and it could reach ninety miles an hour despite the weight of its two machine guns—a fixed, synchronized Spandau and a free Parabellum for the use of the observer.

At the same time the Aviatik C-2 made its appearance at the Front.

Powered also by the superb Mercedes, it was used chiefly for short-range bombing and for artillery observation, but it could fight if need be; twice Aviatiks brought down the great Nungesser, wounding him badly each time. In 1916, a swarm of six Aviatiks was sent to bomb Paris. The raid didn't add much lustre to the name of the aircraft, but it did bring fame to French pilot René Dorme, who, flying a Nieuport single-handed, dived into the formation, brought three of them down and broke up the attack. Two weeks later Dorme emptied his ammunition drum almost point-blank at an Aviatik, but when the sturdy machine refused to go down, the frenzied and frustrated young Frenchman rammed it. He was one of those youngsters who believed in the 'burn wild, die quick' policy, but this time, perhaps to his own surprise, he didn't die. He sheered the top wing of the German aircraft off; Dorme's undercarriage was destroyed, but somehow he made a crash-landing behind his own lines and emerged without a scratch. In 1916, the Allies had nothing in the two-seater category to compare with the Albatros or the Aviatik.

The German public was fed rather fantastic stories regarding the great qualities of the new aircraft and given hints of even greater things to come, but this excitement was stilled and the nation went into shocked mourning when it was announced that Max Immelmann had died.

The first report said that the engine of his Fokker had failed in mid-air and that he had crashed over the German lines at Annay. The legend of his invincibility would have been destroyed had it been admitted that he had been killed in combat; engine failure seemed a better way of ending his glorious career, and everyone was satisfied—except Tony Fokker—to have Germany's foremost hero die because of some deficiency in one of his aircraft. Fokker demanded (and received) permission to examine the remains of Immelmann's machine. Under the eyes of representatives of the General Staff, he and his bright assistants pointed out the obvious fact that the control wires were cut as if by shrapnel—not only stretched as they would have been in an accidental crash. The tail of the fuselage had been found a considerable distance from the machine itself, further evidence that it had not crashed intact. Fokker came to the conclusion that Immelmann had been shot down either by a British aircraft or by German artillery—he had fallen some distance behind his lines. Actually the Fokker monoplane he had been flying closely resembled the French Morane Saulnier, and Fokker believed that German gunners had mistaken it for a French machine. Fokker's explanation was never made public, but the Fokker monoplane was exonerated unofficially and silhouettes of all German aircraft were immediately rushed to artillery commanders.

Coincident with the report of Immelmann's death came an official British report stating that at nine o'clock on the evening of June 18th, Second Lieutenant G. S. McCubbin and Corporal J. H. Waller of No 25 Squadron, flying an FE2B, had shot down a Fokker over Annay. Immelmann had crashed at Annay at exactly 9 pm on June 18th. The British report was published before the victim was known to be Immelmann, and there is no doubt that to Waller belongs the credit for killing one of the Allies' most dangerous foes.

Immelmann's death threw a pall of gloom over all Germany; he had been regarded as the invincible one, and his death generated a tiny doubt in the minds of millions who until then had thought that victory was only a few weeks—or at the worst, months—away. The German High Command sensed this and decided to preserve its one remaining hero—Oswald Boelcke. Boelcke was withdrawn from combat and sent on an inspection tour. He was forbidden to fly, and for a time he made dutiful trips to the various fronts and to factories producing war material, was lionized by the troops and public, but finally rebelled. He insisted upon returning to combat, although he must have known the inevitable result.

Boelcke was not nourished by any flaming anger or hatred of his foes. His heroes were not the militant Prussian warriors; his admiration was reserved for his scholarly father (a schoolteacher) and for men who built houses and bridges, and he wanted to become one of them. But instead of building he was destroying, and his letters home reveal that he was sometimes bewildered at the amazing efficiency he had developed at this distasteful occupation. And now that Immelmann had died this reluctant hero found himself to be the most idolized man in the nation.

Some months earlier Boelcke had made a trip to Berlin to receive a decoration from the hands of the Kaiser. He went into the dining car of the train for lunch. A young German airman entered the car and, of course, recognized the hero. The youngster was Manfred Freiherr von Richthofen, then attached to a bombing squadron.

Young Richthofen, looking younger than his twenty-two years and shy in the presence of greatness, summoned the courage to address Boelcke, who was sitting alone. To his delight, Boelcke smiled, asked him to sit down and ordered a bottle of Rhine wine for them both. Boelcke soon put the young Prussian at his ease by asking him about the work of his squadron, and when they started to discuss flying Richthofen could at least talk of bombing raids without stammering. But he wanted to hear Boelcke talk, and finally he blurted out, "Tell me how you manage to shoot them down."

"Well, it's simple enough," Boelcke said casually. "I fly close to my man, aim well, fire, and then he falls down."

"I have tried this often from my observer's seat," Richthofen said sadly, "but they never fall down."

"What machine are you using?"

Richthofen described the several types of early cumbersome bomber aircraft used by the German air force at this time.

Boelcke nodded in understanding. "It's difficult to get close to them in big, slow machines like that. Half the trick in shooting down an enemy is to have the right kind of aircraft. It is never the pilot alone; it is a combination of pilot and machine. I'm lucky to be flying a fast Fokker."

"One of these days I'll be flying one, too," Richthofen said grimly.

They did not meet again until August, 1916. After winning his successful fight to return to the Front, Boelcke had been given orders to form a Jagdstaffel of his own. He would pick and train the men who would fight under him. His search led him to Kovel on the Eastern Front, headquarters for a bombing squadron. Ostensibly he was merely visiting his brother, who was stationed there. Manfred von Richthofen was an obscure member of the squadron. He had learned to fly the single-seater Fokker, but he was still assigned to observation aircraft. Richthofen was thrilled when Boelcke greeted him and recalled their meeting in the dining car. It was hard for Richthofen and his fellow pilots to believe that this smiling, soft-voiced, almost diffident young man had already shot down sixteen Allied aircraft, but there on his chest was the *Pour le Mérite*, highest of all decorations, nicknamed the 'Blue Max' after its founder, Maximilian Frederick. Many great airmen had stared at death so often that they felt compelled to wear masks, lest occasional human weaknesses betray their almost hypnotic gallantry. They were fighting the cruellest foe in the world—time—and the intelligent among them knew that life was merely lending them a few more casual days or weeks. None of this inner strain showed on Boelcke. He chatted informally with the pilots, drank wine with them and—above all —listened to them; and although they didn't know it, he was mentally assessing them.

Boelcke put them at their ease, and soon they began to ply him with questions, particularly about the air fighting in the Verdun sector during the spring of the year. They knew that when the great offensive began the German General Staff had ordered an 'aerial barrage' to protect the advance. The battle front was divided into four zones, which were to be patrolled by German aircraft from dawn until dark. Theoretically they were to throw up an aerial screen that would prevent French and British aeroplanes from breaking through to observe where the concentration of troops and artillery would indicate the next thrust. The General Staff had assigned 168 aircraft, fourteen balloons and four dirigibles to protect the movements of the German Fifth Army, which was bearing the brunt of the offensive. On paper this seemed an effective scheme, but at best there had to be a whole series of lines, one above the other, to provide any protective scheme.

At the beginning of the offensive an order had come,

'Barrage flying has precedence over all other work.' Three weeks of experience had shown the utter absurdity of the concept—French and British aircraft kept sneaking through —and now the Fifth Army shifted its air tactics. Boelcke and other experienced pilots were given what amounted to roving commissions to knock down enemy aircraft whenever they could find them. Within five days Boelcke had scored four aerial victories and had inspired all of the fighter pilots in the Verdun section to renewed efforts.

All this the young fliers at Kovel knew. They knew, too, that during the first two months of the Verdun offensive the German Air Force had completely dominated the air, and then something happened that lost this advantage to the Germans. Boelcke explained what it was.

"Their losses were so heavy at one time," Boelcke said, "that they were sending out as many as twelve fighters to protect two observation machines. It was seldom that we could get through this protecting screen to reach the observation aircraft."

He then explained that the German General Staff had de-decided to do something similar, and he explained the Jagdstaffel system to them. Each staffel (the literal meaning is 'step') would consist of two 'swarms' of six machines and would be further divided into 'chains' of three machines. Each group of twelve aircraft would be known as a Jadgstaffel—colloquially a 'hunting pack', because it was their assigned task to hunt for and drive enemy observation aircraft from the sky. Boelcke did not say that each Jagdstaffel was to be under the leadership of a pilot whose personal achievements would inspire confidence among his subordinates and fire the imagination of the public; but he added casually that he had been given command of the first staffel. It was to be called the Royal Prussian Jadgstaffel No 2 (No 1 existed only on paper; it was never actually formed), a name which must have displeased the Saxon, who was the negation of everything the word 'Prussian' stood for.

Now Boelcke actually singled out Richthofen and asked him if he had learned to 'get close, aim well', but Richthofen had to tell him gloomily that although he had shot down two enemy aircraft, both had gone down behind the Allied lines, and because there was no independent witness he had not received official credit for the kills.

"Have you the synchronized guns?" Boelcke asked.

Richthofen told him that his squadron had no synchronized guns, but that he had rigged up a Spandau on his upper wing above the propeller and had run a cable from its trigger to the pilot's cockpit.

"You shot down two machines using that gun?" Boelcke asked.

"Yes, he did," one of the other men said proudly. "I was his observer both times, and I saw them crash."

"You must be a pretty good shot," Boelcke said casually to Richthofen.

"I've been hunting all my life," Richthofen answered.

"He keeps our mess in meat," a pilot laughed. "Manfred can hit anything that moves."

Boelcke turned suddenly to the young Prussian. "How would you like to go with me to the Somme and do some real fighting?"

Richthofen could only stammer a delighted acceptance, and with that the fate of at least 200 British and French airmen was sealed.

Three days later he was speeding across Germany in a train toward the Somme to join Jadgstaffel No 2 at Lagincourt, and become a member of what the German public soon began to call 'Boelcke's Own'.

Richthofen was born in Breslau of well-to-do parents. As a boy he was an average student, who lived only for the holidays when his family moved to their country estate where he and his younger brother Lothar could spend their time in the woods hunting.

Young Manfred became a fine shot with rifle and shotgun, and a fair horseman. In 1912, he became a subaltern in the First Uhlan Regiment. This was one of the finest aggregations of riders in the world, and the youngster from Breslau found himself a little out of place. After the war his mother, interviewed by Floyd Gibbons, then perhaps America's best-known foreign correspondent, shook her head when Gibbons asked if her son had won many prizes in regimental competitions.

"No," she said ruefully. "He was always being thrown from his horse, and half a dozen times he wrote me letters from hospitals where broken legs or collar bones were mending. But when he came home on leave, he would usually bring a fellow officer with him. They would talk about Manfred to me when we were alone; they said he was too brave for his own good. He would try anything, but his skill on a horse did not match his courage."

On August 4th, 1915, the blond, pink-cheeked, slim twenty-two-year-old second lieutenant went to war with the Uhlans. Manfred himself couldn't wait for his first engagement; in his letters to his mother he confided that his one ambition was to win the Iron Cross. Late in August he led a cavalry charge against a French group of infantry. When the charge was over ten of his fourteen men were dead, and he and the survivors were riding to the rear at breakneck speed. Slowly came the realization that his cherished concept of war—waving standards, flashing sabres, the excitement of the mêlée and the glorious annihilation of the panicked enemy—was an outmoded concept. One day a shell exploded twenty feet from him and nearly killed him. He was furious. Some unseen, unknown Frenchman, miles away, had pulled the lanyard of an unseen fieldpiece and had sent him an impersonal engine of destruction to deal death to men. This was not his idea of a glorious death or of a glorious war. To make things worse, he was made an ordnance officer and stationed far behind the lines.

Only the killing of wild game seemed to lift him to a new interest in life. Through his letters to his mother there runs a note of joy when there is a prospect of a hunt in which he can bag new victims for his trophy wall and feed the craving which even the war, so far as he then knew it, had failed to gratify. He wrote in March:

Dear Mamma,

    At last I have found a sufficient outlet for my energies. . . . I go hunting. I am rather proud of my bag of three wild boars. The details of these hunting excursions I am writing to Papa.

Three days ago, we had a veritable offensive against wild pigs with thirty drivers and five hunters. I myself was the host of the party. The drivers stirred up eight pigs, but every one of us missed the game. The affair lasted from eight in the morning until seven in the evening. In three days we will have another try, and in ten days, with a full moon, I am expecting confidently to bag a wild boar.

In the same month of the hunting party, his schoolboy friend, Hugo Frei of the Fourth Dragoons, was killed, but his death made only a passing impression on Richthofen, who was incapable of warm friendship. He admired Hugo. Hugo was dead. Well, the best ones are always the first to go.

He was desperately anxious now to see any kind of action, but he felt the war would end before he had a chance to kill an enemy. Richthofen was not the only German, or for that matter the only Allied combatant, who was surprised at the duration. He confided to his mother:

Who would ever have thought that the war could continue so long? Everyone believes that we will win, but no one knows when that will be. Consequently, we have to struggle on.

'Struggling on' was not Richthofen's strong point. He could sit up in a tree throughout a winter night and keep his eyes open watching through the hours for the approach of game. He could track a quarry hour after hour through a forest and never give up the hunt. But he could not play at the war of waiting. It broke his spirit.

So it was that when he received instructions to prepare himself for another duty in the service of supply, still farther back from the front lines, he exploded, and the following day the commanding general of his division probably received one of the shocks of his life when he read the following unmilitary communication from the restless Uhlan.

My dear Excellency,
    I have not gone to war in order to collect cheese and eggs, but for another purpose.

The rest of the letter was an official application for his transfer to the flying service. Richthofen's constructive work in the infantry, the signal service and the supply department seems to have been on a par with his failure as a cavalryman, and it is not recorded that his departure from the old services was accompanied by any great regret on the part of his superiors. His uncivil letter gained his end and his wish. In May, 1915, he was transferred to the flying service and sent to Cologne for training.

With the old cavalryman's contempt for the petrol engine, he knew nothing of what was under the bonnet of a motor car. He was a horseman, and he had held, with other horsemen, that the cavalry would never have to resort to rubber tyres and smelly exhaust pipes. This pardonable ignorance, inherited from the proud spirit of his branch of the service, stood him in bad stead when he began his training for the air. It almost barred him from the pilot's seat.

To him flying offered an opportunity to get in touch with his enemies—to see the man he wanted to kill. But Richthofen was drunk with enthusiasm when he landed after his first flight. In the long glide to the landing field he had been impressed by the heavy silence that followed the din when the motor slowed down and the aircraft skimmed over the ground at express-train speed. But he felt that he could know no fear in the air. It was all so simple, all so clean.

He won his brevet as an observer, and after two weeks of daily flights was sent to the Russian front, where Mackensen was hammering his way through the Russian lines at Gorlice. His pleasure was complete. Action at last—burning towns and fields and the forward-and-backward sway of battle, all unrolled below him every day like some great unnatural spectacle staged to tingle the craving in his heart. The effect of actually seeing carnage was stimulating to the young Uhlan.

His first pilot was Franz Zeumer. Zeumer was a first lieutenant and one of Germany's earliest pilots. He was considered one of the best of Squadron No 69, and his daring was a thing that officers and men alike spoke of when out of the little fellow's hearing. Zeumer did not like them to talk about it in his presence.

He thought they suspected the reason for his bravery. His eyes had a feverish light in them and his sallow skin was drawn tight over his cheekbones and temples. His voice was dry and weak, seeming to come from a mouth that lacked moisture. He frequently wet his lips with his tongue, and sometimes in the upper air he struggled vainly to suppress fits of violent coughing, which shook his skinny shoulders and made it difficult for him to keep his birdlike hands on the flying controls.

Zeumer was dying. Beneath his shrunken chest, slow death gnawed. But his eyes were young and clear, his heart was stout and good, his mind was keen and quick. In the air he was as good as any pair of spotless lungs—better, because he could dare with less to lose and more to gain. To meet quick death in the air as a fighting man would be a victory over the slow death that was gradually killing him from within. Richthofen gained new lessons in fearlessness in those days when he flew with Zeumer (whose merciful release would come twelve months later in the skies over Verdun).

Richthofen immediately persuaded little Zeumer to teach him to fly. Zeumer managed to get hold of a dual-control trainer and now, when the two were not on observation or bombing duty, they were in the air in the trainer. Strangely, the restless Uhlan was not an apt pupil. He handled a plane much as he had once handled a horse. He flew twenty-five hours with Zeumer on dual-control—an inordinate length of time—before the latter felt that his pupil was ready to fly solo.

It was in the stillness of a late October afternoon that the man who was to become the ace of all German airmen took an aircraft into the air alone for the first time. In spite of his long experience as an observer and a student pilot, Richthofen had fears. He did not think he could fly and land safely. His fears were well grounded. He couldn't.

His head was buzzing with Zeumer's parting instructions when he climbed into the pilot's familiar cockpit, tested the controls as he had been taught, made his ignition contact, and felt the vibration of the machine as the motor started in response to a swing on the propeller by a mechanic.

The chocks were removed from the wheels—the aircraft moved off across the field into the wind and, with the motor full on, left the ground. Richthofen was in the air—with the knowledge that his safe return to earth depended solely upon himself. His fear left, however, as the exhilarating tingle of motion stole over him. Acting under Zeumer's last instructions, he circled to the left, and, flying over a ground mark previously arranged, shut off his motor and headed the machine back for the landing field, as he had been told.

Now came the test—the landing. His actions were entirely mechanical. He followed instructions to the letter, but he lacked the 'feel' of the air and of his machine. His flying was by the book and not by instinct. He noticed that the aircraft's responses to his controls were different from what he had expected. Something was wrong. He was not on an even keel, and the machine was careening downwards at a high rate of speed. It met the ground with a crash.

Men came rushing across the field from the hangars as Richthofen, shaken but uninjured, extricated himself from the pile of splintered struts, twisted wire braces and torn fabric. On his first flight he had failed.

Smarting under the gibes and jokes of his comrades, he returned to his quarters and made a vow that nothing would stop his mastering the art of flying. He plunged passionately into studies and instructions, working days and nights on the machines, both in the air and on the ground. After two weeks' intensive cramming, he believed he had overcome his faults, and presented himself for his first formal examination. Again he failed.

Richthofen developed perseverance and grim determination in the weeks of hard training that followed. In spite of his failures, he persisted in his ambition to become a pilot and finally became one on Christmas Day, 1915.

He arrived at the Front in March, 1916, and was assigned to the so-called 'Second Fighting Squadron', then stationed in the line behind Verdun. Richthofen was eager for combat. He wanted a fight in the air, with himself operating both the flying controls and the machine guns. Although he was a pilot, he had not yet achieved his ambition to fly a single-seater machine. He was still restricted to the heavier two-piece aircraft and had to carry an observer with him who, in accordance with German practice, was the superior in command of the machine.

And then, at long last, he was assigned to a single-seater Fokker. Within two weeks he had cracked up two of these machines. Although he emerged unscathed, the single-seater aircraft were too precious to be put into the hands of crude pilots like Richthofen, and he was switched back to flying two-seater bombers and stationed at Kovel on the Eastern Front. For a month he dropped bombs and sprayed machine gun bullets on Russian infantry and cavalry. His letters to his mother and the revealing pages of his diary indicate that Richthofen had an insatiable hunger to kill. He looked upon men on the ground as he had once looked upon boars and deer: they were prey and he the hunter. The Russians had no air protection at all, and Richthofen engaged in wholesale slaughter with no danger to himself. Killing satisfied something in his nature; his letters to his mother tell of his delight in participating in this orgy of blood. When he wasn't flying his two-seater he was borrowing a Fokker, trying hard to improve his technique. He was cold, calm and ambitious.

And then he was given a leave. He boarded a train to Berlin, walked into the dining-car, and fate introduced him to Oswald Boelcke. When he returned to this squadron it was with the fixed determination to become a fighter pilot. Within a month he had mastered the Fokker, but his requests to be transferred to single-seater duty were turned down. He would have perhaps lasted out the war as an obscure pilot of slow observation aircraft, had not fate again taken a hand to direct Oswald Boelcke's search for pilots to the aerodrome at Kovel on the eastern front.

And thus was Manfred von Richthofen, Prussian nobleman, in August, 1916, speeding across Germany to join the one man in the world he idolized.

Richthofen had bright visions of soaring immediately into the air and hurling himself into the midst of a group of British machines; the early dream of leading Uhlans and their flashing sabres against enemy infantry was sublimated to this new ideal. He was a bit let down when he found that Boelcke had no intention of sending him or any of the other young pilots he had gathered into combat as yet. He put them through an intensive period of training, first in the rifle butts, and then he substituted machine guns for rifles. He made them familiarize themselves with the gun; Richthofen had to dismantle one a hundred times and learn why it jammed occasionally and how best this mishap could be minimized.

"Your gun is your friend," Boelcke would say. "Keep it clean, well oiled; it may save your life one day."

This made sense to the young pilot who had, as he had told Boelcke, 'been shooting all his life'. Then there were long sessions with the newly arrived Halberstadts. Richthofen's first landings were clumsy, but Boelcke was a patient man who gave individual instruction to each of his Cubs (as he called them). When the day's flying was finished, he had long sessions with them at the blackboard. He had models of all the British and French aircraft, and he made them learn the strong as well as the weak points of each machine. Germans were taught to hate the British; the French were regarded as reluctant allies forced into war by the former. This line had been pursued in official reports and in the newspapers ever since war had begun, and the feeling had gradually infected even the pilots, who until now had felt that their own air war was something apart from the vicious murderous slaughter on the ground. The feeling of kinship with Allied fliers was gradually being replaced by a feeling of enmity towards the men who had killed Immelmann and so many others. Richthofen found to his surprise that Boelcke had not become imbued with this spirit of all. He talked to them of the bravery and gallantry of their opponents and reminded them that they were as good or better pilots than himself.

For three weeks Boelcke was the only active fighter in his staffel. He felt it would have been sheer murder to send his inexperienced youngsters against the wily British foeman until they had thoroughly familiarized themselves with their new machines and had learned all of the tactics he himself had acquired through experience.

Boelcke had a habit of rising early; each day at dawn he would take off looking for prey. Richthofen wrote enthusiastically to his mother, 'He eats an Englishman every day before breakfast.' It was almost literally true. When he returned from these lone sorties his Cubs were on the field waiting eagerly to hear his report.

"Any luck this morning?" one would always cry out as he stepped from his machine.

"Is my chin black?" Boelcke would ask, grinning.

"Black as ink," they'd yell happily, for then they knew that their idol had shot down at least one Englishman. The grime on his chin was caused by the powder from his machine gun; if he had fired his gun, he had bagged a victim—Boelcke never wasted ammunition.

At breakfast he would give them a detailed account of his encounter. He would tell them what type of aircraft he had brought down and exactly how he had exploited its weakness. The British were having considerable success during the early weeks of the Battle of the Somme with their FEs, a two-seater pusher type which carried four guns—two for the pilot and two free guns for the observer.

"This isn't as fast as their single-seaters," Boelcke told them one morning at breakfast. "But its guns make it dangerous. I've had a couple of close calls fighting these FEs, but this morning I discovered that it has a blind spot. Never dive on one; the observer can tilt his gun up and find you. Never attack head-on, the pilot's two guns will get you. Attack from below; the FE is helpless then, for none of the guns can be brought to bear."

Each morning and afternoon he led them in formation flying. He made each young pilot go through all of the manœuvres each would need when it came to combat. He taught them all of Immelmann's tricks, he showed them a few he himself had evolved.

Gradually Richthofen and the other youngsters became expert under the leadership of the master. They learned to fly in tight formation and to obey the orders signalled to them by Boelcke with his wings. And finally, Boelcke felt that they were ready for combat.

That was the day the long-awaited new Albatroses arrived. There were twelve of them. Boelcke's Cubs stared at the graceful machine in delight. It actually looked like a bird poised for flight. Its sleek, shark-like fuselage was in marked contrast to all contemporary designs. Boelcke, who had flown it and tested it thoroughly at the factory before approving it for his Jagdstaffel, told them its top speed was 110 mph. Its two synchronized Spandaus in the nose made it the most beautiful killer ever to appear in the air. Boelcke immediately assigned a machine to each man and told the squadron to take off. He led them in formations and aerobatics; he climbed to 15,000 feet and they followed him, and then he dived to 1000 feet and every one of his Cubs followed him joyously. This was flying as they had never known it, not even in the Halberstadt. The aircraft landed gently, its steel tubular vee-struts and rubber cord shock absorbers even forgave poor landings. The twelve machines had arrived fully equipped even to the black crosses painted on fuselage and rudder. The young pilots were an exuberant, laughing group at dinner that night. They toasted the new aeroplane, for their flight that day had convinced them that this lovely Albatros made every other fighter in the world obsolete.

"When will you let us fight?" Richthofen asked with feverish impatience.

"Tomorrow," Boelcke said.

The sun shone brightly as the eager Cubs took off the next morning. It was September 17th, 1916. Boelcke led them towards Cambrai, and then he sighted a group of British aircraft. They were far behind the German lines, and Boelcke signalled his men to get between them and the front lines; the British would have to fight their way home. Now it was either kill or be killed.

The British formation contained units of No 11 Squadron, two-seater bombers and an escort of two-seater fighters of the FE type. The British flew steadily on their course, which was a mission of destruction behind the German lines. The German manœuvre seemed neither to startle them nor to deflect them from the object of their regular flight. These were experienced professionals. They kept on towards their goal.

Boelcke and Richthofen and three more of the Jagdstaffel approached the squadron. The altitude was about 10,000 feet. Richthofen and the other Cubs kept their eyes on their leader and hoped for a chance to show their ability under his eyes.

Boelcke approached the first British machine quite closely, but refrained from firing. Richthofen followed immediately behind the squadron leader. The enemy aircraft closest to him was a large two-seater FE painted in dark colours.

At its controls was Second-Lieutenant L. B. F. Morris, and in the observer's seat in front of him was Lieutenant T. Rees. Both were youngsters, but both were veteran airmen. Morris was the son of A. E. Morris of Carshalton, Surrey, and Rees came from Cardiff. Rees manned a Lewis machine gun, mounted on a telescopic tube above and behind the observer's cockpit, and also had another Lewis on a telescopic mounting between the cockpits firing to the rear over the upper main-plane.

Richthofen approached within fifty yards of the British machine and opened fire. At the same instant a stream of lead poured from the rear machine gun on the British plane. Rees was on the job, and his aim was good because Richthofen was forced to change his position immediately. He dived out of range, but zoomed upwards again and regained his position above and in the rear of Morris and Rees.

Whenever he approached within range, Rees opened fire, and Richthofen could see the British tracer bullets zipping through the air quite close to him. The British aircraft with its forward and after machine guns could shoot in almost all directions.

Appearing to accept failure for the time being, Richthofen changed his tactics and banked into a cloud. He made a large circle and returned at a lower altitude. With his speedy machine he soon had the enemy in view again and noticed that Morris was now flying straight on instead of twisting and turning. From this he presumed that the two British fliers had lost sight of him.

He recalled the instructions of Boelcke about the 'blind spot'—a small angle of vision which would be covered neither by the pilot nor the observer nor their guns. He had man-œuvred himself into this safe angle, and Morris and Rees above him were unaware that he was 'under their tail'.

He pulled up on the stick sharply and, with his motor roaring under a wide-open throttle, zoomed upwards under the dark red belly of the British machine. In a flash of a few seconds he was within thirty yards of his quarry. His finger pressed the trigger button, and the twin Spandaus poured forth a stream of lead which raked the underside of the enemy aircraft from nose to tail. The first part of the stream shattered the crankcase of the engine, releasing the compression and destroying the motor. The spray next ripped through the fabric and wooden bracing above which Morris was seated. The last of the stream sewed a long seam of lead under the cockpit.

After delivering the burst of lead into the bottom of the British machine, Richthofen found himself so close under the FE that he had to swerve suddenly to one side to avoid colliding with it. As he came out from under and swept by, he saw that the propeller of the British plane had stopped. 'I nearly yelled with joy,' he wrote his mother that night.

The British machine reared and sideslipped. Morris at the stick had received some of the bullets from below and was, temporarily at least, out of control. As the machine fell, Richthofen dived on it and, looking down into the after cockpit, saw Rees crumpled up on his seat. He was either dead or unconscious. The disabled FE plunged downwards in a mad spiral towards the earth—almost two miles below.

Morris revived sufficiently to bring his shattered aircraft to a safe landing in a field. Richthofen, his heart pounding and his eyes burning with the excitement and exhultation of the moment, had never let the stricken enemy out of his sight. So great was his eagerness that he landed in the same field and almost smashed his own machine. He wanted to be sure of his prey.

He jumped out of his Albatros immediately and rushed over to the British aircraft. The field was behind the German third line, and reserve infantrymen were running towards them from all directions. Morris and Rees were unconscious. Richthofen's shots had gone home with telling effect.

With the assistance of the soldiers, Richthofen lifted his two victims from the bloodstained cockpits. He laid them on the ground and loosened the leather flying coats and the collars of their tunics.

Rees opened his eyes at once with a boyish smile and died.

A medical officer and two stretcher bearers arrived; Morris was placed on the stretcher and carried to a dressing station. He was dead when he arrived there.

Returning to his aerodrome, Richthofen found Boelcke and the rest of the Jagdstaffel in the midst of a joyous victory breakfast. He proudly reported his 'kill' and learned that Boelcke had 'had another Englishman for breakfast'. Four other pilots had earned their first victories that day.

Boelcke was proud of his young pupils; not one of them had been touched by an enemy bullet. In the mess were a dozen or so large silver mugs of medieval German design. He had them filled with champagne and he and the staffel drank a toast to the five men who on that day had tasted blood. Then he presented each of the five with the silver mug from which he had been drinking. They were intensely proud of this mark of honour from their leader, but the cup wasn't enough for Richthofen. That night he wrote to a jeweller he knew in Berlin, asking him to send him a silver cup two inches high with engraving on the outside. The engraving was to read:

1. Vickers 1.   17/9/16

This would always remind him that his first victory was over a British aircraft and that the date was September 17th, 1916. (The FE 26 was sometimes confused by German pilots with the earlier Vickers FB5 as the Vickers type). In his letter to the jeweller, Richthofen advised that he would forward successive orders for more cups, and he warned the craftsman to preserve the same design and type of engraving, as he desired to build up a uniform collection, one for each aircraft he would shoot down. Six days later he wrote the jeweller a brief note:

One more cup, please, just like the last one ordered. Engrave it with the following:
2. Martinsyde 1.   23/9/16

He would keep the jeweller busy for nearly two more years.

Chapter Six

THEIR FINEST HOUR

THE GREAT struggle of 1916, the one on which both sides staked everything, was the Battle of the Somme. It even eclipsed the furious fighting in the Verdun sector in the early spring of the year. The Somme valley has always been, geographically, a line of defence for Paris, a great natural military barrier. From June, 1916, until the heavy rains of the late autumn made artillery transport, troop movements and flying literally impossible, a series of tremendous engagements took place.

The Somme, after flowing north from Ham to Peronne, takes a giant bend west to Amiens, whence it follows the general lines of the rivers in this part of France in a north-westerly direction to the sea. Some seven miles before the river enters Amiens it receives the water of its tributary, the Ancre. Between the two rivers is a deserted, arid country of wide, monotonous uplands and shallow depressions. An observer flying over the district would be struck by the absence of habitation outside the towns and villages. This was open, unobstructed country where lines of trenches could be sited almost anywhere to give a wide, clear field of fire, and there were the clustered villages which could be fortified as strong-points. Into the slopes about the towns, deep and secret hiding-places had been tunnelled in the French wars of religion, and these catacombs were to serve their turn as a protection for German soldiers from British shells.

Much of the Somme country was once covered with thick forest, and the continuous clearing which had gone on down the centuries for the purpose of agriculture left only patches here and there where trees were embedded in this unfriendly clay and flint. Many of these patches of woodland were to earn world notice for the bloody fighting that would mark their capture. To name some of them: Mametz, Railway

Copse, Fricourt, Bernafay, Trones, Delville, Bazentin, High Wood.

By September the full strength of all opposing air forces had been thrown into the desperate battle, in order to attain the aerial supremacy which would allow accurate observation of enemy movements. This aerial supremacy was never a permanent possession of either side. The Allies were not only up against the new Halberstadts and Albatroses; the Germans had perfected an excellent 3·7 cm rapid-fire anti-aircraft gun which was deadly against low-flying French and British machines. By September, the Germans had 885 aircraft of all types on the Somme front (including Boelcke's new Jagdstaffel) and the Allies had 760.

The most important part of the aerial battle was the development by the Allies—particularly the British—of strategy and tactics designed to go beyond fighter activity. It now was realized that aerial bombing was necessary.

Besides attacking billets and dumps immediately behind the battle lines, destroying material and wearing down the spirit of resistance of the German troops, Allied bombers attacked rail junctions and lines. The effectiveness and potential danger of these raids forced the Germans to employ their air strength in defence.

The French and British finally realized that basically an air force was an offensive weapon and made its greatest contribution to victory by attacking. At the Somme, the German bombers had to fly on defensive patrols instead of being able to strike at vital British centres. The German fighters were compelled to give battle far behind the lines, and although this gave them an immediate advantage in the air, their passive role diverted the German Air Force from its primary missions and sapped its strength. The effect of the Allied bombing was supplemented by direct action against the German Air Force through the strategic offensive carried out by the fighters seeking and destroying the enemy machines wherever they could be found.

It is difficult to over-emphasize the importance of this development in the employment of the air weapon. When the direct action against the enemy Air Force was extended to include raids against all establishments contributing to the maintenance of that Air Force, the Allies had the basic strategy which brought them air superiority and victory in 1944–45.

The air war on the Western Front had progressed beyond the stage of individual combat. Yet the French aces in their striving for fame persisted in their understandable, but wasteful, desire to fly alone in the blue. Their commanders ranted and the Army directed otherwise, but they managed to pursue their individual ways. An instruction issued by the commandant of aeronautics of the Sixth Army defined the unit of combat to be an element consisting of two machines, while the unit of manœuvre was to be a flight consisting of three elements. In practice this rule was followed until the machines were in the air, but it was forgotten once German aircraft were sighted. Then every individual concentrated on running up his own score of victories. But French losses began to grow when opposed by the German combat teams.

In fact the thrilling aerial exploits of individual pilots such as Nungesser, Guynemer, Foncke and Dorme, captured the imagination of the French public in 1916 to such an extent that the country's real poverty in front-line aircraft was ignored. General Roques, Minister of War, boasted that although the country began the war with only 272 machines, there were now 1530 operating at the front. This sounded reassuring, but the balloon sent up by the Minister was rudely punctured by Air Minister Daniel Vincent who, in making a report to the Chamber of Deputies on budget requirements for the Air Force, said bluntly that in reality there were only 1149 aeroplanes at the front. They included:

Maurice Farman	379
Voisin	184
Caudron	309
Nieuport	210
Caproni	7
Breguet	33
Morane-Saulnier	18
Spad	4
Ponnier	5

There were only four of the new fighter Spads, and the small number of Breguel models illustrated the downfall of French bombardment aviation. The Capronis had been imported from Italy to supplement the unsatisfactory Breguets but were too slow for use at the Front.

During the summer of 1916, England was still dependent to a great extent on France for high-grade engines, and when she asked for immediate delivery of 150 Le Rhône motors, only twenty-four were allotted and of these only ten actually delivered. The French aircraft industry was not geared to mass production.

By the autumn of 1916, however, production had increased to the point where the Minister of War could state that there were now 2203 aircraft at the front. This sounded fine until the discouraging Monsier Vincent broke the figure into its component parts. He said that 196 of these were used only for training and 409 of them were held in reserve as replacements. Of the remaining 1418 there were 328 *avions de chasse*. 837 reconnaissance machines and 253 bombers. He further pointed out the unhappy news that only eighty-two of these aircraft were the latest models (there were still only twenty-five Spads in action). Of the 837 reconnaissance machines, 488 were Maurice Farmans and 324 Caudrons—ancient pusher types, absolutely helpless if attacked. It was a depressing picture, made endurable only because of the excellent front-line organization headed by Colonel Bares and the almost superhuman efforts of the fliers themselves. It is true that most of them were non-conformists who disliked hiding their identities under the anonymous cloak of formation flying, but their courage, endurance and flying skill was unquestioned.

Of these new Allied machines, the early French Nieuports and Spads attracted the most attention—even though there were too few of them. Captain H. A. Cooper and Sergeant Foster of No 11 Squadron, RFC, devised an ingenious sliding-rail gun mounting for their Nieuport fighters. The Lewis gun could be brought down on a curved rail for reloading and for upward firing. Towards the end of the year, eight Le Prieur rockets were usually fitted to the distinctive 'V' interplane struts. These were fired electrically and were fairly effective against balloons at short range. The Spad was capable of 119 miles an hour, and was armed with a single synchronized Lewis gun mounted above the engine cowling. It could climb faster and had a higher ceiling than the Nieuport, though it wasn't as manœuvrable. But whereas Nieuports of all models had an unfortunate tendency to shed their wings in a speed dive, the stronger Spad could be dived without fear. Its one drawback for most pilots was its lack of dihedral, which made it more difficult and sensitive to fly than most reconnaissance aircraft; it had literally to be 'flown in' to a landing.

The British produced several new aircraft now and several improved version of older ones. Much was expected of the FE2, a two-seater, improved version of the first aircraft Richthofen had shot down. It got off to a dismal start. The very first one to be flown to France in 1916 lost its way over the Channel and landed quietly and obligingly behind the German lines. Before the rest arrived the Germans knew everything there was to be known about the machine. It gained one distinction, however. The only VC to be awarded to a non-commissioned air officer during the war went to Sergeant Thomas Mottershead, an FE2 pilot, who brought his flaming machine to a safe landing despite frightful burns.

Almost any ex-RFC pilot on being asked to name the aircraft which had the most delightful flying qualities and was most devoid of vices and bad flying habits would unhesitatingly cite the Sopwith Pup. Its Le Rhône rotary engine developed only eighty horsepower, but its structure was sound, its elevators powerful and it maintained its manœuvrability up to 15,000 feet. Its light wing-loading allowed forced landings on the smallest of fields and also enabled it to hold its height better than most of its contemporaries. In all-round performance it almost compared with the German Albatros.

During World War II, the American fighter pilot had an average of nearly 300 hours of flying before his first combat. By the time he took his place in a fighting squadron, he was an expert on navigation; he knew his engine as well as he knew the back of his hand; he had more than a smattering of the science of aeronautics and he was a past master of both offensive and defensive aerial acrobatics. It was a bit different in the autumn of 1916. Major-General (later Air Marshal) Hugh Montague ('Bloom') Trenchard had been put in charge of the RFC. The confidence and affection he inspired among British pilots could well be compared to similar feelings of American troops and officers, twenty-five years later, towards a general named Eisenhower. 'Boom' Trenchard had a perfect understanding of the part aircraft had to play in warfare, and he constantly cried for more machines, more pilots from home. If the Somme were to be the decisive battle (as well it might have been), Trenchard knew that aerial supremacy was vital and he told London that he just damn well didn't have enough pilots or aircraft.

The training of pilots was stepped up under the urging of Trenchard. A seventeen-year-old boy could now join the RFC. Suppose we follow the career of an English youngster who wanted to wear the bright wings of the RFC, from the time he passed a recruiting station in London until he arrived at the Front. We might consider Cecil Lewis, who, although a prototype of the British teenager of the day, is by no means a fictional character. Cecil Lewis is one of those incredible men who survived two wars without ever losing his sense of humour or his life. He and a pal slipped away from the prep school which was teaching them to memorize the dates of the Battle of Hastings and the signing of Magna Carta and went to the War Office in Whitehall to apply for entrance in the RFC. Lewis was a string-bean of a boy, six-foot-three, and he weighed under nine stone.

"I don't think you could get into an aeroplane, you're too tall," the recruiting officer said doubtfully.

"I'd like to try, sir," the earnest schoolboy said.

"Well—I'll at least accept your application. How old are you?"

"Nearly eighteen," Lewis said. (His seventeenth birthday was only three days behind him.)

Within a few weeks the boy was making his first aeroplane flight in a Maurice Farman Longhorn. He was given six weeks' training at Brooklands, flying successively the Longhorn, the Shorthorn, the BE2C, the Avro and then, after one and half hours of dual instruction, was told casually to take the Longhorn up alone. He survived the solo flight and by the grace of God and by appointment of the King was certified as an RFC pilot. A bit more training at Gosport and he was off for France. His flight commander took a look at his logbook, which showed only twenty hours of solo flying, and he winced. He was not a murderer at heart, so he told young Lewis to take an aeroplane and fly all day—every day. Ten more hours of flying alone and the harassed CO had to use him as he had to use everyone who came to him with wings. The Battle of the Somme was on and everyone who could fly an aeroplane was needed. Four months later the boy was still alive; he wasn't eighteen yet, but he had 300 hours in the air, most of it over the active Somme. Like every other youngster, he shrugged off the statistics which showed that the life of the average pilot in the autumn of 1916 was three weeks.

Lewis, an exceptionally intelligent youngster who afterwards became well known in two civilian fields, writing and broadcasting, believed that the law of averages were merely the arithmetic of statistics. It was not a law that applied to everyone or, for that matter, to any individual. If some conformed to it, many did not; it was a law for a mass of people, not for any one person. Lewis had only to look around at his squadron mates to prove his case—many of them had been fighting for more than a year without bearing a scar. The statistics also revealed that most who were killed met their deaths during the first week or two of combat. If you survived that long, it showed that you had an aptitude for this strange trade and there was no reason why you shouldn't survive indefinitely. If such reasoning is faintly reminiscent of the irrational logic practised by the Mad Hatter, it was nevertheless a comforting one and a very common one.

Friends, drinking companions, confidants would go out on patrol and never return, and often the manner of their going was never known. You sat down at dinner faced by the empty chairs of those you had laughed with and joked with at lunch; the next day new men would be there in those same chairs laughing and joking. You either accepted the spurious but comforting belief that you were invulnerable, or the alternative—that it was merely a matter of time before your turn came. If you accepted the latter, you were passing a death sentence on yourself, for such an attitude slowed your reflexes in combat and clouded your judgment.

It was their attitude that made the men of the Royal Flying Corps the most outstanding. If testimony is needed, one need only go to the official records of the German Air Force, written by its commander, General von Hoeppner, or to the diaries left by German pilots. But young Cecil Lewis was perhaps an average pilot (he would not thank me if I presented evidence to the contrary), and there were others who had reached combat-flying maturity when he arrived in France. Already they were fighting Germany's first team.

With the arrival of Boelcke's Jagdstaffel and its new fighters, the air supremacy which Britain and France had enjoyed during the summer of 1916 came to an abrupt end. During those three months, British and a few French aircraft had roamed far into German territory, giving the artillery the information it needed to maintain the offensive. Their methods of observation had revolutionized the art of gunnery, and their bombing, if primitive by modern standards, had at least the merit of being directed wholly at military targets behind the lines—ammunition dumps, railways, bridges. Since July 1st they had hit 298 targets with 17,600 bombs totalling 292 tons, and they had learned at least the fundamentals of bombing at night with the aid of flares which they dropped. But the ground victory so doggedly sought after had eluded the British and 343,000 men had already been lost in the suicidal but necessary attempt to relieve pressure on the French at Verdun by forcing the Germans to withdraw large forces from there to defend the Somme area. Throughout, on ground and in the air, the Germans fought a defensive battle.

British aircraft were bringing back the information so sorely needed by ground forces, but this couldn't be done without high casualties. The Germans knew that swarms of enemy aircraft would cross their lines every day; they only had to perch high in the heavens waiting for them to appear. The observation machines were always well escorted, but the advantage was with the defenders, who had more mobility and who, in case of mishap, could with luck land in their own territory. The British escorts, committed to remaining close to the two-seaters they were assigned to protect, took a grim beating. The risk they took was a calculated one and the losses had been anticipated. If their losses were much higher than those of the enemy, their accomplishments were far greater, for their bombing was putting relentless pressure on front-line supply lines, and their observers who survived the hazardous missions were able to return with accurate reports as to German tank and artillery positions.

The autumn of 1916 was perhaps the most glorious period in the history of the German Air Force. In September they brought down 123 Allied aircraft over the Somme (mostly British, for the French were at Verdun) with a loss of only twenty-seven of their own. In October, the Allies lost eighty-eight machines to the Germans' twelve. The total number of RFC aircraft in action in the Somme area on October 1st was 563, the Germans had but 434. However, by now it had been clearly established that mere numerical superiority did not mean air supremacy. A good portion of the British strength consisted of two-seater observation machines, vulnerable to fliers of Boelcke's calibre, and during the autumn they were falling like the leaves of the forests in the wooded Somme district.

Boelcke himself accounted for twenty victories in five weeks, and his Jagdstaffel posted fifty-one kills during that time. Boelcke and Richthofen were not the only ones emerging as great fighters; Max Mueller, Werner Voss, Erwin Bohme, Franz Hoehe and young Karl Immelmann (a cousin of the late ace) had developed under the leader's tutelage into skilful, resourceful handlers of the Albatros. 'Boom' Trenchard sensed the growing aggressive spirit of the German Air Force, for by now Boelcke's squadron was being allowed to make forays into Allied territory. The British were fighting desperately on the ground, hoping to resolve the four-months-old battle before the rains came in November. Trenchard knew that he would need more aircraft to keep the sky even reasonably clear of Germans. He made an earnest plea to the War Office for help. He wrote:

Throughout the summer the Royal Flying Corps in France maintained such a measure of superiority over the enemy in the air that it was enabled to render services of incalculable value. The result is that the enemy has made extraordinary efforts to increase the number, and develop the speed and power, of his fighting machines. He has unfortunately succeeded in doing so. . . . Within the last few weeks the enemy has brought into action on the Somme front a considerable number of fighting aeroplanes which are faster, handier, and capable of attaining a greater height than any at my disposal with the exception of one squadron of single-seater 'Nieuports', one of 'FE Rolls-Royce', and one of 'Sopwiths',— the last mentioned being inferior to the enemy's new machines in some respects though superior in others. All other fighting machines at my disposal are decidedly inferior. The result of the advent of the enemy's improved machines has been a marked increase in the casualties suffered by the Royal Flying Corps. The situation threatens to be very serious unless adequate steps to deal with it are taken at once.

By now, every British airman knew the name of Oswald Boelcke, and every pilot wanted the supreme honour of killing him. But Boelcke beat them all, including some of the best. In a spectacular duel lasting nearly half an hour, he met Captain G. L. Cruikshank, leader of 70 Squadron. Cruikshank was a pre-war flier who, since August 1914, had done everything that a pilot is supposed to do and a great many things besides. He had even landed spies behind German lines. Witnesses (both German and British) have recorded that the duel between the two was productive of more sheer flying genius than any they had ever seen. Each was a master of his machine and each knew every feint and parry ever devised by man. But Boelcke finally fired a burst that disintegrated the Sopwith in mid-air, and Cruikshank fell to his death in Havrincourt Wood.

British planes twice dropped bombs on Boelcke's aerodrome at Lagincourt: it was the highest compliment they could pay him, for aerodromes were well protected by anti-aircraft guns. And then, ironically, Oswald Boelcke was killed by his best friend in an almost incomprehensible accident. Boelcke and five of his pilots (including Richthofen) were out hunting in gusty weather on October 28th, 1916. They came upon two British aircraft and Boelcke gave the signal to attack. Richthofen re-created the tragic incident in his diary that night:

Had they been twenty, Boelcke would have given us the same signal. I attacked one aircraft and he the other. I had to let go because one of the German machines got in my way. I looked round and noticed Boelcke settling his victim about 200 yards away from me.

It was the usual thing. Boelcke would shoot down his opponent and I had to look on. Close to Boelcke flew a good friend of his. It was an interesting struggle. Both men were shooting. It was probable that the Englishman would fall at any moment. Suddenly I noticed an unnatural movement of the two German flying machines. Immediately I thought: collision. I had not yet seen a collision in the air. I had imagined that it would look quite different. In reality, what happened was not a collision. The two machines merely touched one another. However, if two machines go at the tremendous pace of flying machines, the slightest contact has the effect of a violent concussion.

Boelcke drew away from his victim and descended in large curves. He did not seem to be falling, but when I saw him descending below me I noticed that part of his aeroplane had broken off. Now his machine was no longer steerable. It fell accompanied all the time by Boelcke's faithful friend.

When we reached home we found the report 'Boelcke is dead!' had already arrived. We could scarcely realize it. The greatest pain was, of course, felt by the man who had the misfortune to be involved in the accident.

It is a strange thing that everybody who met Boelcke imagined that he alone was his true friend. I have made the acquaintance of about forty men, each of whom imagined that he alone was Boelcke's intimate. Each imagined that he had the monopoly of Boelcke's affections. Men whose names were unknown to Boelcke believed that he was particularly fond of them. This is a curious phenomenon which I have never noticed in anyone else. Boelcke had not a personal enemy. He was equally polite to everybody, making no differences.

The only one who was perhaps more intimate with him than the others was the very man who had the misfortune to be in the accident which caused his death. I don't know who can ever replace him. We always had a wonderful feeling of security when he led us.

The Germans gave their distinguished ace a funeral worthy of a crowned head, and from every British aerodrome within reach warplanes flew over the German lines on peaceful errands. 'To the memory of Captain Boelcke, our brave and chivalrous foe', is a typical inscription on one of the wreaths they dropped. It was the beginning of a tradition; thereafter both sides observed the custom of honouring distinguished enemies who had died after valiant service.

Neither Richthofen nor any member of the squadron ever mentioned the name of the pilot who had so tragically killed their leader. Neither did they mention the fact that on the day of the funeral he attempted suicide, but was prevented by men of the squadron. He had been a careful, methodical fighter, eight or ten years older than the others, and he had absorbed the philosophy as well as the skill of Boelcke. Like his leader he was a killer not by nature but by force of circumstances. He never said much after the fatal accident; the others did their best to cheer him by telling him, quite truthfully, that his handling of the Albatros had not been at fault. It was the capricious, gusty half-gale that had caught his machine and had thrown it against Boelcke's. But he refused to be comforted. The careful, methodical pilot now became a reckless, impetuous fighter who seemed grimly determined to keep an early appointment with death. Not long afterwards they met and Lieutenant Erwin Bohme probably welcomed the meeting.

On October 30th, Lieutenant Hans Kirmaier formally took over the leadership of Jagdstaffel No 2, which by Imperial decree was henceforth to be known as the Boelcke Jadgstaffel, so that all its pilots, old and new, might be inspired to valiant deeds by the constant memory of the founder who had launched it on its career of fame.

The twenty-five new victories during the month after his death showed that Boelcke's spirit still lived in his staffel. Most of its encounters with British opponents were successful. For a week after Boelcke's death, however, Richthofen failed to bring down a single enemy; then he increased his efforts and on November 20th 'shot a double', which, in the parlance of the corps, meant that he brought down two enemy aircraft in one day. The first was a two-seater bombing machine, and the second was a single-seater fighter. Both were British.

This success set his mind running back to his trophies in quest of some means by which the double victory could be symbolized in a manner to distinguish it from single affairs. His first thought was to mark the double event with a cup twice the size of the eight little cups that now formed his collection. But, by doing so, he would reduce the number of trophies by one, and this would conflict with the original purpose of the collection. He pondered this and then abandoned the idea for a compromise.

Writing to the jeweller, he ordered two more cups, the first one, after the usual fashion, to be inscribed:

9. *Vickers 1.* 20/11/16

The second was to be of the same design but just twice as big and was to bear the inscription:

10. *BE1.* 20/11/16

The similarity of the dates registered the fact that both were brought down in one day, and the double size for No 10 would mark the passing of his first ten. He also instructed the jeweller that, hereafter, every tenth cup was to be just twice the size of the little ones that commemorated the intermediate victories.

The little bespectacled jeweller in Berlin chuckled when he received the new orders and exhibited them and the cups to his customers. His pride in the collection was almost as great as Richthofen's, and he wrote a magazine article to gain a little vicarious fame; how droll, how carefree, how happy these knights of the air who faced death aloft every day and then joked about their risks. The Fatherland would be for ever safe with sons like these to protect it. The jeweller, with the wartime spirit of the land, gloried in his task as a maker of silver tombstones for the enemies of his country.

If any one of Richthofen's conquests in the air deserved distinction above the others, it was the next one, his eleventh, which occurred a few days later—on November 23rd. On that day he killed the first and foremost ace of the Royal Flying Corps, an accomplished air fighter of long experience and fame, and one who carried on his breast the purple ribbon of the Victoria Cross. His victim was Major Lanoe George Hawker, VC, DSO, RE, RFC.

Hawker was a pre-war pilot and was one of the first to emerge from the anonymity which cloaked the early performances of RFC pilots. He had dropped four twenty-five-pounder bombs on the airship sheds at Cologne from a height of 200 feet. The flying débris resulting from the explosions peppered his craft and the blast bobbed it about like a cork in a storm, but he flew home safely. In the spring of 1915, when aerial fighting really began to be taken seriously, he received the Victoria Cross for downing three Germans in one day—the first time this feat had been accomplished. He became a notable squadron commander, impatient of routine but brilliant in the important phase of innovation. He inaugurated a system of co-operation with the British anti-aircraft batteries which saved his squadron hundreds of fruitless hours of patrol. He asked the battery commanders to report to him every time they saw German aircraft flying over the lines. He found that the German aerial activity fell into a defined pattern; they came over each day about the same time, at the same altitude, and in about the same numbers. He arranged the schedule of his squadron accordingly, and gradually its total of kills began to mount.

It was seldom that Richthofen found himself alone in the sky; Boelcke's training had always emphasized formation attacks, and Richthofen adhered closely to the teaching of his master. But one day he did become separated from his staffel and that was the day he met Hawker. By now, of course, the name of Hawker was as well known to the German pilots as the name of Boelcke had been to the British, but naturally Richthofen when he joined combat with the de Havilland did not know its pilot. That night he confided details of the fight to his diary:

The Englishman tried to catch me up in the rear while I tried to get behind him. So we circled round and round like madmen after one another at an altitude of about 10,000 feet. First we circled twenty times to the left, and then thirty times to the right. Each tried to get behind and above the other.

Soon I discovered that I was not meeting a beginner. He had not the slightest intention to break off the fight. He was travelling in a box which turned beautifully. However, my packing-case was better at climbing than his. . . .

When we had got down to about 6000 feet without having achieved anything particular, my opponent ought to have discovered that it was time for him to take his leave. The wind was favourable to me, for it drove us more and more towards the German position. At last we were above Bapaume, about half a mile behind the German front. The gallant fellow was full of pluck, and when we had got down to about 3000 feet he merrily waved to me as if he would say, Well, how do you do?

The circles which we made round one another were so narrow that their diameter was probably no more than 250 or 300 feet. I had time to take a good look at my opponent. I looked down into his carriage and could see every movement of his head.

My Englishman was a good sportsman, but by and by the thing became a little too hot for him. He had to decide whether he would land on German ground or whether he would fly back to the English lines. Of course he tried the latter, after endeavouring in vain to escape me by loopings and such tricks. At that time his first bullets were flying around me, for so far neither of us had been able to do any shooting.

When he had come down to about 300 feet he tried to escape by flying in a zigzag course, which makes it difficult for an observer on the ground to shoot. That was my most favourable moment. I followed him at an altitude of from 250 to 150 feet, firing all the time. The Englishman could not help falling. But the jamming of my gun nearly robbed me of my success.

The following day, when he learned the identity of his distinguished victim, Richthofen flew to the site where he had crashed and wrenched the machine gun from the wreckage. He sent it home to his mother and asked her to have it attached over his bedroom door. Henceforth he would always try to get some memento from an aeroplane he downed, and soon his home was filled with grisly souvenirs.

Hawker was given a burial with full military honours by Richthofen's flying mates. Richthofen, usually completely insensitive, remained away from the funeral: this, like the wreaths dropped by the British when Boelcke was buried, would be part of the gradually forming tradition of air fighters.

Richthofen personally dropped a note from the air behind the British lines addressed to Hawker's comrades of the Royal Flying Corps, stating briefly the death of the British ace and expressing the widespread admiration of German airmen for him as an exceptionally brave airman and a chivalrous foe.

In the last attack of the Somme battles in November, 1916, when the western outskirts of Grandcourt were reached, the elements played their final and decisive part. A thaw set in, changing the battlefield into a sea of mud, and mixed rain and snowstorms shrouded the movements of the infantry from the eyes of the observers who were flying low over them. So ended the greatest continuous battle which the world had yet seen. It was a battle of limited objectives against intricate defences. An autumn of average wetness might have seen the campaign develop according to plan. But to some degree the great struggle achieved the three main objects for which it had been waged. It not only removed the tension at Verdun, but it also enabled the French to turn on the enemy and, before the year had ended, sweep the German armies back almost to the positions from which, in February, 1916, they had sprung with such advertised confidence. It kept the main German forces pinned to the Western Front at a time when France was fighting with her back to the wall. Finally, it dealt a blow at the morale of the enemy troops from which they never recovered.

In the air, despite the dreadful casualties, the RFC had always maintained the offensive. From the beginning to the end of the battle, the air war was fought for the most part over enemy territory. Even when the hostile aircraft increased to the point when they were nearly equal in numbers and often superior in performance to those of the Royal Flying Corps, the German air policy remained, except for the occasional exceptions made to Boelcke's Jagdstaffel, a defensive one. As the enemy air service multiplied, so did British casualties grow,

The Caudron G-2 was a useful trainer in 1914

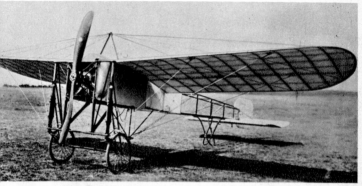

The Blériot monoplane, also used for training
in the early days of the War

One of the most versatile early warplanes,
the Maurice Farman Shorthorn

A Morane Bullet of 1915, a well-liked French single-seater

The Bristol Bullet, a delight to fly, could remain aloft for 2½ hours

The Caudron G-3, a development of the G-2

Germany's Halberstadt CL II of 1916

The 1916 Albatros was a favourite German general purpose aircraft

The Nieuport biplane, a very successful French fighter

The German Aviatik C-2, a short-range bomber also used as a fighter

Britain's Sopwith Pup fighter, brought into service in 1916

The British FE2b, slow but respected by German airmen

Gotha bombers like this one raided Britain in the last years of the War

The Fokker triplane, deadly in the hands of the 'Red Baron'

The Sopwith Snipe was the last word in fighters when introduced in 1918

American pilots were trained in this Curtiss JN-4D 'Jenny'

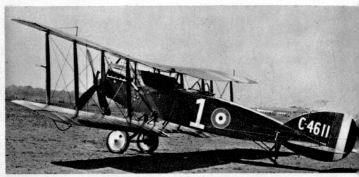

Most of the virtues were combined in this Bristol Fighter of 1917

Fokker used the best features of this 1917 Sopwith in his own triplane

Ernst Udet and his Fokker, 1918

Ypres, 1918; early aerial photographs like this one were obtained at
heavy cost in aircraft and lives

Captain Albert Ball, VC, the first pilot to be idolised in Britain

Captain 'Billy' Bishop, the Canadian VC with 72 victories to his credit

but in retrospect they were not heavy in view of the great volume of work that was done day after day to further the task of the Army.

Chapter Seven

THEY COULDN'T WAIT

O N May 18th, 1916, Corporal Kiffin Yates Rockwell of Asheville, North Carolina, flying with No 124 Squadron (French) shot down a German aircraft over the lines in Alsace-Lorraine. It was the first time he had flown in combat; it was the first time he had fired a gun at an enemy machine. His tactics in this victory were typical of those he would use henceforth in the forty aerial combats in which he would engage. He aimed his aircraft at the German, ignored the enemy fire until he was within one hundred feet of the machine, gave it a short burst and then just before colliding with it zoomed upwards. On this occasion the short burst was short indeed; only four bullets streaked from his machine gun, but they killed the pilot and sent the aircraft crashing to the ground.

The victory by Rockwell received wide notice, for No 124 Squadron was better known as the *Escadrille Americaine*, a title which, under the pressure of neutral-minded politicians at home, was shortly changed to the *Escadrille Lafayette* and which finally grew into the Lafayette Flying Corps. Rockwell's victory turned the spotlight on this small band of Americans, who felt from the very beginning that this was their war, too. Before they were incorporated in the United States Air Force (February 18th, 1918) as the 103rd Pursuit Squadron, these men would score 199 confirmed victories over German aircraft. But the squadron would perform a far more important mission. The influence of the Lafayette Flying Corps had a tremendous effect on public opinion at a time when America was neutral and under heavy pressure to maintain that status.

The idea of a group of young American pilots fighting in

the uniform of France was a brain-child of Norman Prince of Pride's Crossing, Massachusetts. He began planning it during the early months of the war, but more than a year passed before he was able to overcome the many diplomatic obstacles. To begin with, when a citizen of a neutral country enlisted in either the French or British armed forces, he had to take an oath of allegiance to the country he wished to serve. Any American taking an oath of loyalty to another country immediately forfeited his American citizenship. Norman Prince went to Paris to ask for the aid of a highly successful American doctor practising medicine in the French capital. Dr Edmund L. Gros had already been instrumental in forming the American Ambulance Service, which presented no problem because as non-combatants the ambulance men did not have to sign any oath of allegiance. Gros had been thinking along the same lines as had Norman Prince, and now they were joined by two Americans of influence also residing in Paris, Robert W. Bliss and Robert Astor Chanler. In Jarousse de Silac, a member of the Air Ministry, they found an important French ally. He pleaded their cause before the War Department and eventually a method of circumventing the oath of allegiance was found: about a dozen Americans were serving in the French Foreign Legion, a peculiar organization which demanded no oath of allegiance to the country but merely an agreement that the volunteer would obey the orders of his superior officers. Several of them had used the device of a technicality to transfer to the French Flying Corps. This became standard procedure for Americans wishing to fight for France.

The indefatigable Dr Gros combed the Foreign Legion and the ambulance corps for men who were pilots or who wished to be pilots, and as soon as they were found he had them 'detached' to the French Air Force, with the idea of eventually making them the nucleus of an American group. William Thaw became a bomber pilot; Jimmy Bach and Bert Hall were flying Nieuports; Prince, Cowdin and Lufbery were with escadrilles flying Voisins; Jimmy McConnell and Victor Chapman were flying Maurice Farmans. All of them, however, were dreaming of the day when they would be members of a purely American fighter group. The report that such a project was in the final stages of development spread to England, and several youngsters who had gone to London to enlist in the RFC, but who were frustrated by the prerequisite oath of allegiance to the Crown, hurried to France, were taken in hand by the ever-helpful Dr Gros, joined the Foreign Legion and were then detached to the Air Force. They went to Pau for their training. Many others came to France directly from America for the same purpose.

On April 17th, 1916, all difficulties had been cleared away and the Escadrille Americaine was officially born, with seven men comprising the original membership: Norman Prince, William Thaw, Victor Chapman, Kiffin Rockwell, James McConnell, Elliot Cowdin and Bert Hall. Only Hall, Cowdin and Thaw would survive. The next day they were sent to Luxeuil and assigned to the job of escorting and protecting one of France's most illustrious bombing groups. They were given Nieuports. One of them, James McConnell, wrote the story of the arrival of the young escadrille:

On our arrival at Luxeuil we were met by Captain Georges Thenault, the French commander of the Escadrille Americaine —officially known as N124—and motored to the aviation field in one of the staff cars assigned to us. I enjoyed that ride. Lolling back against the soft leather cushions, I recalled how in my apprenticeship days at Pau I had had to walk six miles for my laundry.

The equipment awaiting us at the field was even more impressive than our automobile. Everything was brand new, from the fifteen Fiat trucks to the office, *magasin*, and rest tents. And the men attached to the escadrille! At first sight they seemed to outnumber the Nicaraguan Army—mechanicians, chauffeurs, armourers, motor-cyclists, telephonists, wireless operators, Red Cross stretcher-bearers, clerks! Afterward I learned they totalled seventy-odd, and that all of them were glad to be connected with the American escadrille.

Rooms were assigned to us in a villa adjoining the famous hot baths of Luxeuil. We messed with our officers, Captain Thenault and Lieutenant de Laage de Meux, at the best hotel in town. An automobile was always on hand to carry us to the field. I began to wonder whether I was a summer resorter or a soldier.

Among the pilots who had welcomed us, we discovered the famous Captain Happe, commander of the Luxeuil bombardment group. After we had been introduced, he pointed to eight little boxes arranged on a table.

"They contain Croix de Guerre for the families of the men I lost on my last trip," he explained, and he added: "It's a good thing you're here to go along with us for protection. There are lots of Boches in this sector."

I thought of the luxury we were enjoying; our comfortable beds, baths and motor cars, and then I recalled the ancient custom of giving a man selected for the sacrifice a royal time of it before the appointed day.

To acquaint us with the few places where a safe landing was possible, we were motored through the Vosges Mountains and on into Alsace. It was a delightful opportunity to see that glorious countryside, and we appreciated it the more because we knew its charm would be lost when we surveyed it from the sky. From the air the ground presents no scenic effects. The ravishing beauty of the Val d'Ajol, the steep mountainsides bristling with a solid mass of giant pines, the glittering cascades tumbling downward through fairylike avenues of verdure, the roaring, tossing torrent at the foot of the slope—all this loveliness, seen from an airplane at 12,000 feet, fades into flat splotches of green traced with a tiny ribbon of silver.

Within a few days Raoul Lufbery, Chouteau Johnson, Clyde Balsley, Dudley Hill, Lawrence Rumsey, Didier Masson and Paul Pavelka arrived from the French groups for which they had been flying. Like the original seven they were all experienced pilots. It was a typical American group. In it were sons of wealth like Prince, Cowdin, Thaw and Chapman; there were gay adventurers like Lufbery, soldiers of fortune like Hall, and there was Pavelka, who had spent most of his life as a common seaman. They all became first-rate pilots, and the American characteristic of team-work in sport was, surprisingly enough, developed superbly by their French CO, Captain Thenault. The escadrille was transferred to Bar-le-

Duc, closer to the Verdun front, and they had hardly settled down when Bert Hall and William Thaw brought down their first victims.

That same day Thaw and Rockwell were wounded. Thaw was hit in the arm, the bullet severing an artery. He bled profusely and just managed to make a safe landing before blacking out. An explosive bullet detonating on Rockwell's windscreen tore several gashes in his face. Almost blinded by blood, he was still able to land and was flying again within twenty-four hours. The French mechanics idolized Rockwell. They knew that he had been badly wounded during his stint as an infantryman with the Foreign Legion, and now he had stopped German lead again. They chuckled when they saw him, heavily bandaged, walk towards his Nieuport twenty-four hours after his painful wound, and said proudly, '*Il ne lâchera pas; c'est un bagarreur.*' In truth, he had come to fight and fight he did with every bit of energy and courage he had. But fighting came naturally to the soft-spoken young Southerner; an ancestor was a captain on George Washington's staff and both of his grandfathers (Captain Henry Rockwell of North Carolina and Major Enoch Shaw Ayres of South Carolina) had been officers in the army of the Confederacy. He was a complete idealist, with unbounded faith in the justice of the cause for which he was fighting. After he was wounded he wrote to his mother, 'If I die, you will know that I died as every man should—in fighting for the right. I do not consider that I am fighting for France alone but for the cause of humanity, the most noble of all causes.'

A week later Victor Chapman was wounded.

Chapman was considered by his fellow fliers to be the most courageous of them all. The son of a well-to-do family, he had been educated at Saint Paul's School, Harvard, and then had studied architecture and painting in Paris. As soon as war broke out he joined the Foreign Legion and saw considerable service. He spent one hundred consecutive days in the front-line trenches and saw half his comrades killed. He and Kiffin Rockwell became fast friends during these days. Chapman earned the whole-hearted admiration of the hardened men of the Legion. Gay, in love with life, he nevertheless constantly courted death. Those with whom he fought said that he was never completely happy unless he was in danger. When he finally transferred to French aviation, his exuberant letters to his parents, his friends and to his uncle (William Astor Chanler) indicated that he was actually grateful to a capricious fate which had supplied this war—at last his singing spirit, his courage and his perhaps subconscious fascination with danger had found a satisfying outlet. Finally the universe, which until now had rather bored him, had provided him with the most exciting of all gifts, a full opportunity of realizing the potentials which had for so long lain dormant in him.

He had never cared for sports or for books or for studying. He had loved the bright colours of nature and had often painted them, and in Paris he had grown fond of the old and beautiful buildings; but these interests were only evidences of something deeper within his nature, something that had to accept painting and architecture as substitutes for the real and as yet unrecognized fulfilment. Flying was the answer; it even satisfied his love for colour. He once wrote his father:

Everyone says they get tired of flying, 'It's monotonous'. I don't see it, but on the contrary, an infinite variety in this, when there is a slight sprinkling of clouds. Clouds are not thin pieces of blotting paper; but liquid, ceaselessly changing steam. I played hide-and-seek in and out of them yesterday; sometimes flat blankets like melting snow on either side below me, or again, like great ice-floes with distant bergs looming up, and 'open water' near at hand, blue as a moonstone cloud, floating full, for all the world like a gigantic jellyfish (those that have red trailers and a sting). In the nearer pools the mottled earth, piebald with sun and shadows, showed through; and it was thanks to these I knew my whereabouts. I was going from below the clouds to above them, circling in some hole; thus I realized the size and thickness of the walls 300 metres sheer from top to base of dazzling whiteness. Some have many feathery, filmy points and angles, others are rounded and voluminous, with cracks and caverns in them. These are all the fair weather, fleecy clouds; for there are the lower, flatter, misty ones, and the speckled, or mare's tail clouds, above which one never reaches. There are such a lot of trumpet-shaped and wind-blown clouds this evening I should like to go out and examine them; but it's a bore for my mechanic, and I doubt if I could go high enough to warrant crossing the lines.

Your loving
Victor

Captain Thenault gave the free spirits under his command a great deal of latitude. Chapman took full advantage of this to fly constantly. He had become a fine pilot, more reckless than most, and as often as not he'd return to the base after forays over German territory with his wings and fuselage perforated with bullets. The day he was wounded he attacked four German aircraft. They scattered and a Fokker got behind him. His machine was riddled and a bullet cut deep into his scalp, but he swerved away, emptied his ammunition drum at his attacker and headed for home. A stability control had been severed, but Chapman held the broken rod in one hand, somehow managing the machine with the other. He landed, received medical attention, allowed a doctor to bandage his head and then, after repairing his Nieuport, immediately took off again.

A few days later Captain Thenault, Rockwell, Clyde Balsley and Norman Prince became involved in a serious encounter. They found themselves surrounded by at least fourteen German machines which, circling about them, fired at long range. Thenault knew their only slim hope of salvation was to break through this ring, and he signalled his men to attack the Germans, flying between them and the French lines. Thenault, Rockwell and Prince broke through successfully, but Balsley found himself hemmed in. An explosive bullet hit him in the thigh. He tried to get away by a vertical dive, but his Nieuport went into a corkscrew and swung over on its back. Somehow he righted his staggering, violently shaking aeroplane and landed in a meadow just beyond the firing line.

He was hustled to a field hospital and ten fragments of the explosive bullet (technically outlawed by the Geneva Convention) were removed from his body. For days he lingered between life and death. He developed a terrible thirst, which he could only satisfy by sucking oranges. One afternoon Chapman decided to carry a bag of oranges to his friend. He took off just after Prince and Lufbery had left. They were far ahead of him when a squadron of Fokkers fell on them from above. It was a desperate fight for survival. Chapman saw the mêlée and hurried to help his two escadrille comrades. Lufbery and Prince managed to stay intact. They hurried back to the field to tell how Chapman's diversion had saved them. They waited for him to check in—he was always the last to land, so at first they weren't worried. Then a phone call came from another escadrille. A pilot said he had seen a Nieuport fall. A second call verified the fact that it had been Chapman. James McConnell wrote of what the escadrille felt:

> We talked in lowered voices after that; we could read the pain in one another's eyes. If only it could have been someone else, was what we all thought, I suppose. To lose Victor was not an irreparable loss to us merely, but to France, and to the world as well. I kept thinking of him lying over there, and of the oranges he was taking to Balsley. As I left the field I caught sight of Victor's méchanician leaning against the end of our hangar. He was looking northward into the sky where his patron had vanished, and his face was very sad.

Chapman's death made a deep impact on his flying colleagues. Because he was the first American pilot to meet death, the French and American newspapers gave considerable space to the sad event. An American correspondent interviewed Captain Thenault, and the commanding officer of the Escadrille Americaine said:

> Our grief was extreme, for we loved him deeply. At the moment of greatest danger in the air we could always discover the silhouette of his machine, that machine which he managed with so much ease. One of my *pilotes* has just said to me, "Would that I had fallen instead of him." With the Army at Verdun his bravery was legendary, and hardly a day passed without some exploits from which he returned with his machine pierced by bullets and sometimes slightly wounded

himself. He was to have received the *Medaille Militaire* when death took him. A citation with the *Croix de Guerre* will speak for a small part of what he did.

Perhaps the greatest tribute to the dead airman was penned by Kiffin Rockwell, who wrote to the pilot's mother. It read in part:

There is nothing that I can say to you or anyone that will do full credit to him. And everyone here that knew him feels the same way. To start with, Victor had such a strong character. I think we all have our ideals, when we begin, but unfortunately there are so very few of us that retain them; and sometimes we lose them at a very early age, and after that, life seems to be spoiled. But Victor was one of the very few who had the strongest of ideals, and then had the character to withstand anything that tried to come into his life and kill them. He was just a large, healthy man, full of life and goodness toward life, and could only see the fine, true points in life and in other people. And he was not of the kind that absorbs from other people, but of the kind that gives out. We all had felt his influence and seeing in him a man, made us feel a little more like trying to be men ourselves.

For work in the escadrille, Victor worked hard, always wanting to fly. And courage! He was too courageous; we all would beg him at times to slow up a little. We speak of him every day here, and we have said sincerely among ourselves many a time that Victor had more courage than all the rest of the escadrille combined. He would attack the Germans always, no matter what the conditions or what the odds.

He died the most glorious death, and at the most glorious time of life to die, especially for him, with his ideals. I have never once regretted it for him, as I know he was willing and satisfied to give his life that way if it was necessary, and that he had no fear of death. It is for you, his father, relatives, myself, and for all who have known him, and all who would have known him, and for the world as a whole, I regret his loss. Yet he is not dead; he lives forever in every place he has been, and in everyone who knew him, and in the future generations little points of his character will be passed along. He is alive every day in this escadrille and has a tremendous influence on all our actions. Even the *mécaniciens* do their work better and more conscientiously. A number of times I have seen Victor's mécanicien standing (when there was no work to be done) and gazing off in the direction of where he last saw Victor leaving for the lines.

I must close now. You must not feel sorry, but must feel proud and happy.

Kiffin Rockwell

To say that Chapman was perhaps the best-loved man in the squadron would be no exaggeration. Those who survived and who are alive today will smile gently when you mention his name, and the floodgates of their memories will open and you'll hear them speak of him as a symbol of American idealism. One of them might still have a copy of the verse written about Chapman by John Heard, Jr:

> Great-hearted, loyal, reckless for a friend;
> Not counting risks, cool-headed, clear of sight,
> He gave himself to serve a lofty end,
> And, like an eagle soaring in the light,
> On wings unruffled by the wind's chance breath
> He sought, and seeks his goal with steadfast flight,
> ——Victor, indeed, in name, in life, in death!

During the Verdun battle the Escadrille Americaine came of age. In the beginning, the French looked upon the young Americans more as valuable instruments of propaganda than as first-class fighting men; but the reports of Captain Thenault to the Air Ministry were highly enthusiastic, and finally the escadrille was accepted not as a curiosity but as a first-rate fighting unit.

By now the escadrille had been transferred back to Luxeuil where it had begun its combat life only five brief months before. It was a quaint and quiet Vosges town, and for a week, while waiting for the new, improved Nieuports to arrive, the escadrille took the opportunity of getting acquainted with the Royal Naval Air Service unit stationed at Luxeuil. There were fifty pilots and 1000 enlisted men in this bombardment group which had been detached from the British forces and was, like the escadrille, serving under French command. The Americans and British, helped to some extent by huge quantities of champagne and Hall's Manhattans, became firm friends. They took over the Hôtel Lion d'Or and threw a joint party, during the course of which every dish, cup, saucer and bit of furniture was hilariously broken. At the height of the party, shots were heard outside. A dozen pilots rushed to investigate, only to find that they had been fired by a former Canadian Mountie. He and Lufbery had been discussing shooting, and the exuberant Lufbery had suggested that they have a little target practice. Lufbery held a book out at arm's length, and from thirty paces the Canadian was hitting beautifully. Even Lufbery admitted that this was the best shooting he had even seen in view of the fact that the Canadian had a very unsteady target at which to aim. The book was a thin volume of British drill regulations.

When Lufbery, now recognized as the most skilful pilot of them all, wasn't flying or raising hell, he was, incongruously enough, picking mushrooms, for which he had an inordinate passion. Bill Thaw was keeping the mess supplied with fresh trout from a nearby stream, but it was Bert Hall who became the hero of the hour. He went fishing as no man had ever fished in the Vosges district. He scorned the use of pole, lure, or hook. He merely rolled up his sleeves and waited. When a trout swam within his reach he'd pounce, hook his fingers in the gills of the fish and haul it out. He caught one five-pound trout this way, the largest ever taken from the stream. It was a trick, Hall said, that he'd learned in Missouri as a boy.

By that time the escadrille had a mascot, a lion cub called Whiskey. Thaw, Hall and Lufbery had bought the animal for 250 francs in Paris. The cub took an immediate fancy to Thaw and soon became a valued and accepted member of the escadrille. Finally the Nieuports arrived and the men were delighted with the machine's high performance and its Vickers machine gun which could fire 500 rounds a minute. Then the fighting was resumed. The gaiety, the fishing, the hunting for mushrooms were forgotten.

But there were still occasional trips to Paris for a day or two of what the British, with their wonderful capacity for phrasemaking, called 'fun and games'. Usually the men would first contact the generous Dr Gros, who would smile and immediately say, 'I know how much you boys make; now here's 20,000 francs. Have a good time while you can.' There is no record that Dr Gros ever turned down the unuttered request of an American pilot for the wherewithal to enjoy the 'fun and games' which were available in Paris to young and acquiescent Americans. Jimmy McConnell, Raoul Lufbery, Bert Hall and Bill Thaw were four men who were always ready for a fight or a frolic, and in the course of their Paris peregrinations they were often joined by Charles Nungesser, now on his way to becoming one of the greatest of French aces. One evening he introduced them to a beautiful girl.

"A big steel millionaire from Pittsburg," Nungesser said, indicating Hall, and the eyes of the girl kindled with interest. She invited a few friends to the table, and when it was time to leave, Hall found that Nungesser and Lufbery had quietly disappeared, leaving him with an enormous bill.

He found Nungesser and Lufbery back at the hotel enjoying a nightcap and he stormed at them for leaving him holding the baby.

"And damn it all," he added, "I don't even know the girl's name."

"She calls herself Mata Hari," Nungesser laughed. "You usually see her with some cabinet minister or general. Some people actually think she's a spy."

"All she asked me about was the profit a man could make out of steel," Hall snorted.

Nungesser was recovering from a bad crack-up and he had been grounded for two months. He liked the carefree young Americans—and especially the murderous Manhattan cocktail Hall concocted in a water-bucket—and suggested that he return with them to their base. He did, and he remained for nearly a month, flying and fighting with them, and when he downed a Fokker one afternoon, Lufbery was host at a tremendous party in his honour.

The Americans were also beginning to have great respect for both French and British pilots. They agreed that the French were natural pilots. An aeroplane seemed to obey Nungesser's thoughts rather than the controls, Jimmy McConnell wrote. The Americans felt that they could spot a French pilot no matter what type of machine he was flying; the French flier added a few extra frills to the ordinary acrobatic manœuvring.

The British pilots always carried out his mission calmly, methodically, seriously; he never indulged in aerial dramatics. To the Americans he was the best. The American seemed to be a combination of both—neither better nor worse than the others. The men of the escadrille didn't have nearly as much respect for the German fliers. They flew by the book and had little talent for improvisation. In his judgment, however, they always excluded Oswald Boelcke.

With the death of Victor Chapman the war had become personal. Combat flying was no longer an exhilarating game; it was not even a sacred crusade as it had been with Chapman. Chapman was dead and the rest of the escadrille was grimly determined to avenge his death. Norman Prince and Kiffin Rockwell in particular flew long and hard, for Chapman's death weighed heavily upon them. One day Rockwell wrote to his brother (then training to be a pilot), 'Prince and I are going to fly ten hours tomorrow, and we'll do our best to kill one or two Germans for Victor.' They each did get a German that day. The following day Rockwell went up with Lufbery as his flying partner. Over the Vosges they separated, each to engage a Fokker, and it was at 10,000 feet above the ground that the brief and splendid life of Kiffin Rockwell came to an end. He fell behind the French lines, and when his body was recovered a huge, gaping wound in his throat made by an explosive bullet indicated that death had been instantaneous. That evening Thenault had to announce his death to the squadron. "The best and bravest of us all is no more. . . . When Rockwell was in the air no German passed, and he was in the air most of the time."

He was buried with full military honours and with the whole British and American personnel attending the rites. Dozens of French pilots flew to Luxeuil for the funeral. When it was over, Prince and Lufbery, without even exchanging words, hurried to take off in their Nieuports. During the next two days, Prince, flying with reckless abandon, downed two Germans which were confirmed and at least two more so far behind the German lines that there were no witnesses. A few days later these two brilliant fliers were sent out to protect some bombing machines which were due back from a long-range mission. They cleared the sky above the airport of enemy aircraft, and then went searching for the returning bombers. Darkness fell rapidly that afternoon. Lufbery managed to land all right at a small field near the lines called Corcieux, but when Prince tried to come in, the darkness had deepened. He did not see a high-tension cable stretched above the treetops bordering the field, and his undercarriage struck it. The Nieuport snapped forward and hit the ground on its nose. Prince was thrown far from the wrecked plane. Both of his legs were broken and it was obvious that he had sustained internal injuries, but before losing consciousness he managed to gasp, "Light some petrol flares; other aircraft may be trying to come in." They placed Prince in an ambulance and with Lufbery holding the hand of his pain-wracked friend it hurried towards a hospital at Gerardmer.

Three days later Prince died. He had been a brilliant organizer, a stabilizing influence on younger men and a skilful pilot, with a great capacity for improvisation. He was one of the few who had been successful in shooting down observation balloons, a difficult task, for they were well protected by anti-aircraft fire. He had rigged up some rockets (really glorified fireworks) on the wings of his Nieuport and found that if he could get close enough to the sausages, his home-made weapons were highly effective.

A few days after Prince's death the escadrille was moved to the Somme, where the greatest battle of the war was in progress. During the six months of its existence the American squadron had done well; it had participated in 156 combats and had (officially) destroyed seventeen German aircraft. And it had captured the imagination of the American public to such an extent that the German Government had lodged a protest in Washington against the use of the term Escadrille Americaine as being a violation of the neutrality of the United States. Pressure was such that the French Ambassador in Washington was asked to take official action, and he notified the Ministry of War that a change must be made in the name of the squadron. The French Ministry of War called Dr Gros in for consultation. He heard without enthusiasm the suggestion that the name be changed to *Escadrille des Volontaires*, and then made a suggestion of his own. It was that the squadron be henceforth known as the Escadrille Lafayette. His suggestion was adopted, and under that name the escadrille achieved enduring fame.

More and more recruits were arriving from the United States now. Dr Gros had obtained financial backing from William K. Vanderbilt and several other wealthy Americans, and he paid the passage of new recruits from America, bought them uniforms, gave them spending money and impressed upon the more irresponsible newcomers the deadly seriousness of their mission. The publicity received at home was perhaps out of proportion to the importance of the American group, but it was calculated propaganda and successfully aroused public sentiment for France in the United States, which was making a brave show of being neutral. At home the public knew that in the autumn of 1916 American pilots were fighting in the great battle of the Somme; they knew that they were holding their own against the most skilful fighters in the German Air Force.

During the latter part of 1916, more than fifty Americans arrived in Paris to join the Escadrille Lafayette. James Norman Hall, later to achieve literary fame with his *Mutiny on the Bounty* and other wonderful tales of the South Seas, was one of them. He had served with the First Hundred Thousand (Kitchener's Mob) as infantryman, had been honourably discharged and had returned home for a breathing spell. Commissioned by *Atlantic Monthly* to do a series on the American group, he returned to Paris intending to write his articles quickly and re-enlist in the British infantry. He visited Dr Gros, who suggested casually that instead of joining the infantry he might like to throw in his lot with his fellow Americans.

"But, Dr Gros," Hall protested, "I know nothing about flying. I've never even been up in a plane."

"Few of our men know anything about flying to begin with," Gros smiled.

"And I know nothing about engines. I don't even know how to drive an automobile."

"There are expert mechanics at the front to care for the

engines. Your only duty would be to learn to fly and to fight in the air."

A few days later Hall found himself at the *École Blériot* at Buc (not far from Versailles) learning to fly the aptly named Penguin, a Blériot whose wings had been clipped. He found a great many other fellow countrymen at Buc in various stages of training: Stephen Bigelow of Boston; Ray C. Bridgemen of Lake Forest, Illinois; Courtney Campbell, Jr, of Chicago; Charles Dolan, Jr, of Boston; William E. Dugan, Jr, of Rochester; Willis B. Haviland of St Paul; Dudley L. Hill of Peekskill, New York; Chouteau Johnson of St Louis; Henry S. Jones of Harford, Pennsylvania; Walter Lovell of Concord, Massachusetts; Kenneth Marr of San Francisco; David Peterson of Honesdale, Pennsylvania; Robert Rockwell of Cincinnati; Robert Soubiran of New York City; Harold B. Willis of Boston; and Douglas MacMonagle of San Francisco were among them. Campbell, MacMonagle and Peterson would die before the war had finished; Hall and Willis would be shot down and become prisoners of war.

Chapter Eight

THE GREAT ZEPPELIN SCARE

DURING THE four years devoted to organized slaughter by most of the world's civilized nations, there were 8,538,315 men killed and 21,219,452 wounded. There was one further casualty, a significant death, because out of it arose the pattern of warfare conformed to since then, and the pattern of warfare for the future. The corpse was Article 25 of the Land War Convention of 1907, commonly known as the Hague Conference. This conference, attended by representatives of forty-four countries for the purpose of drawing up ground rules for the unscheduled but inevitable war that they all knew lay ahead, inserted in Article 25 a sanctimonious embargo against any bombardment of undefended places 'by any means whatever', and when the 1914 war arrived it was clear enough to all concerned that this phrase expressly forbade the aerial attacks against centres of civilian population.

On December 21st, 1914, at 1 pm, a German aircraft dropped a bomb on the town of Dover. The bomb neither killed nor wounded anyone, it merely shattered some glass—but it destroyed Article 25

Gradually, as the war grew more bitter, there came the realization that there was no room in modern battle for such peacetime luxuries as chivalry, decency or respect for contracts and international agreements. By 1916 both sides had to a great degree adopted the theories of General Guilio Douhet. If examples of German 'frightfulness' in attacking undefended centres of population far outnumbered Allied examples, it was only because they were better equipped for the job. It was also part of the calculated Allied propaganda drive to arouse America's sympathy that gave such wide circulation to German atrocities. It is, of course, true that Germany began fracturing all tacit rules of accepted warfare early in the game. When it was all over and a peace treaty was being negotiated, the German Prime Minister asked Clemenceau, "I wonder what history will say of this frightful war?" The doughty Clemenceau said dryly, "History will never say that Belgium invaded Germany." Nor will history ever deny that the Germans from the beginning treated civilians as military targets.

This philosophy of warfare was demonstrated most dramatically by the Zeppelin raids on England. In a way, the spiritual godfather of the Zeppelin was Abraham Lincoln, who, after watching Thaddeus S. C. Lowe demonstrate his captive observation balloon which was moored in the grounds of the Smithsonian Institute, became an enthusiast for the lighter-than-air contraption. Send it up 200 feet and a man with a good telescope could tell you about enemy positions five miles away. Lowe also devised a telegraph connection for the use of the observer, who could make immediate reports to men on the ground. Lincoln's Civil War army chiefs were doubtful of the value of the balloon, but the President overrode their objections, ordered a fleet of them and made Professor Lowe chief aeronautical engineer.

A young German military attaché, Count Ferdinand von

Zeppelin, went to the front and received permission to ascend in one of the balloons. He was wildly enthusiastic in praise of this new type of aerial observation post, and he speculated on the enormous possibilities of making such a post mobile and navigable. After the Civil War had ended, Zeppelin returned home filled with ideas on the subject. He received financial backing from the Government, and with the help of some of Germany's finest engineers developed a navigable airship. He began with the basic assumption that 1000 cubic feet of air weighed eighty pounds; 1000 cubic feet of hydrogen weighed five and a half pounds. Enclosed in a bag, the hydrogen would float in air just as a piece of wood would float in water. From the beginning he was committed to the proposition that the airship must be rigid in order to keep its streamlined shape, despite variations in the pressure of the hydrogen. The French, already experimenting with airships, put their hopes on the semi-rigid airship; that was, a flexible balloon which could contract or expand as heat or cold affected the hydrogen, and was attached to a rigid keel or body. The British clung to the idea of an entirely flexible airship, suspending their observation car from a gasbag which had no rigid framework to hold it in shape.

One of Count Zeppelin's greatest contributions was the latticework of aluminium alloy, which formed the framework, and the sixteen compartments, each of which held a large hydrogen gasbag. His first two airships left much to be desired, but when he flew 750 miles non-stop in his third lighter-than-air craft, not only the Government but the whole German public acclaimed him and poured funds into his enterprise.

He was ready when war came to turn his ships over to the Army. At that time, Germany possessed the Z-4, 5, 6, 7, 8, and 9, which were Zeppelins. There were three others named *Saxony*, *Victoria Louise* and *Hansa*, and the Navy had one lone ship, the L-3. From the very beginning the German public, led before the war to expect great things of its airship fleet, pressed for attacks on England. It was not until 1915, however, that the 'fleet' really came into existence. Now the Army had added the Z-10, Z-11; the LZ-34 and LZ-35, and five more dirigibles had been built for the Navy.

The Kaiser, giving way to public pressure, specifically sanctioned airship raids on England, and the deluded nation waited in happy anticipation for the spectacle of London, Liverpool and Manchester in flames.

The Navy made a few unsuccessful raids on England and then in May 1915, the first bombing by a military dirigible of London occurred. It was made by the LZ-38, with Hauptmann Linnarz, experienced and skilful mariner of the air, in command. Linnarz had tried twice, unsuccessfully, to reach London before he made it. The first time, he got as far as Southend and dropped several incendiary bombs close to the moored hulk of the ss. *Royal Edward*, which he had no way of knowing housed nothing more important to the British war effort than German prisoners of war. He also dropped 120 incendiaries on Southend itself which killed one woman, injured two men and set a timberyard on fire. In addition, he dropped one large cardboard placard on which was something seemingly more suited for today's comic strips than anything else. It read, 'You English. We have come, and will come again soon. Kill or cure. German.'

He finally reached the capital on May 31st, just before midnight. The Zeppelin was at a great height, and although in his official report Linnarz said solemnly that he dropped bombs only on London docks and military establishments, it was of course impossible for him with the crude bombsights at his disposal even to approximate where his bombs would fall. Actually the bombs killed seven people, injured thirty-five more and did damage estimated at £18,000 to houses and business premises. Following the raid, the gun defences of London were increased and a squadron of light cruisers based on the Humber were armed with anti-aircraft guns to intercept any Zeps cruising over the North Sea en route to the capital.

The traditionalists in the Navy probably winced at the thought of the senior service having to play nursemaid to the civilians of London, but Winston Churchill was First Lord of the Admiralty and he had a doughty right arm in the person of Lord Fisher, whom he had brought out of retirement at the age of seventy-four. Lord Kitchener, the great professional soldier, was England's foremost popular hero, but he was respected rather than liked; Churchill, the loquacious, ingratiating rebel, was disarming, but he was relatively young and there were those who thought he had too little respect for tradition and the established military and naval way of doing things—but everyone loved Lord Fisher. He had the humour and warmth which Kitchener lacked, and he had the experience and calm judgment which at that time often obscured the true greatness of Churchill. Churchill and Fisher made an excellent team—each complemented the other. Churchill liked to work late at night; Fisher liked to be at his desk at five am. He'd arrive in his office to find the ink barely dry on dozens of Churchillian memoranda. He'd depart in the afternoon, leaving an equal amount of notes for Churchill signed merely with the green-inked 'F' which became famous in the Admiralty. The two made a formidable team, and if they said that it was necessary to divert important naval vessels for the odd duty of shooting down Zeppelins, not even the most hidebound traditionalists could object. And so a squadron of light cruisers joined the defence of London.

A few weeks later a fleet of four airships was sent to bomb London. None of them reached the city. One of them, the L-12, lost so much gas that it fell into the sea; engine trouble and hits from anti-aircraft guns forced the others to turn back. In all they dropped sixty-eight bombs on English soil, but casualties were few and the damage inconsequential. The panic which the Germans had anticipated among the people of Britain never materialized. The raids were frightening enough, but the capacity for panic has always seemed to be lacking in the British public. The War Office, however, realized that the Zeppelin was potentially a mighty weapon that could do severe damage to London, and the defence of the city was put into the capable hands of Sir Percy Scott, a gunnery officer of wide experience.

Although the appointment of Sir Percy Scott reflected the faith of the War Office in the gun as the effective anti-aircraft weapon, Sir Percy Scott himself had, or quickly developed, faith in the aeroplane. He urged that night flying by the naval aircraft on the east coast should be taken in hand seriously. Aircraft, he said, when their pilots had been trained for night flying, were going to be 'the Zeppelins' worst enemy'. They would, in the future, play a much more important part in the defence of London than people thought. He held the view that the defence of London by aircraft started at the Zeppelin sheds, and that the defence by gunfire began on the English coast. The mobile defences in the country should be increased so that they could turn back any attempted air raid and, while no Zeppelin should ever be allowed to reach London, there should be sufficient heavy guns strategically distributed near the capital to make hitting a certainty if an airship got through.

Sir Percy Scott, indeed, soon began to make his presence felt. It was not long before he wrote to Winston Churchill threatening to resign unless he was given a free hand in getting what he wanted. He promptly discarded all the pom-pom guns, which, he held, were useless and dangerous, and put forward detailed proposals for new gun stations, which would require an extra 104 anti-aircraft guns, and at least fifty searchlights. He pressed the First Lord to divert guns and searchlights from the Fleet, which, he suggested, had fifty more guns of suitable calibre than it required. He at once began the preparation of a number of additional gun and searchlight stations, and sent Lieutenant-Commander A. Rawlinson to Paris to bring back a sample of the best existing French anti-aircraft gun. By September 19th Rawlinson was back in London with a 75-mm gun on a special motor-mounting, complete with equipment. This gun, manned by ratings from the disbanded armoured-car squadrons, was the nucleus of the London Mobile Section which was formed under Lieutenant-Commander Rawlinson. By 1916 its strength had been increased by six three-pounder high-angle Vickers guns, mounted on Lancia light lorries, and by two mobile searchlights. Two of the guns were temporarily detached for the defence of the Hampton Waterworks, and one each to the waterworks at Kempton and Surbiton. The remainder moved to pre-allotted positions on the receipt of a raid warning.

Forty aircraft were assigned to the London area for the specific purpose of defending the city against Zeppelins, and this to some extent did justify the enormous expense and risk incurred by the Germans. The Germans had always hoped that a good portion of the RFC and a great number of guns would be diverted from the Front to protect not only London but other industrial centres.

Until now, a rather curious misconception had been prevalent as to the defensive strength of the airship. It had been thought that each Zeppelin was protected against fire by a layer of non-inflammable inert gas. It was believed that the only way for an aeroplane to destroy a Zeppelin was to bomb it. Each plane carried two twenty-pounder Hales high-explosive bombs, and two sixteen-pounder incendiaries. These proved spectacularly unsuccessful. It was difficult enough for an aeroplane to find a Zeppelin and get above it; it was virtually impossible to score a direct hit upon it. Actually the only targets these bombs found were targets on the ground. No one thought that a Zep could be destroyed by ordinary machine gun fire. Even if a dozen drums of Lewis gun ammunition were fired into the body of an airship, it was felt that only some gas would be lost and the ship might be forced down before returning to its base.

Lieutenant Leefe Robinson was the first pilot to bring down a raider, and vindicate Sir Percy's new techniques. He caught sight of one of the wooden-framed Schutte-Lanz ships over Essex. His two machine guns were fitted with both incendiary and explosive ammunition. He managed to get above the huge airship, and dived, emptying two drums of ammunition into it. It immediately caught fire and fell in flames, the first German airship to fall on British soil. Robinson received the Victoria Cross for this exploit, and the whole English public breathed a collective sigh of relief: aircraft could get above and destroy heavily-laden dirigibles. A few days later two Zeppelins came to grief; the L-33, hit simultaneously by gunfire from the ground and by bullets from an aircraft piloted by Lieutenant A. de B. Brandon, came down in a field near Little Wigborough almost intact. The L-32 was destroyed by Lieutenant F. Sowery.

In October, Kapitanleutnant Heinrich Mathy, the most resolute and successful of all Zeppelin commanders, met his death in the L-31, and the shock to the German public was similar to that felt by the death of Immelmann several months previously. Mathy was born in Mannheim in 1883 of an old Baden family. He had served in airships since the inception of the service and was worshipped by the men who served under him.

He had made repeated and often successful attempts to bomb London. On this occasion he was caught near the capital by Second Lieutenant W. J. Tempest, who had taken off from North Weald at about ten pm. He soon saw Mathy's Zeppelin about fifteen miles away, caught in a cone of searchlights, and set off immediately in pursuit, flying through the whole London barrage in, so he says in his report, 'a very inferno of bursting shells'. When five miles away, his mechanical pressure pump broke and 'I had to use my hand pump. . . . This exercise at so high an altitude' (he was flying at 15,000 feet) 'was very exhausting, besides occupying an arm and thus giving me "one hand less" to operate with when I commenced to fire.' Despite this disadvantage and the barrage, he held on until he got within range, when the Zeppelin, having now jettisoned her bombs, was 'mounting rapidly. I therefore decided to dive at her. . . . I accordingly gave a tremendous pump at my petrol tank and dived straight at her, firing a burst straight into her as I came, I let her have another burst as I passed under her and then banked my machine over, sat under her tail, and flying underneath her pumped lead into her for all I was worth.' Tempest's resolution soon had its reward. 'As I was firing,' he says, 'I noticed her begin to go red inside like an enormous Chinese lantern.' He had set her on fire and for a moment seemed likely to be engulfed by his victim. 'She shot up about 200 feet, paused, and came roaring down straight on to me before I had time to get out of the way. I nosed-dived for all I was worth, with the Zeppelin tearing after me. . . . I put my machine into a spin and just managed to corkscrew out of the way as she shot past me, roaring like a furnace.' Tempest watched the L-31 strike the ground in a shower of sparks and 'then proceeded to fire off dozens of green Very lights in the exuberance of my feelings.' The Zeppelin fell at Potters Bar.

The Germans, however, had not abandoned all faith in their airships. On March 16th, five naval Zeppelins were sent to bomb London and southern England. They were met this time by the forces of nature rather than those of man. A forty-mile-an-hour wind which got up shortly after their take-off rendered this mission hazardous. The L-39, whose captain had been unwise enough to stop his engines, drifted helpless over France, for the motors had become frozen and his ship was eventually destroyed by French gunners. This was their only casualty, but the next German attack was equally unsuccessful. The British had their troubles, too. In an endeavour to intercept one of the Zeppelins taking part in that raid, a naval pilot flying a Sopwith seaplane fell into the sea but was found by a ship and towed into port. Another pilot from the same flight, Flight Sub-Lieutenant Morris, with his observer, Air Mechanic G. O. Wright, went out to look for him and was forced down into the North Sea by engine failure. The two airmen clung to the remains of their machine for five and a half days, subsisting on a few malted milk tablets. They were eventually rescued by a flying-boat from Felixstowe.

On the next Zeppelin raid, the L-48 met her end at the hands of Captain R. H. M. S. Saundby and Lieutenant L. P. Watkins. It fell near Theberton in Suffolk and its crew were buried in the local churchyard, upon their grave being inscribed the text: 'Who art thou who judges another man's servant? To his own master he standeth or falleth.'

It was on the night of October 20th, however, that the Zeppelins suffered their greatest disaster of the war. Eleven naval Zeppelins attacked England in curious weather conditions. Up to 10,000 feet the winds were light, but above that height they were blowing at forty miles an hour, and at 20,000 feet there was a full gale. The Zeppelins started at a comparatively low altitude, but in order to reduce the risk of air attack gained height as they neared the English coast. They at once found themselves in the grip of the gale. Four of them, the L-44, 45, 49 and 50, never saw Germany again. The first, after dropping bombs which just missed an ammunition dump between Elstow and Kempton, drifted across France, was hit by anti-aircraft fire and destroyed. The second, the L-45, had suffered a similar fate. She left Tondern at eleven-twenty-five am on October 19th and crashed near Sisteron in southern France at ten am on the 20th having, among other feats,

Manfred von Richthofen, greatest of the German aces, shakes hands with General von Hoeppner, commanding the German Air Force

Max Immelmann, an early German master of aerobatics

Oswald Boelcke, the first German ace. Unlike Richthofen he was a man of humanity and feeling

Werner Voss, who shot down more than 30 Allied aircraft

Anthony Fokker with two of the men who flew his machines: *left*, Bruno
Loerzer; *right*, Hermann Goering, who flew with Richthofen's Circus

A great French ace,
Charles Nungesser.
Wounded seventeen
times, he survived
the War

Guynemer, the French ace
who destroyed more than
50 enemy aircraft and
became a legend in France

Rene Fonck, an outstanding
French fighter pilot
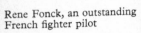

Major James T. McCudden, VC, who won 58 victories

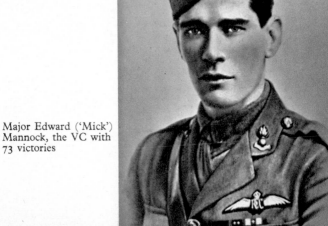

Major Edward ('Mick') Mannock, the VC with 73 victories

Major W.G. ('Billy') Barker, VC, one of Canada's most distinguished pilots

Captain L.G. Hawker, VC, one of Britain's first heroes

Lieutenant Rhys-Davids, who brought down Werner Voss

Captain Roy Brown, who brought down the great Richthofen

Raoul Lufbery, most
skilful of the veteran
American pilots

Eddie Rickenbacker, the
foremost American ace

dropped a bomb on Piccadilly Circus. The L-50 followed closely in the track of her ill-fated colleague. Driven southwards by the high wind, she made an effort to land about midday near the trenches in France. Being fired at, she made off, came down again, and grazed the top of a wood, losing her forward car with its crew. Thus lightened, she shot upwards and disappeared. She later passed over the crew of the L-45, who were by then prisoners of war at Sisteron, and went out to sea pursued by French pilots. She was finally lost to sight and knowledge far out over the Mediterranean. The L-49 also drifted over France and was forced down near Neufchâteau and captured intact. Once again the elements had come to England's help, for not one of the seventy-three pilots who went up against the Zeppelins that night was able to reach them at the height at which they flew.

Such was the end of the Zeppelins. They had been mastered as much by the weather as by the defence, for though a high proportion were shot down, had they been able to make better use of their climbing powers they might, at any rate in the later stages of the war, have outmanœuvred the defence because there was no aircraft capable of reaching their ceiling. As it was, the results they achieved in fifty-one raids, during which they dropped 196 tons of bombs, were not commensurate with the great efforts made: 557 persons were killed and 1358 injured. But seventy-seven of the big ships were lost before the raids were abandoned.

The fact that the raids were completely unsuccessful, in view of the huge expenditure of time and money which went into the construction of the ships and the training of the crews, should not obscure the fact that Germany did earn some dividends on the investment. The threat of the raiding potentialities of the airship fleet did compel England to set up a huge defensive organization which diverted aircraft, guns and men from the important theatre of war on the continent. By the end of 1916, 17,340 officers and men were serving in the home anti-aircraft services, and twelve Royal Flying Corps squadrons comprising 200 officers, 2000 enlisted men and 110 aircraft, were stationed in England despite the desperate need for them in the Somme battles. When raids were threatened or in

157

progress, vital war work was held up all over the country and trains hurrying war material to ports were stopped. But this is about all the twenty-two Zeppelin raids of 1916 accomplished, and the German public was never able to realize its early dream of seeing all England in flames.

Once the German High Command realized that airship raids on London were too costly, they decided to try the long-range bombers.

The Germans always claimed—with some justification— that the French were the first to bomb an open city and that their subsequent attacks were nothing but retaliatory measures. Early in the war the French actually did drop a few bombs on Freiburg, a city that was well behind the battle line. This incident is mentioned in nearly every official German chronicle of the war as complete vindication of the Zeppelin raids and the aeroplane raids which replaced them. Exactly what was meant by open cities was not certain. The capital of a great nation at war can scarcely be described as an open city when it houses, as did London, all the machinery of government and many of the staff directing operations, both on sea and on land. There is not the slightest doubt that the RFC would have bombed Berlin at that moment had the means to do so been available. But in 1916 'total war' was a phrase unknown save to a few students of German psychology.

The first attempt to hurt London by daylight was made by Deck-Officer Paul Brandt and Lieutenant Walther Ilges in an LVG powered by a 170-horsepower Mercedes. They had orders to bomb the Admiralty offices in Whitehall, and they tried to hit the target assigned to them. The aeroplane flew high and wasn't observed until it was over the city. It gave notice of its presence by dropping six bombs which fell near Victoria Station. The observer took twenty photographs of aerodromes, military installations, and ammunition factories en route to London, but the pictures were destined never to be developed. On the way home the LVG developed engine trouble but although evading the Royal Flying Corps, it was shot down by a French anti-aircraft battery near Dunkirk; the photographs were captured.

Then came a really serious raid. Fourteen Gothas of the Third Bombing Squadron, under the experienced command of Captain Brandenburg, were based at Ghent about 170 miles from London, with orders to bomb the British capital. The Gotha was a three-seater with two 260-horsepower engines, a wing span of seventy-eight feet, and it was capable of carrying a bomb-load of 1000 pounds to 12,000 feet. This squadron was named the *England-geschwader*, and when fourteen of them, flying in diamond formation, reached London in daylight and gave the East End docks and Liverpool Street station a severe beating, the Government knew that a more effective weapon than the Zeppelin had arrived on the scene. On this raid alone seventy-two bombs fell on the city, killing or wounding 594. Ninety-four interceptors went up to repel the invaders, but only five managed to find the bombers and these did nothing but engage in ineffective and isolated combat after the bombs had been dropped. The bombers flew too high to be reached by anti-aircraft fire and all of them returned to Ghent untouched.

The complete failure of the defences and the sight of a formation of German planes calmly bombing the heart of the country in broad daylight aroused feelings of intense indignation. To quell public clamour and to stiffen the defences the Air Ministry brought No 56 Squadron, equipped with SE5s, from the Western Front to guard London. A few weeks later twenty-two Gothas hit London again. Brilliant Captain Brandenburg, anticipating that the aerial defences would be better this time, wisely lightened his bomb-loads to give his machines more speed on their trip home, and there were only 250 casualties among the people of London. This time ninety-five RFC and RNAS aircraft went up after the raiders; a Navy machine shot one down and a second, developing engine trouble, fell into the sea. The Germans had really touched the nerve-centre of the Empire and now the Government decided to combine all the elements of defence, both on the ground and in the air, under one head. Brigadier-General E. B. Ashmore, then commanding the artillery of the 29th Division in the line north of Ypres, was selected to head the new defensive organization. Ashmore (and Trenchard and Haig) were understandable reluctant to withdraw fighter squadrons from France. Trenchard at a Cabinet meeting emphasized that this was the main object of the German raids. Above all, the Germans wanted to weaken the RFC in France. The only alternative was to adopt the plan advocated for some time by Lieutenant-Colonel M. St L. Simon, the anti-aircraft chief on London, to ring the city with guns capable of reaching the high-flying raiders. Ashmore urged that Simon's plan be adopted, and it was.

Captain Brandenburg, about this time, broke his leg in a landing accident and while he was in a hospital recovering (and incidentally falling in love with and marrying his nurse), the bombing of London was put into the rash hands of Captain Kleine, a courageous but reckless leader, who sent his men out in just about any kind of weather. So many Gothas fell victims to the weather and to Ashmore's guns that the Germans decided to hold daylight bombing to a minimum and concentrate on night bombing.

The aerial barrage thrown up by the guns kept the bombers high, and accurate bombing of specific targets was out of the question. Before the war ended, there were fifty-two aerial raids on England; the bombers dropped seventy-three tons of bombs, killed 857 people and injured 2058 more. These, in the objective military sense, were mere pinpricks on the sturdy body of England, but the raids again had the result of keeping hundreds of aircraft, men and guns from the Western Front, as well as reducing the effectiveness of workers in war plants.

Winston Churchill, who had become Minister of Munitions, reported to the Cabinet that after one heavy raid on London only twenty-seven per cent of the workers in Woolwich Arsenal had reported for duty and that on the following day only sixty-four per cent showed up. Then there was the matter of replacing the anti-aircraft guns. The life of the usual gun was only 1500 rounds—after that they were useless and plants which had been making fieldpieces and machine guns for the Front had to be hurriedly reconverted to producing the anti-aircraft guns.

But the raids had one effect that the Germans had not foreseen. From the very beginning, Trenchard, a thorough realist, had insisted that the only way to deter the Germans was to bomb their own cities. "Reprisals on open towns," he told the Cabinet when asked for his view, "are repugnant to British ideas, but we may be forced to adopt them and if we do, half measures are useless. We will have to pursue the policy to the bitter end."

The Cabinet had previously heard Colonel Bares of the French Air Force express the same view. Sir Douglas Haig objected strenuously on the grounds that long-range bombing of German cities was a luxury that could not as yet be afforded. The Admiralty, which, of course, exercised autonomous control over the RNAS, liked the idea enormously. The War Office, which controlled the RFC, was dead against the policy on the grounds that its implementation would mean that a large number of long-range bombers would have to be produced at the expense and maintenance of the seventy-six fighter reconnaissance and night-flying squadrons then operating.

The discussion was typical of the muddled situation which had inevitably resulted when the air services were divided into two separate units with only the Air Board having a loose power of recommendation and no executive powers at all. Obviously the only sensible solution was the creation of an Air Ministry which was being advocated by the doughty Boer, Lieutenant-General Jan Smuts. But both the Admiralty and the War Office resisted any move to take away their sovereignty. Sir Douglas Haig warned the Cabinet against what he called 'the grave danger of an Air Ministry which would assume control with a belief in theories not in accordance with practical experiences'. In 1914 no one had wanted the stepchild—now its foster parents were so fond of it that neither wished a third party to interfere with its raising.

Even after two years of combat, dreadful mistakes were being made by both War Office and Admiralty, which existed in a welter of confusion, rivalry and incompetence. The War Office placed orders in the most haphazard manner for Avros, Farmans and Blériots long after they had outlived their usefulness. Only 600 engines were being produced each month at the end of 1916, and many of these were of poor quality and too big for existing air frames. The War Office ordered 3000 eight-cylinder engines (later called the Sunbeam Arab), despite a warning by the manufacturers that the engines were untried and that many of the parts, being of aluminium, would probably be difficult to cast properly. This order immediately absorbed the full producing capacity of two large factories, and when the engine appeared, its aluminium cylinders and crank chambers did, in fact, prove to be unequal to the strain put upon them. The engine was useless. The Deasy Company had received an order for 2000 BHP engines which in their early stages were as inefficient as the Arab. On delivery of one consignment ninety per cent of the cylinder blocks were found to be defective. The 200-hp Hispano-Suiza being manufactured by the Wolseley Company was at first equally unsuccessful. At a bench, one test engine broke four crankshafts in succession in four hours. Eventually all of these would be modified and improved, but there was no time for experimentation then.

The Admiralty avoided many mistakes by tying up with Rolls-Royce, a company which during its history seems to have been incapable of producing an inefficient engine. Both air services were in constant rivalry for priority on the production of aircraft and engines and this type of competition, although the breath of life in peacetime free enterprise, often choked the continuous flow of material from plant to Front. By the end of 1916, the bugs had been removed from the Hispano-Suiza, and the naval staff ordered 8000 of these now-reliable engines to be constructed in the Mayen company plant in France. Lord Curzon objected to the size of the order on the extraordinary grounds that by the end of 1917 every warring country, including Britain, would be so exhausted and its material of war so depleted that the war would just peter out and 'to be left with a large number of aircraft would be highly inconvenient'. Luckily he was overruled.

At last the complaints of pilots themselves as to the inferiority of their flying equipment began to reach the ears of the public—and in Britain, above all countries, public opinion can be a mighty force. The War Cabinet finally took cognizance of the resentment against the confusion and downright incompetence by setting up an Aerial Operations Committee to decide the whole question of priorities in the matter of all equipment and munitions. The ex-enemy of England, Lieutenant-General Smuts was made chairman and Winston Churchill placed on his committee. No one could appeal from a decision made by this board: even inter-departmental enemies recognized the vision, the excellent judgment and absolute impartiality of Smuts, and his decisions were accepted without murmur. The name of the board was changed to the War Priorities Committee and it grew in power. Out of it (if indirectly) would emerge an Air Ministry with the power to co-ordinate the air services, and out of the Air Ministry would eventually come— eight months before the end of hostilities—the Royal Air Force.

It is conceivable that there never would have been an Air Ministry or an RAF until far too late had not the bombing of London so aroused the public that the War Office and the Admiralty had to abandon reluctantly their private war to become allies in the fight against a common foe.

Chapter Nine

A YEAR OF HEROES

DURING THE winter of 1916–17 the RFC tried desperately to restore its ranks, so sadly depleted during the bitter four months of the Somme struggle, which cost Britain the lives of 867 airmen. Trenchard had asked for an air force consisting of 106 active and ninety-five reserve squadrons. This was to include two squadrons of night fliers. His request, seconded by the powerful voice of Haig, was granted, but carrying it out was a different matter. By the early months of 1917, there was little new manpower available in Britain apart from youngsters leaving school. There were many men in the military services who were willing to transfer to the RFC, but the Army was understandably reluctant to let them go. Finally, in desperation, the War Office ordered regimental commanders to make an appeal to their men for flying volunteers. Many of the officers did their best to disassociate themselves with this compulsory depletion of their forces, but orders were orders, so they had to obey the letter, if not the spirit, of the command. They left the appeal for volunteers to their sergeant-majors, who were astute enough to sense that the fewer the volunteers, the more happy the commanding officer would be. One infantry man who transferred after hearing the 'appeal' by the sergeant-major of his regiment preserved for posterity the words of the stirring announcement.

"If any of you wants to go to 'eaven quick, now's your chance," the sergeant-major roared. "They're askin' for volunteers to learn to fly and become orficers in the bloody RFC. So if any of you feels like committing suicide, step two paces forward out of the ranks and I'll take 'is name. But remember it's an 'ell of a long way to fall and you only falls once."

In spite of this enthusiastic invitation to oblivion, hundreds of adventuresome young men showed their preference for death in the air over death in the mud. The infantry and artillery commanders had enough influence to keep a string to these volunteers. They would keep them on the regimental roster, allow them to be attached temporarily to the RFC, but if the volunteers did not show the specialized qualities necessary for air service they insisted that the men be returned to their regiments. The volunteer was granted the status of the mistress of a married man—attached but not engaged. However, if the volunteer did show an aptitude for air duty the attachment became more than a temporary liaison; it became a marriage to be dissolved only by the termination of hostilities —or by death, the usual outcome.

Hundreds of volunteers also arrived from Canada. By arrangement with Washington the Canadians had been allowed to train in flying schools opened in Texas. The sovereign state of Texas is virtually one huge landing field and it provides flying weather for twelve months in the year. The Canadians were greeted with joy by the hard-pressed RFC leaders. In England training was usually interrupted by unflyable weather during all but the summer months; these Canadian pilots, after intensive and uninterrupted weeks of Texas training, were not only thoroughly schooled in aerobatic flying and in gunnery, but they had learned to fly almost any type of aircraft. They would make their presence felt very quickly.

For several months there had been reports that a new two-seater fighter, superior to the great Albatros, was about to join the ranks of RFC aircraft. It finally appeared early in 1917 in time to join the fighting above Arras. It was the Bristol Fighter, powered by a 275-hp Rolls-Royce engine. This biplane combined the best features of the sturdy reconnaissance machine and the fast, manœuvrable single-seat fighter (a word, incidentally, that by now was replacing the earlier designation, 'scout'). In adition to the synchronized Vickers machine gun it carried two machine guns in its fuselage for the use of the observer.

Six Bristols were hurried to No 48 Squadron and experienced Captain Leefe Robinson, VC, immediately sallied forth with five of his men, flying the new aircraft. They hadn't really had time to familiarize themselves with the potentials or the flying habits of the Bristol, and they were unfortunate enough to meet Manfred von Richthofen leading a flight of five Albatros fighters.

It was a short and bitter battle. Four of the Bristols were shot down, the other two limped home. Leefe Robinson landed his badly crippled machine behind the German lines and spent the rest of the war in captivity. A few days after this encounter Richthofen, interviewed by a Berlin newspaper, dismissed the new British machine with contempt. It did not compare with the Albatros, he said, and his words were quickly carried to all front-line German pilots. Richthofen had unwittingly passed a sentence of death on dozens of his fellow pilots, who for a long time treated the Bristol lightly and had to pay the price.

The RFC was on fairly friendly, if watchful, terms now with the Royal Naval Air Service and the latter had some months before obligingly given the RFC some of its fine Sopwith Triplanes and Sopwith Pups. These were easy to handle, and the first men to be given the Bristols assumed that the new machine would be as accommodating as these two reliables. The Bristol wasn't that amenable; you had to woo it before it allowed you to take liberties. But once you had mastered the new craft, you had an aeroplane under you which many pilots still declare to be the best all-round fighter-reconnaissance machine the war produced.

Despite the presence of the Bristol and the two Sopwiths, casualties during the spring of 1917 were horribly high. This was due to a number of causes. In the first place there just weren't enough high-class machines, the result of muddle and delay in production. There was, too, the prevailing westerly wind, which often meant a long struggle home after a fight which had drifted far over the enemy's lines. But the chief cause was the implacable determination of the Royal Flying Corps to pursue the offensive no matter what the cost. Every one of its pilots was well aware that to practise the doctrine of attack day in, day out, meant heavy losses, especially against an enemy as skilled and resolute as, for example, Werner, Voss, Richthofen, Schleich, and their Jagdstaffels. But these losses were accepted without flinching. The mood of the officers and men of the Royal Flying Corps can best be depicted by a phrase used a generation later to describe the British people in a crisis even graver. They were grim and gay. The first quality was displayed in the air, the second in mess. However many empty chairs there might be, the spirit of relaxation, which tradition decreed must prevail after toil, was never allowed to depart from the board.

The work of the RFC during both phases of the Battle of Arras in 1917 was essentially the same. It maintained contact patrols whenever possible in order to report the progress of the infantry; it bombed back areas without very great success; it did valuable spotting for the artillery; and it did its utmost to prevent the German Air Force from crossing the lines.

Another duty which the RFC fulfilled, whenever the weather made it possible, was the interminable task of photographing the enemy's positions. This was accomplished mostly by the RE8, an aircraft which on entry into service immediately acquired a bad reputation. It mounted a Vickers gun, operated by the pilot and firing through the propeller, and a Lewis gun fired by the observer in the rear. The early models showed a tendency to spin and there were a number of fatal accidents, so many, in fact, that pilots began to show a distinct lack of confidence when called upon to fly it. Lord Cowdray, then President of the Air Board, forthwith caused an exhaustive series of trials to be made, with the result that the design was so successfully modified that before the war was over, 2000 of them appeared on the Western Front. It remained in the service till the end as the standard corps reconnaissance machine.

By 1917 the names of the German and French air heroes were well known to the world. The deeds of Guynemer, Nungesser, Navarre, Fonck, Richthofen, Udet, Voss, Lowenhardt and a dozen others were chronicled in newspapers in Peoria, Illinois, as well as in Paris and Berlin. Only by slow degrees was the British public becoming aware that the RFC had more than its quota of great war heroes. When a high military award was given an airman, a brief story of his exploit was printed in the *London Gazette*, but the names of individual pilots never appeared in the daily GHQ communiqués. The RFC firmly set its face against the canonization of the individual, but in 1917 nothing could prevent the names of Albert Ball, James McCudden, Mick Mannock, Donald McLoren, Phillip Fullard, the Canadians Billy Bishop, Billy Barker, Raymond Collishaw and others from being known the length of Britain. Pilots at home on leave talked glowingly of these men when confronted with familiar tales of French and German aces; this word-of-mouth praise carried the names everywhere, and in the dark days of 1917 the brilliance of these bright stars relieved some of the gloom.

The RFC felt that it was unfair to the men who lived and fought in the miserable squalor of the trenches to spotlight the achievements of a a relatively few airmen who were fighting a clean, relatively comfortable (if hazardous) war. It also believed firmly that the lionization of a few heroes was bad for the morale of the service as a whole. In France, for instance, where the official policy was to publicize sensational airmen, a great deal of jealousy had resulted and many pilots, in disgust, had transferred away from the escadrilles in which the great heroes flew. Many excellent pilots of bombers and observation aircraft insisted upon transferring to single-seater fighters in an effort to gain the fame and adulation given to the fighter heroes. Many first-rate French combat pilots—in desperate efforts to catch up with Guynemer, Nungesser, Fonck and the other leading aces who were so lionized by the public—threw caution to the winds and fell victims to German aircraft. It appeared to be contrary to the Gallic nature to fight in anonymity.

1917 was the year of heroes. To the men in the RFC, Albert Ball embodied all of the qualities of the truly great fighter. He was a deeply religious youngster with a passion for playing the violin and with an abhorrence of killing. He believed in the righteousness of Britain's cause, and he was quite willing to die for it. In 1916 he arrived in France with No 13 Squadron, which flew two-seater BE2s. Although young Ball (he was nineteen then) was primarily engaged in artillery observation, he managed to down three Germans during his first two months at the Front. It was recognized that he had the temperament and the ability to fly a fighter, and he was transferred to No 11 Squadron and given a Nieuport. During the Battle of the Somme he developed the tactics which were to gain him fame a few months later. To begin with, he liked to fly alone, and his skill at lone forays was such that he was generally given a roving commission. He perfected a highly dangerous but effective manœuvre which few pilots had the hair-trigger judgment to use safely. He would often deliberately allow a German to get on his tail, for he had the uncanny ability of gauging just when the German was about to open fire; then he would turn sharply, come up underneath the German and attack him in his blind spot. Another of his favourite methods of fighting was not unlike that used by Oswald Boelcke so successfully. Ball liked to fly head-on against an enemy in the certainty that if he held his course the German, just before what appeared to be an inevitable collision, would turn away. As the German turned he was vulnerable for perhaps one second; that was all Ball needed to send an accurate and lethal burst from his gun.

In 1917, Ball was serving with No 56 Squadron with such outstanding pilots as Crowe, Meinties, Bowman, Rhys-Davids and McCudden, and even those looked upon Ball with awe. He was a diffident, smiling youngster who seemed immune from the doubts and tensions that at times possessed all pilots. Completely lacking in self-consciousness, he never sought fame or recognition; as his victories piled up, both came to him and he received them with modest reluctance. It is almost traditional to endow a great hero with noble qualities and say of him that he set a standard of valour which was accepted by his fellows as the measure to emulate—but all this really was said of Albert Ball during his lifetime and is preserved in the diaries of men who fought with him; encomiums to his decency, his courage, his complete disregard for his own safety were not meaningless sentiments expressed in a funeral oration by a member of the family. The men of No 56 Squadron were talking of him in these terms in the spring of 1917. If you pressed them for evidence, one might tell you of how Ball actually challenged two German fighters to personal combat, of how a trap was set for him and finally how the combat was resolved.

One afternoon Ball encountered two Albatroses over the lines. He opened the attack, gave each machine minor wounds, and both headed for the safety of their home base. Ball followed and then ran out of ammunition. He took out his revolver and pursued them, but they managed to land safely. Ball, enraged and disgusted that any fighting airmen would act in what he felt to be a craven manner, wrote a note on the pad all pilots carried strapped to the right thigh, weighted it and dropped it on the airfield. He said that he would be over the base the next day at the same time, and he challenged his two late opponents to come up and resolve the battle.

Ball arrived promptly the next day and to his delight he found the two aircraft circling slowly. He flew straight towards the nearest one, intending to rely on the near-collision manœuvre which had stood him in such good stead, but before he could close in he heard machine gun bullets whistling all around him and he knew that he had flown into a trap. He zoomed upwards and to the left, and now he saw that there were three uninvited guests at the joust. It was five against one now. He tried hard to get close enough to pick off one or two, but the Germans were wily fliers; they swerved away, merely waiting for the chance to close in and finish him off. Ball chased them furiously, firing at longer range than he liked, but he always had to break off his run as one or two of the others manœuvred above and behind him. Then he ran out of ammunition. Theoretically he shouldn't have remained alive for more than a minute. If he lit out for his own territory, he would be as vulnerable as a sitting duck, for always three of the five Germans stayed between him and Allied territory. Then he improvised perhaps the most unorthodox and apparently suicidal manœuvre ever attempted by a cornered airman. He put his plane into a crazy spin. The Germans, of course, were sure that he had been hit. Ball had observed a large open field below; he brought his Nieuport out of the spin and fluttered towards the ground. He landed. The Germans knew that this was Albert Ball; taking him prisoner would be an even greater triumph than killing him. Two of the German aircraft swooped down to land on the field; the other three flew over it, wagging their wings in derisive triumph, and then went on to their nearby airfield to spread the story. Ball was slumped over the seat of his little Nieuport but his engine was still idling. The German pilots hopped out of their respective machines and ran toward the Nieuport and its presumably wounded pilot. As they approached Ball opened his throttle, pulled back his control stick and the little aeroplane shot down the field, rose in the air and Ball headed for home without having received a scratch.

This story became a legend in the RFC, and if there are those who believe it to be only a legend, it is written in the memoirs of German pilots who were in the squadron with the five embarrassed fliers who had Britain's great fighter all wrapped up and sealed for delivery to eternity, and who allowed him to escape. Ball could—as just demonstrated—think with amazing quickness in an emergency but actually his record was the result of sheer, blazing courage; he wasn't the cool, calculating technician that Mannock was; he wasn't a deadly shot as McCudden and Billy Bishop were; he didn't handle a plane with the intuitive grace of a Rhys-Davids; and he lacked the guile and cunning of a René Fonck. His only thought was to get close to the enemy and kill or be killed. Time after time Ball returned to his field with dozens of bullets in his machine. On many, many occasions he almost rammed enemy planes, and some of his squadron mates felt that more than once when out of ammunition he actually tried to accomplish this suicidal feat. He was the only pilot who never wore goggles or a helmet. He used to explain a bit apologetically that he liked to feel the wind in his hair.

Ball was the first fighter pilot to be an idol in England. After the Paris and the American newspapers had written at great length about his exploits, the RFC relaxed its traditional policy, and the British learned that they too had a hero as great as Guynemer or Richthofen. Reporters rushed to Nottingham and pleaded with his father, asking for excerpts from his son's letters. The proud father smilingly refused, but the letters would perhaps have been disappointing to the journalists and the public. One asked for garden seeds and explained that he had moved out of the barracks into a tent pitched right at the edge of his squadron's flying field. He lived in this tent because he wanted to be close to his aircraft; when Germans approached he wanted to get into the air as quickly as possible. Besides, he told his father, alone in the tent at night he could practise on his violin to his heart's content without disturbing the sleep of the squadron. He seldom went into details about his air battles, but he did tell with pride of the forty square yards he had fenced in and how the seeds his father had sent him had blossomed.

When reporters pressed the father for details of his son Albert, he could only tell them quite honestly that he thought the boy would develop into a fine businessman once this war was over. He himself was an estate agent with a large interest in a Nottingham construction firm. His son had suggested that he buy up all the old copper he could find: there would be a big market for it after the war. He also said in a letter that he had sold options to some of his fellow pilots on plots of land owned by his father—but the reporters weren't interested in such mundane details.

The nineteen-year-old youngster was made a captain and

given a flight to lead. He had an idea that he could improve the speed of his Nieuport by streamlining the propeller hub. He found a large aluminium bowl and covered the hub with it. When he was in the air, this bowl spun and he called it his Spinner. RFC pilots were not allowed to paint their machines with distinctive markings, but Ball painted the Spinner a bright red and there was no reprimand. The Spinner soon became known to the Germans as a feature of the machine piloted by their most feared enemy, and henceforth he was, he wrote happily to his father, a marked man.

Once, he wrote ruefully, he really met his match in the air. He and an unknown German pilot were alone in the sky. Each went for the other full out. Each tried his favourite tricks in succession, only to find that the other knew his counter-moves. Each fired at the other from many angles. Each tried to get on his opponent's tail, but neither could outmanœuvre the other enough to get into position to fire the mortal burst. Neither attempted to break away. It would have been fatal for either to have made the attempt with such a superb duellist as foe. At last both had fired all their ammunition. Each seemed to realize what had happened. Each looked at the other and began laughing uproariously. They flew side by side for a few seconds, waved to each other, then broke off, each returning to his own aerodrome. Ball wrote that the Hun was a 'real sport'.

Ball's squadron had been organized and was led by the slightly built, energetic Major Bloomfield. He had hand-picked every man in it and had raided every training centre in England searching for mechanics, mess attendants and cooks who were also saxophone players or violinists. He wound up not only flying with a fine flying squadron, but a fine band led by a former professional orchestra leader. When the hard, tense days of fighting began he would order the band out, and his theory that music relaxed men who were taut and whose nerves were on edge was completely vindicated. When a squadron member received a decoration, he would order a celebration and drinks, and the singing of old favourites and new irreverent flying songs written by talented men of the Air Force filled the night. Ball, of course, would always join in with his violin. If a man didn't come back and dark gloom enveloped the squadron, Bloomfield would order the same kind of celebration.

With a total of forty-three victories Ball was now four ahead of Guynemer. General Trenchard telephoned that Ball was to be presented to Field-Marshal Sir Douglas Haig, commander-in-chief of the British armies. On May 5th, Ball wrote to his fiancée: '. . . won't it be nice when all this beastly killing is over, and we can just enjoy ourselves and not hurt anyone? I hate this game, but it is the only thing one must do just now.' And on the same day he wrote to his father: 'Am indeed looked after by God, but Oh! I do get tired of always living to kill, and am really beginning to feel like a murderer.'

On the evening of May 7th, the drinks flowed freely and the squadron band played as it had never played before, and if voices raised in song were at first a bit tremulous, they soon gained in strength and volume. Late that afternoon eleven aircraft had gone up—only five returned. Albert Ball had flown into a heavy white cloud and it was as though the cloud had taken him and kept him, for he was never seen again. There were no tears shed for Ball or the other five that night, no one mentioned the names of those who had laughed at lunch and who would laugh no more. That was not in the tradition of No 56.

One oblique reference was made to the tragedy of the day. Major Bloomfield asked Lieutenant Cecil Lewis (one of the five who had returned) to sing the Stevenson *Requiem*. There wasn't a sound as his clear young voice sang:

> Under the wide and starry sky,
> Dig the grave and let me lie.
> Glad did I live and gladly die,
> And I laid me down with a will.
>
> This be the verse you grave for me:
> 'Here he lies where he longed to be;
> Home is the sailor, home from the sea,
> And the hunter home from the hill.'

The men applauded and shouted huskily this tribute to The Hunter, then the band struck up *Tipperary*. After that a Lancashire corporal did a comedy turn, and then they all shouted the words of a song borrowed from No 54 Squadron and sung to the tune of 'John Peel':

When you soar into the air on a Sopwith Scout,
And you're scrapping with a Hun and your gun cuts out,
Well, you stuff down your nose till your plugs fall out,
'Cos you haven't got a hope in the morning.

For a batman woke me from my bed;
I'd had a thick night and a very sore head,
And I said to myself, to myself I said,
"Oh, we haven't got a hope in the morning!"

Three days later the Berlin *Tageblatt* announced triumph-antly that Manfred von Richthofen had shot down Britain's greatest fighter pilot. A few days after that the German Air Force announced that it was his younger brother, Lothar, who had killed Ball, to score his twenty-second victim, although Field Headquarters, which exercised control over the Rich-thofen Jagdstaffel, said frankly that details of Ball's death were unknown. The men of No 56 Squadron somehow didn't think that either could have done it; they were convinced that the impetuous Ball had either penetrated so deeply into German territory that he had run out of fuel and crashed, or that he had been hit by anti-aircraft fire.

After the war was over, Manfred von Richthofen's diary was published. So was a biography, *The Red Knight of Germany*, written by Floyd Gibbons. Both diary and book agree that on May 7th, the day on which Ball met his death, Manfred was on leave in Berlin and Lothar was in a hospital recovering from wounds received on May 7th.

So the art of German propaganda was not introduced into Germany by Dr Paul Joseph Goebbels in the 1930s. Berlin was pretty good at it in 1917, and it seems obvious that the authorities thought that the rather ragged morale of the public would be revived by the announcement that Ball was killed by one or other of the illustrious Richthofens.

Major James T. McCudden's admiration for the dashing courage and the headlong attacks of Albert Ball was touched with awe—though it wasn't his way of doing things. But no one flew harder or fought more fiercely than did this little Irishman, one of the few pilots who had risen from the ranks of enlisted men. McCudden joined the RFC before the war, and, following the classic pattern, became a mechanic, an observer and eventually a pilot. His formal education had been scanty, but during his apprenticeship in the RFC he learned everything there was to be learned about these things: an engine, a machine gun and an aeroplane. More than most, he was a professional pilot who looked upon his calling as a trade and who worked hard to become proficient at it. His tactics were completely cerebral; to dash recklessly alone into a large formation of German machines was to him the sign of inexperience.

McCudden always flew the SE5a, which reputedly presented the most stable gun platform of any World War I aircraft. Its 200-hp Hispano-Suiza motor gave it a speed of 132 miles an hour. Its ceiling was 20,000 feet. Ball always preferred the Nieuport; McCudden liked the SE5a. In many ways the SE5a was like McCudden himself; it was steady and yet spectacular because of the superb planning that went into its design. McCudden, a technician to his fingertips, could never accept an aircraft as it was delivered. Before flying in combat he would test it thoroughly and then invariably improve it. To begin with, he got rid of every ounce of superfluous weight. He tuned up the engine much as young sports-car devotees of today get extra power from their motors.

He had special high-compression pistons installed in his SE5a and tested the engine on a work bench to see if its performance was improved. When he found that the engine now produced many more revolutions per minute than with the standard pistons, he put the motor back into his SE5a, which now had an extra ten miles an hour added to its top speed.

'I've done so many things to my plane,' McCudden wrote to his brother, 'that I can take it up to 20,000 feet easily. I take a lot of interest in my engine, my gun and the plane itself, and keep making adjustments to get more speed and higher altitude.'

McCudden was never consumed by blind hatred of the enemy; he always felt that he was fighting machines—not men.

One day just after Ball's death he had an experience that for the moment disturbed his calm detachment. At 11,000 feet he engaged an Albatros and sent a burst into it. A small trickle of flame appeared, and the aeroplane began to go down. McCudden followed it. The flames enveloped the whole fuselage and tail assembly, and suddenly McCudden saw the doomed pilot writhing in agony as the fingers of fire reached him. McCudden didn't sleep much that night, but the next morning the Irish ace recovered his composure and confided to Rhys-Davids that a man had to ignore such incidents if he was 'to do his work properly'. This was work, it was a trade like that of watch repairing, and you had to exercise full control over emotions and nerves to do a proper job.

"Until yesterday I never looked upon a German plane as anything but a machine to be destroyed," he told Rhys-Davids. "When I saw the flames touch that German pilot, I felt sick for a minute and I actually said to myself in horror, 'There's a man in that plane.' Now, I realize we can't be squeamish about killing. After all, we're nothing but hired assassins."

McCudden, like Ball, often flew alone. Every morning German two-seater observation aircraft came over the lines to take photographs. Primarily, the job of the fighter was to prevent these machines from doing their job. McCudden liked to go up to 20,000 feet and, like a spider, wait quietly until a victim appeared. No Rumpler or LVG, which usually crossed the lines at 17,000 feet, ever expected to find any British aircraft above it. The only warning they had was the rattle of machine gun fire from the diving SE5a piloted by McCudden. One morning in the space of twenty minutes he bagged three; the next day he added four more. Unlike Ball, he didn't try to close in on enemy aircraft. McCudden was perhaps the best shot in the RFC—he shot one German down at 400 yards with only one short burst. It was rarely that his machine ever came home scarred by bullet holes. When it did, he was disgusted; a careful, skilled craftsman had no right to let a German aeroplane get close enough to hit him.

Often he would return and on his combat report say, 'Almost had an Albatros but noticed that the wind was strong from the west, and I might have trouble getting home, so I broke off the engagement. Or, 'Found myself above two slow observation planes and was about to dive when I saw I was running a bit short of petrol. I immediately turned away and returned to base.' He took no unnecessary chances, and what in another man might be thought of as excessive caution or temerity was recognized in McCudden for what it really was —the mark of the skilled professional. During 1917, forty victims fell to the skill of the Irish ace. His example was one which young pilots were asked to follow. Those who followed his admonition to be cautious at all times lived much longer than did those who tried to emulate Albert Ball.

"The best way to get a Hun is to find him before he sees you," he'd tell pilots who asked his advice. "Sure, I hate to shoot a Hun down without him seeing me; it's against what little sporting instinct I have. But it is in accordance with my doctrine and theory of fighting, and it seems to work pretty well."

There was one man in the squadron who just didn't have the temperament to emulate McCudden. Lieutenant A. P. Rhys-Davids, a handsome young Etonian, was the prototype of Ball. Often he and McCudden flew together, and the latter would always return shaking his head sadly and pointing out the dozens of holes in the aircraft flown by his friend.

One day McCudden came back and made his report. He had been engaged in a mêlée with three Germans, but running out of ammunition he had hurried home. Rhys-Davids had not as yet returned and the squadron commander was a bit anxious.

"I saw him fighting like hell against four Huns," McCudden said.

"You sure it was Rhys-Davids?"

"Who in God's name but him would be going after four Huns all by himself?" McCudden exploded. "And who else would be handling his plane as beautifully as Rhys-Davids?"

Richthofen's squadron was directly opposed now to No 56, and there were daily fights against these superb fliers. When Boelcke had the flight, the aircraft were painted in neutral colours in an effort to camouflage them. Now that Richthofen had his own Jagdstaffel, he had his Albatros painted a bright red so that it could easily be recognized by friend and foe. His men painted part of their machines red, but each added distinguishing marks. It was a good fighting group. Lothar von Richthofen was making a name for himself and his elder brother in his letters home occasionally showed twinges of jealousy. There was Gussmann and little Wolff, the hard-luck man of the outfit; three times he had been shot down behind his own lines and much of his time had been spent in the hospital. There was Weiss, a really gifted flier, who was already credited with shooting down fourteen British machines but who probably had at least ten more. Weiss was not only a modest man, he never thought of the war or of air fighting as a race for individual honours. As often as not he neglected to put in claims for aircraft destroyed until comrades who had seen his victory insisted. There was one-armed Karjus, the miracle man of the whole German Air Force. Shot down early in the war, he had lost his right arm, but he persuaded a Berlin aircraft designer to work out a rearrangement of controls and triggers, and he learned to operate them with the steel hook he now used for a hand. There was Lowenhardt, with forty victories already. There was a short, gay, spirited young man named Ernst Udet, who would survive the war and fly in World War II.

But the British reserved much of their admiration for Werner Voss. One day Voss, out alone, engaged a British BE. He hit it and the aircraft wobbled towards the ground. The pilot made a landing of sorts in No-Man's-Land, but quite close to the British lines. He and the observer climbed from their wrecked machine and ran to the safety of their lines. Voss was bitterly disappointed; he had shot down a British aeroplane, but there was no one to give evidence of his victory. He knew that the German infantry had retreated that morning, so he couldn't call upon them for verification. There was only one thing to do. He cut his engine and glided down to land in the crater-dotted, torn land beside the wreckage of the British machine. He hopped out and wrenched the machine gun from the mounting of the BE and lugged it back to his aircraft. A rattle of rifle fire came from the British trenches; now mortar shells were landing and machine gun fire opening up. Somehow he bumped over the uneven ground and forced his aeroplane into the air. He returned triumphantly with very tangible evidence of his victory. Shortly afterwards Voss was given a staffel of his own which was stationed not far from Richthofen's. The British pilots felt that in every way he was as skilful as Richthofen; he was easily identified by the skull and crossbones painted on the red nose of his silvery-blue machine. He had shot down about thirty British aircraft and had fought some magnificent battles (many against odds), but he never fought as brilliantly or as bravely as he did on the day he died.

He had attended a party the night before in Berlin. It was held at the Bristol Hotel on the Unter den Linden, and the host—Tony Fokker. Fokker's new triplane had brought him into favour again and now, in addition to several suites upstairs, he maintained three large rooms on the ground floor of the hotel for entertaining pilots and their friends. Known as the Weissensaal, it was especially decked with flowers for this occasion. Bruno Loerzer, one of the most popular of all staffel leaders, was to be awarded his *Pour le Mérite* here. Fokker had told the Viennese maître d'hôtel, never known as anything but Herr Anton, to spare no expense to make his party a success, for every great fighter who could be spared would be present to pay tribute to handsome, laughing-eyed Loerzer. Herr Anton was a resourceful man; he even knew ways of getting food out of Switzerland and Holland. A huge table groaned with *paté de foie gras*, hams, bologna, cheeses, salami, turkey and game not only from the Black Forest but also from the Black Market. Bartender Ernst Gentsch, too old to serve in the Army but not too old to serve drinks, presided over an assortment of German wines, Munich beers, Scotch and American whiskies, cordials, English gins, and both French and German champagne. Wide-eyed, sixteen-year-old Otto Siefert was his *Bargehilfe*, and the assistant bartender found it hard to take his eyes off his country's greatest heroes. General von Hoeppner himself put the decoration around the neck of the smiling Loerzer, and then they toasted him in the champagne of France. Bartender Gentsch, who by now knew the individual taste of every guest who was present, had mixed

Fokker's favourite drink himself. It was coffee and hot milk, well sweetened, but Herr Anton had managed to find some real coffee and the little Dutchman drank half a dozen tall glasses of it in delight. Nervous, excitable, flushed with triumph, he was the only man there who appeared to feel his drinks.

Hoeppner left and a three-piece band played the songs the fliers liked. Schleich, Loerzer, Hermann Goering and Voss hovered over the piano singing lustily as they sipped champagne. Ernst Udet, a truly fine artist, sat with two others at a table, smiling gently and between drinks making sketches of his fellow pilots. Manfred von Richthofen sat alone nursing one glass of wine. As always, he seemed to dwell in some secret silence, unable to unbend or raise his voice in song. He frowned when he saw one of his pilots unbutton the collar of his tight tunic; even at a celebration he felt that a German officer should maintain his dignity. His young brother Lothar joined the group at the piano and Manfred frowned again as his clear young voice rang out. There were those who said that he was jealous of the youngster's popularity, for if Lothar had not earned from his colleagues the awed respect which they granted to the elder brother, he had earned their warmhearted affection.

Herr Anton approached Richthofen to whisper that a huge crowd had collected outside; the people of Berlin had heard that he was in the hotel. Would he just show himself to the crowd? Richthofen told Anton curtly to have his car come to the side entrance. He would not show himself to the crowd and he'd had enough of this party. He said a formal goodnight to Tony Fokker, nodded briefly to the pilots and left. No one asked where he was going—not even those closest to him took such liberties. Richthofen was never concerned with the mystery he created, and he discouraged speculation as to what kind of personality lay hidden under his rather austere exterior. He was usually courteous enough, but it was an aloof and distant courtesy that discouraged intimacy.

When he had left, the restraint was gone, too, and Goering and Loerzer called for more champagne, and young Otto Siefert's small legs hurried to keep up with the orders. Girls had appeared and there was dancing and laughter, and men who had lived so long and at such close quarters with death forgot for a time the inevitable destiny that was waiting for them, perhaps tomorrow; tonight at least they could enjoy the illusion of immortality. No one was gayer than Werner Voss. He had enjoyed phenomenal success during the past few weeks with the Fokker Triplane, and he saw no reason why it shouldn't continue. He led a toast to Tony Fokker, drained his glass, and announced with regret that his twenty-four-hour leave was about to expire and he had to go back to the front. Fourteen hours later he was once again flying high over the lines in his triplane.

He was out alone when he ran into McCudden, Rhys-Davids, Lewis and four other machines from No 56. Instead of trying to scoot home, he attacked. Wise McCudden, heading the flight, led his men in a circling movement; they had Voss in the middle now, taking the brunt of their concentrated fire. But he performed one miraculous manœuvre after another. Twice he escaped from McCudden by going into a quick, flat half-spin—a tactic McCudden confessed he had never seen before. For ten minutes this incredibly courageous and skilful flier kept seven of Britain's finest fighter pilots at bay, and then Rhys-Davids got him in his sights and the uneven battle was over. Voss died fighting.

Rhys-Davids was given a shower of congratulations on his return to the base, but he only said ruefully, "I wish I could have brought him down alive." All agreed that Werner Voss on that day had proven to be the finest fighter pilot any of them they had ever seen. They felt that in holding off seven of them he had done something that no flying man alive could match—not even Richthofen or Guynemer.

They talked, too, that night, about the aircraft Voss had been flying. It had made its appearance only a few weeks before; Voss had been the first to fly it, and he had shot down twenty-two British pilots in the space of three weeks before Rhys-Davids put an end to his career. It was a triplane, and it was Tony Fokker's latest and proudest creation. Actually the British had a three-wing machine, the Sopwith Triplane, but the RFC pilots were suspicious of it. They preferred their more conventional fighters, and the Sopwith was given to the RNAS where it performed very well. Fokker didn't exactly copy the Sopwith, he merely borrowed the theory that an aircraft with three short wings would be more manœuvrable and able to climb faster than a machine with one or two wings with larger spans. The result was the amazing Fokker Triplane, never called anything but 'The Tripe' by the British fliers.

Fokker, still unable to get the powerful Mercedes engines, had decided to concentrate on designing a plane whose manœuvrability would compensate for its lack of speed. He reasoned that the defensive tactics used by the German Air Force did not call for tremendous speed; they seldom had to chase British aircraft—the latter were only too eager to cross the lines looking for trouble. His intensive study of aerial fighting tactics and his close relationship with the great pilots had convinced him that the machine that could climb quickly, turn sharply, and even go through improvised stunts in combat, was more effective than the aircraft that relied merely upon sheer speed. The Fokker Triplane filled the bill perfectly, but the pilots at first were suspicious of its banked wings. Fokker persuaded Voss to try it out and for three weeks he enjoyed phenomenal success. The story of Voss's great fight against hopeless odds confirmed Fokker's estimate of his creation, and Richthofen demanded that his whole 'circus' be equipped with the new machine. Fokker's star was in the ascendant again.

He took special care with the aircraft that the Red Baron would fly. He had it painted bright scarlet except for the white rudder and the white squares backing up the black crosses on fuselage and upper wing. It was a beautiful if unconventional-appearing machine, and the first day Richthofen took it up he shot down a British aeroplane with the expenditure of only twenty rounds of ammunition.

The Triplane had its limitations; it wasn't, of course, as fast as either the Sopwith Camel or the Spad, and its fuel capacity was limited. In a long dive the fabric of the top wing had a tendency to peel off, but a clever pilot seldom had to resort to long dives. It made a tighter turn than any other aircraft in the air, and in the hands of Richthofen and his superb fliers it was deadly. During the following weeks the Baron's red three-banked machine became only too familiar to the men of No 56 Squadron. But they were great fighters themselves, and it wasn't long before they learned how to minimize the advantages of the Tripe.

A few weeks after Voss had been killed, a batch of decorations arrived for the men of No 56 Squadron. Ball received a posthumous Victoria Cross, Rhys-Davids received the DSO, and Barlow received a Bar to his MC, as did McCudden. It was a joyous occasion and the band was in fine fettle. Rhys-Davids was the special hero of the occasion; even men like McCudden, usually wary of giving their affection lightly, loved the impetuous, generous, warm-hearted young Etonian. They all felt that the mantle of Albert Ball had fallen on his shoulders; if he lived, they thought that he would be the greatest of them all. Rhys-Davids was incapable of meanness or guile or dislike even for the enemies he fought every day. He respected them, and above all he respected Richthofen, who had claimed sixty victims. As the celebrations reached its climax, McCudden began chanting for Rhys-Davids to make a speech. Others joined in the clamour, and the embarrassed pilot had to rise to his feet and say something. He stood there for a moment and then, as complete silence fell upon the mess hall, he said slowly, "I'm very happy to receive this decoration, but I'm not going to talk about that. I've been thinking of the great bravery of the men we fight, men like Werner Voss. We are fighting against magnificent men of courage, and I'm going to ask you to do an unprecedented thing. I'm going to ask you to rise and drink a toast." He filled his glass and held it up. "Gentlemen, I drink to Manfred von Richthofen—our most worthy enemy."

They drank the toast enthusiastically, except for one man. He remained seated and said bitterly, "I won't drink a toast to that son-of-a-bitch."

The spotlight here played on No 56 Squadron doesn't mean that there weren't other squadrons every bit as good. The presence of Ball, McCudden and Rhys-Davids in it and the fact that it fought directly against Richthofen's men merely dramatized its activities. In every other way it was a typical fighter squadron, and a similar story could have been written about virtually every other RFC squadron doing long, sustained fighting. Ball and McCudden were outstanding, each great in his own way, but in 1917 there emerged a man who in retrospect seems to have been greater than either; now that all the evidence is in he seems, in fact, to have been the greatest fighter pilot of World War I.

His name was Edward Mannock, and, like McCudden, he was an Irishman born on the wrong side of the tracks. He joined the Army before the war, and served his apprenticeship first in the ambulance corps, then in the engineers and finally in the RFC. Mannock was a tall man with blue-grey eyes, and a thin face; he seemed to wear an expression of perpetual disapproval. His father had been a Regular Army man before him, and Mannock's early life had been confined by the limitations of his father's pay as a corporal.

Edward never forgot the gallant efforts of his mother, his elder brother and elder sister to make a home for the family. He had to leave school and help out. He worked as a delivery boy for a grocer in Canterbury, became a barber's assistant at fifteen, and finally got a job he liked; he became a linesman for a telephone company and was transferred to Wellingborough. He boarded with the Eyles family, and to Jim Eyles he transferred all of the affection he would ordinarily have given to his father. It was undoubtedly the warm personality of Jim Eyles which kept the boy from becoming an embittered man, for the early responsibilities and the poverty of his childhood left scars on him that would have remained open wounds, had it not been for the affection given him by Eyles and his wife. They called him 'Pat', though most of his friends would always know him as 'Mick'. Mannock was a devout member of the local Labour Party, which he felt epitomized the underdog in the country. Mannock was an articulate critic of the Government and of the *laissez-faire* policy practised by the men in power. But he was a sturdy patriot, and he felt that political fights, no matter how bitter, were still family fights. Then his restless spirit prompted him to leave the country; he travelled in the Middle East and Turkey for five years doing odd jobs, and in a very real sense, growing up. But when he felt that war was inevitable, he hurried to the country he loved (even though he liked to criticize it).

He disapproved of a great many things, wealth, social position, sham, and finally the Germans. He requested transfer from the hospital corps to which he had first been assigned, because he felt that fate might some day order him to care for a wounded German, and he had the deep conviction that the only way to beat Germany was to kill, kill and kill. Only combat would give a man a chance to do this. And finally he was accepted in the RFC despite a very bad left eye.

James McCudden was given a brief assignment to teach the neophytes advanced combat tactics, and Mannock was lucky enough to be assigned as one of his pupils. Mannock was always very proud of the fact that the great McCudden had saved his life during this period.

"What do I do if I go into a spin?" he had asked McCudden.

"Put all controls central and pray like hell," McCudden said laconically.

That afternoon Mannock's aircraft did go into a spin; he centralled his controls and he prayed like hell and the machine came out of it. From that time on the two Irishmen were great friends; they shared their leaves together, and if McCudden—who Mannock called Old Mac—could never quite share the bitter hatred his friend had for the Germans, they had much else in common including a great mutual respect.

Mannock arrived in France early in 1917 at the advanced age of thirty. He was assigned to No 40 Squadron, which numbered among its pilots such redoubtable fighters as Bond, Keen, MacKenzie, Mulholland, MacLanachan, Godfrey, McElroy, Cecil Lewis and a fine commanding officer, Major Robert Lorraine, who had been one of England's best actors in peacetime. Mannock's first day was marred by an incident that bothered his fellow pilots but didn't even cause him to frown. On the night of his arrival he went into dinner to find his new squadron mates all seated. There was one empty chair, and he moved hesitantly towards it.

"This belong to anyone?" he asked quietly, and was startled at the sudden silence which fell.

"Sit down," one of the pilots said gruffly.

"You sure it isn't someone else's chair?" Mannock asked.

"It was. It belonged to Pell. He didn't come back this afternoon," one of the pilots said curtly.

Mannock nodded coolly and sat down. He was never superstitious, and for a long time he had no thought that death would ever claim him. He remembered not only the lessons but also the fighting philosophy of James McCudden. Recklessness and boldness had no place in air fighting, he felt; the man who won was the man who had mastered both strategic and tactical skill. Of course, there were desperate situations which called for foolhardy boldness, but even then an intelligent pilot should temper this recklessness with reliable, sound judgment.

Mannock was not a natural flier; he had to practise long hours to get the hang of formation flying. Nor was he a good shot. This deficiency was due in part to his badly astigmatized left eye which an alert examining doctor would have spotted and immediately disqualified him from flying duty. To make up for this natural defect he spent hours in the gunnery pits, improving his aim, and he soon became a better than average shot. During his first weeks with the squadron some of his mates thought him to be over-cautious. He hadn't even got close enough to a German machine to open with his guns, and there were those who wondered if he didn't have a yellow streak. Mannock knew what they were thinking, but he also knew what he was about; he proceeded along the tedious path of caution and perseverance, and gradually he became proficient in formation flying and a master of both offensive and defensive tactics.

The squadron was flying Nieuports, and a question often discussed in the mess was, 'How steep can you dive a Nieuport without having the wings come off?' One day Mannock took his aircraft up over the field and went into several steep dives. He came out of each one, and now the whole squadron was out watching, wondering what he was up to. Finally he held his dive until the lower wing turned in its fastening and started to disintegrate. Somehow he managed to right the machine and land in a soft, newly ploughed field half a mile from the aerodrome. That night at dinner he told his fellow pilots calmly just how much diving a Nieuport would take. Mannock was a man who had to do things and find out things for himself.

Captain 'Zulu' Lloyd, a veteran of No 60 Squadron, joined the squadron about this time and grew very friendly with Mick Mannock. Mannock, usually rather reserved, opened his heart to this friendly, experienced pilot.

"I know what they are saying about me," Mannock confessed, "and they are partly right. I've had a few bad scares . . . I mean I've been frightened against my will. This is a nervous reaction and I've studied it and conquered it, I believe. I think, too, I've mastered the science of air fighting."

Mannock had met a stubborn enemy—his own inherent fear, but he had conquered it and now he went after a lesser enemy—the German.

It was two months before he shot down his first German, but during those two months he had perfected his skill. And now, within three weeks he had shot down five more and the squadron realized that his previous caution was merely his way of learning this most difficult of all professions. He was made a flight commander, and pilots found they enjoyed following him. He attacked with superb skill, never losing his head, always using tactics which minimized the odds against him and his men, and, if he took risks, they were carefully calculated.

Like McCudden, he was always working on his aircraft, his engine or his gun, trying to make each more efficient. By inserting a washer on the front of his Vickers gun barrel, he increased its rate of fire. Major J. L. T. Pearce, Chief Armament Officer of the RFC, had devised an electric gadget to warm the gun so it would not freeze at high altitudes. Mannock adopted it with great success. He always arranged the sights of his own guns and invented a special sight of his own. He placed good shooting above good flying. 'Good flying,' he would say, 'never killed a Hun yet. And when you shoot, don't aim for the plane—aim for the pilot.' Now his victories increased day by day.

"You know," he said to 'Zulu' Lloyd, "There is room for brains in this game, and I've been working out a set of new tactics. I'm really going to bowl over some Huns from now on." He did.

He had one motto which he repeated over and over. "Always above, seldom on the same level, never underneath." By the autumn of 1917 he had twenty Germans to his credit, he had completely conquered all fear, and he was as good a tactician as his friend McCudden.

When a friend in the squadron was killed, Mannock was not ashamed to weep, but his tears were only in part for his departed friend; they were also tears of rage because he couldn't kill enough Germans to satisfy the implacable urge that was in him. But when he was leading a patrol, Mannock the individualist ceased to exist. He was especially skilful in nursing newly arrived pilots through their first trying weeks. Often, after hitting an enemy aircraft, he would veer off to allow one of his new men to give it the *coup de grâce*, and that night he'd insist that his bullets had missed and that the youngster get credit for a kill.

Mannock feared only one thing—death by fire. Always, just before he took off for combat, he would check his revolver to see that it was loaded and in good working order. A visiting pilot from another squadron, not knowing about his obsession with fire, noticed his care with the revolver and asked. "What's wrong with your Vickers; are you going to tackle a German with that little peashooter?"

Mannock shook his head. "No," he said, "This little gun is for me if I ever catch fire. Then I'll put a bullet through my brain. They'll never burn me."

They never did burn him, but he burned many of them, and every time it happened he came to his base joyously and cried out, "Sizzle sizzle sizzle. . . . I sent one to hell in flames today." Mannock kept a diary and he wrote nearly every week to his old friend James Eyles. Happily, these frank, honest letters have been preserved, and are available to anyone who wants to know what manner of man this was—perhaps the greatest killer any war ever produced. Why, for instance, did he have this almost pathological hatred for Germans? You have to search carefully, but if you read the things he wrote that still survive, and read the various books later written about him and talk to some of the men who knew him and who fought with him in those days, you can find a rational motivation. To begin with, Mick Mannock loved his country, not with the synthetic, spurious love of some born to wealth and social position but as the pub owner loved it, as the workman loved it, as the small shopkeeper loved it, as the man in the street loved it. And Mick Mannock was desperately afraid that the great German war machine would destroy the England that he loved. His life hadn't been easy, and he had supported himself and helped support his mother since he was fifteen, but he felt that it was a better life than any other country offered, and now it was in jeopardy. Mick Mannock was a patriot. His hatred for anyone who tried to destroy his England was intense, and he felt that the danger to his country lessened with every German he and his squadron mates killed. His country wasn't perfect, God knows, but it was his country and it was the best Goddamn country in the world (he'd tell McCudden when they were alone on leave in London), and any man who wasn't ready to die for it had no right to call himself an Englishman.

This estimate of Mick Mannock has been read by men who flew with him; they agree that it is an accurate appraisal of a man who was outwardly simple and uncomplicated but who within was a mass of unresolved contradictions, doubts, hatreds and fears. Not fears in the conventional sense, for these he had conquered, but fears for his country—and to his hatred of Germans there was added his hatred of injustice and poverty. He was seldom preoccupied with the thought of his own death; by now he felt that his specialized skills were proof against any mishap in the air. And he fought on as perhaps no man in the history of mankind ever fought on, never with blind rage but with controlled fury. The man who, during his first two months in combat, had been thought by some to be a coward, now, in late 1917, warned his own pilots that the only excuse he would accept if a man fell out of formation was engine trouble. Once a veteran pilot did duck out when the going was bad, and Mannock, who saw him cut short his attack upon the enemy, turned and fired a burst at his own squadron member. He always regretted that he didn't bring him down.

The man lived to get back to the base, and after Mannock examined his engine and found it in good working order, he told his commanding officer quite simply to have the man transferred somewhere else or he, Mannock, would have to kill him. Yet he would excuse any mistakes made by a new pilot and fly close to him, protecting him, teaching him by example and advice how best to master the trade of killing Germans while remaining unhurt.

Mannock was probably the only pilot in the RFC who never knew exactly how many Germans had fallen to his blazing guns. He was conscious of the number only when a new decoration arrived to be celebrated by the whole squadron, for by now he was loved as well as respected. 'At one time or another Mick saved the life of every one of us,' a member of his squadron wrote home, and it was almost literally true. But one day, in writing to his friend Jim Eyles, Mannock did mention his total of enemy aircraft shot down, but only to poke fun at his friend McCudden.

Mannock had one small, almost childish conceit. Whenever possible after he had shot down a German behind the British lines, he would hurry to the spot to collect some souvenir of the kill, and this he would always send to Jim Eyles. He would take a piece from a smashed propeller, a boot from a dead German pilot, a map case, a magneto or a sparking plug from the engine; had custom allowed, he probably would have scalped any German whose death he had caused, and sent the scalp lock back to Eyles. In his letter he wrote:

'Same Place'
1 August, 1917
Raining like hell.

Dear Jim,

Your last letter to hand. Glad to hear that all at home are well and in fine fettle. Plenty of scrapping in the air now every day. Three of us went up and ran right into nine Hun machines yesterday. We had a glorious 'schemozzle'. They gave us a hell of a time, although we held our own. I made the old bus do some horrible things on that occasion. I believe the whole front from Lens to Arras was looking at us. They hopped it in the end, and I hadn't a bullet-hole anywhere on the machine. . . .

I sent the parcel off to you yesterday. Pilots' boots which belonged to a dead pilot. Goggles belonging to another. The cigarette holder and case were given to me by the Captain Observer of a two-seater I brought down. The piece of fabric with the number on it is from another Hun two-seater. . . . The other little brown packet is a field dressing carried by a Hun observer for dressing wounds when in the air. I got it from a crashed bus. I have several other things which I cannot send home, they will do later. . . .

We have only lost six of our original squadron and have brought down about forty-five Huns. My total is now forty-one, although you may not believe it, and they have given me the DSO. I'm expecting the Bar at any moment, as I have brought down about eight since I was recommended for the DSO. If I've any luck, I think I may beat old Mac. Then I shall try and oust old Richthofen. . . .

His next letter two weeks later read:

Secret: Got the MC, old boy, and made Captain on probation. *Don't tell anyone* and still write me as the usual Lieutenant. Had some more luck, only bad this time. Busted two buses during the last three days. Engines broke in two places in mid-air. Got down all right. Some pilot! The Old Man congratulated me. "Damn good work, Mannock, you did well." Hurt myself a little bit on the second occasion, but not much. Send Mrs E's letter on if she's not yet returned. . . .

One day last week I had five scraps on my own and fired off 470 rounds of ammunition. Got one.

Lost some fellows during the last week. Rotten. Hit by 'Archie' direct. Went down in a spin from 7000 feet. . . .

Thanks for the French quotation. As you say, there *is* a good
time coming.

Yours,
Pat.

During the latter part of 1917, Mick Mannock was averag-
ing a victory a day, and by his example encouraged hundreds
of young pilots to follow his tactics rather than the suicidal,
if gallant, methods of Albert Ball. And because of this, many
of them are alive today. Before 1917 had ended, Mannock had
surpassed Old Mac with fifty-six victories. No one was hap-
pier about it than the Irishman who had taught him so well
in the almost forgotten days of the dim past—nearly ten
months before.

But his greatest days lay ahead.

Chapter Ten

BRIGHT WINGS—AND TRAGIC GLORY

THE YEAR 1917 saw Death reap a fiendish harvest in the
air. British fliers, still relentlessly pursuing the effective
but costly offensive tactics that had become the trademark
of the RFC, were the chief sufferers. During the first half
of the year official figures issued by both sides agree that
Allied air losses were exactly four times as great as casualties
among German fliers.

The Fokker Triplane and the Albatros were demonstrating
their superiority, and during one five-day period in the spring
they accounted for seventy-five British aircraft, with a loss
of 105 men. During those same five days, fifty-six British aircraft were lost because of flying accidents. This was due not
only to the limited training given to new pilots, but also to
the nervous strain which had gripped so many of the veteran
airmen. Often an experienced pilot would suddenly lose his
fine, sure touch, crash on takeoff or landing, make elementary

and tragic mistakes in combat, and commanding officers could only shake their heads in bewilderment. The strain on pilots engaged in constant fighting was unbearable, but it was also unseen, and even the pilots themselves were often unconscious of it until it was too late. Doctors were equally puzzled; aviation medicine was not yet the science it would be in World War II, and the expression 'combat fatigue' had not yet crept into the airman's vocabulary. Not even the greatest of the French and British pilots were immune from this strain.

There is no question, for instance, that Georges Guynemer had reached the breaking-point during September, the month in which he kept his long-deferred appointment with eternity. Guynemer was never a clever virtuoso of the air like Captain Heurtaux, leader of the Stork Escadrille. He didn't have the calm detachment of the great René Dorme who, a fellow pilot wrote, 'went to battle as a fisher goes to his nets'. A modest, quiet, gentle man, Dorme kept his hatred for the enemy where the Germans had put it—in his heart. When the invaders captured his own countryside of Briey, they held his parents in custody for six months. But Dorme's intense feelings never interfered with his brilliant manœuvring in combat. Most opponents in the air were bewildered by his flashing tactics. He would present them with what they thought to be an easy target and then, even as they pressed the trigger, the target would veer, zoom upwards, dive or slip to either side. He induced sheer frustrated exhaustion in his foe; in trying desperately to follow his amazing and, to anyone else, suicidal aerobatics, a German often would stall, lose control of his plane and crash.

It was easy for Dorme to evade the rudimentary aggressions of the ordinary enemy pilot; in more than a hundred air battles he received only three bullet holes in his Nieuport. He seemed invulnerable; he was sustained by the strength of his inner hatred, and in him there was no room for uncertainty or the fears which took possession of even the greatest fighters.

When he attacked in single combat, his first pass was tentative, almost disinterested; he was like a sleepy cat striking at a butterfly. And then he and his Nieuport, acting in perfect harmony, would suddenly turn in furious but always calculated attack. The second time a cat slaps at a butterfly he means it. He would return from combat, give his report casually, acting, a pilot wrote, 'as though he had just returned from the theatre after watching a performance that was interesting enough but hardly worth talking about.'

René Fonck, destined to perform two miracles—he would eventually shoot down seventy-five German aircraft, and he would live to celebrate Armistice Day—was, like Dorme and Mannock, a master of self-preservation. He fought cerebrally, never emotionally, and he had a technical answer for every new German attack manœuvre. He could only shake his head helplessly at what he considered the wild impetuosity of Guynemer. Fonck was the smallest, the youngest, but perhaps the most mature of all French fighter pilots.

Guynemer was invariably as taut as a violin string stretched to its limit; but he lacked the robust extrovertism of Charles Nungesser, who could spend a day of desperate fighting in the air, then sneak off to Paris for a night with convivial souls and be relaxed and ready to fly again at dawn.

During one two-month stretch of the Somme fighting, the official report accompanying a decoration said that Guynemer 'waged 388 combats, brought down thirty-six German aircraft, three balloons, and compelled thirty-six other badly damaged aircraft to land'. He fought much as Ball had fought. Although he was a fine mechanic, a gunsmith and a master of aerial aerobatics, in actual combat he seldom used the skill he had acquired. Not for him the delicate manœuvring before joining the battle; he used what in the French school of fencing is called 'the thrust direct'.

Guynemer had an insatiable appetite for flying and for fighting. Nothing else seemed to exist for him. To the slim, frail pilot with the black burning eyes this was his war, and he begrudged every moment that he wasn't in the air. Each morning he walked silently to his machine and examined it. He had three aeroplanes which he used according to the mission of the day. He had a standard Spad, a high-compression Spad and a third aircraft made especially for him by the same factory, which was fitted with a 200-hp Hispano-Suiza engine and was unique in that it mounted a four-pounder pom-pom in addition to an ordinary machine-gun. He used tracer bullets in the machine gun to sight the pom-pom; when his tracers were hitting the mark, he'd release what he always called his 'cannon', firing explosive shells. His aircraft, a Spad VIII, was one of the very few to use such a weapon in World War I.

Having looked gun and engine over carefully, he would check the fuel, talk briefly to his mechanics and then slip into the fur-lined *combinaison* he wore, don his tightly-fitting woollen head-covering, the *passe-montagne*, and over this put on his leather helmet. He would step into the cockpit and, ready for battle, his whole expression changed. Plutarch spoke of the terrible expression on the face of Alexander when he went into combat. One of his escadrille mates wrote that when Guynemer was ready to fight, 'the look on his face was appalling; the glances of his eyes were like blows'. It was as though he had passed a sentence of death on adversaries he would meet that day, and he was on the way to carry out that solemn sentence.

When he returned from combat, his machine usually bore marks of the struggle, and he himself was still in the grip of the tension engendered by the fighting. No matter how many he had shot down, he could not celebrate joyously as could most pilots; if he was satisfied with what he had done, he confided only to his inner self. He had already been wounded eight times, but although he shrugged off these mishaps as unimportant accidents, the men of his squadron noticed that he was becoming more and more withdrawn and showing an irritability that was not like him at all. His eighth accident was a painful but not serious flesh wound in the right arm. He spent only a week in the hospital and then left, with his arm half healed, to fly again.

The first flight after a man has been hit is always a significant one. Had he lost his nerve? Were his reflexes still working? Sheer courage wasn't enough any more. A wound or a crash often did something to your co-ordination, and a man with four unco-ordinated limbs and a mind to match seldom lived long. Guynemer resolved whatever doubts he had in a highly unorthodox manner.

He returned from the hospital to his base, flew alone for

two hours, and that night hurried to the home of his parents at Compiègne. His sister Yvonne was his closest confidante, and to her he poured out the story of what he had done that afternoon.

"As long as you have never been wounded, you think that nothing can ever happen to you," he said. "But once you are hit a few times, it is difficult. Today, when I saw a Boche in the sky, I felt quite differently than I ever felt before. I was uncertain, hesitant."

"What did you do?" she asked.

"I ordered myself not to shoot," he said tersely. "The Boche attacked and I merely manœuvred; he emptied at least 500 shots from his guns and I never answered his fire. That is the way to master one's nerves, little sister. Mine now are entirely mastered. I am now in absolute control."

His wise father was not so sure. He urged his son to rest until his arm was completely healed.

"You need strengthening," his father said earnestly. "You have done too much. If you go on now, you will be in great danger of falling below your high standard; you wouldn't really be yourself. You have given enough of yourself."

"We have given nothing as long as we have not given everything," the flier replied.

He continued to fight and, as his victories mounted, he became the most worshipped hero in France, the Ace of Aces. When he visited Paris, he was mobbed by crowds; women pressed close, vying for his attention, for a souvenir of some kind. He brushed them aside petulantly. Not only France but Britain gave him the highest decorations. His father, feeling doubts about the capacity of his son to resist the heady intoxication caused by the fact that every beautiful woman in Paris seemed hysterically eager to climb into bed with him, pleaded with him to keep a sense of proportion.

"Don't worry," Guynemer laughed. "I am watching my nerves the way an acrobat watches his muscles. I have chosen my mission and won't allow anything to interfere with it."

But with his added victories came an increased irritability. Aviation medicine hadn't advanced to the point where this was considered a danger-sign; he was a law unto himself, and his fellow pilots shrugged it off. They did not recognize it for what it was—a sign that an invisible master was beginning to control the frail fighter; an enemy he didn't even know existed.

After his fifty-third victory he went to Paris for a visit to the Spad works, where he often conferred with the great engineer, Bechereau, who had so improved the little aeroplane. That evening he was somehow inveigled to attend a social function and he was subjected to the inevitable hero worship which by that time completely bored him.

"You have every honour now that your country can give you," a woman gushed. "What new decoration is there left for you to earn?"

"The wooden cross," he said simply.

He almost earned it after a fight with three Germans. On this occasion they had penetrated into French territory, and the fight took place in full view of thousands of infantrymen stationed between Peronne and Montdidier. Always meticulous in his combat reports, he noted that at eleven-twenty he had 'asphyxiated a Boche in flames beyond our lines'. He then noted that at eleven-twenty-one he had 'disabled Boche aircraft, killed pilot', and then in his final victory at eleven-twenty-five, 'brought down Boche in flames from upper storey'. The whole engagement had taken five minutes, but a shell from his own anti-aircraft fire had smashed his water reservoir and thrown his machine into a sharp tailspin. He rushed towards the earth, but succeeded in getting the aircraft out of the spin and into a glide. He hit the ground hard, rebounded and then pancaked into the shell-pocked earth. He climbed out of the wrecked Spad, dizzy and with a cut knee. The infantrymen crowded around him, recognized the Ace of Aces and carried him off in triumph to their commanding general. The general, as excited as his men to meet the great flier, immediately gave orders for a military salute to be given him by the division.

"You will review the troops with me," the general announced proudly.

"But my knee is paining me," he protested.

"Nonsense," the general replied. "When a man falls from

the sky without being broken to bits, he is a magician and he cannot feel pain."

Dizzy from what afterwards was diagnosed as a brain concussion, and in agony from the wrenched and bleeding knee, he had to stand in front of the troops and take their salute. And then spontaneously there came a song from a few throats; it grew into a roar and was taken up by the whole division—the surging battle-cry of France, the *Marseillaise*. Guynemer stood there, frail, his body wracked by pain, but now he was sustained by his pride and the worship of fighting men, which was different from the cloying lionization of the women of Paris, and he saluted; afterwards the general said in wonder that tears had been in the eyes of the great Guynemer.

He had to rest for a few days after that, and he wrote his sister the full story. 'During my long fall down I was planning how best to hit the ground. I made up my mind, but there were still ninety-five out of a hundred chances for the wooden cross. But I did not earn it that day.'

He never did earn it. This last honour escaped him. He was shot down on September 11th, 1917. He fell between the lines and his only requiem was the dirge of artillery fighting for the few feet of ground where he lay. His body was never found, and even though the Paris newspapers proclaimed sadly, 'The Knight of the Air is Dead', thousands of worshipping school-children never believed it; out of their firm belief in his immortality they created the legend, 'He flew so high that he just could not come down again.'

In April, 1917, the United States entered the war, and within twenty-four hours French and British airmen began scanning the skies, hoping to see the vast air armada from the world's great industrial giant. On the day America joined the conflict her vast air armada consisted of 109 aircraft; fify-five were the Aviation Section of the Signal Corps—fifty-four were with the Navy. All were training machines of venerable vintage and quite innocent of the various accoutrements of combat.

Washington was crawling with headline-hunting optimists secure in the smug belief that 'one Yankee is equal to fifty Germans'. 'The day after war is declared,' one patriot cried, 'a million men will spring to arms overnight.' He omitted one detail—they would have no arms to spring to for more than a year, and then it would be a bit late for springing. Another politician let his enthusiasm get the better of him by declaring, 'Within a short time we will darken the skies with our airplanes.' All of these phrases sounded soothing to the war-weary people of France and England, and the newspapers of Paris and London displayed them prominently. Significantly, no American military figures of stature made any predictions; they were all too appalled at the country's state of military unpreparedness.

Only a few months before war was declared in 1914, an evaluation of air power showed the distressing fact that the most progressive country in the world stood fourteenth among the world's nations in the amount of money spent on aircraft for military use, and twelfth in the number of aircraft attached to its army. About this same time, the American Secretary of War made the astounding statement regarding his request for funds to be allocated for military aeroplanes: 'It has seemed wise to me this year, in view of other more urgent necessities, not to ask for any large appropriation for these services.' And he presented a modest demand to Congress for $125,000. There were angry officers like Billy Mitchell and Henry Arnold and others who were shocked at this criminal pusillanimity, but their protests were but feeble cries shouted against the wind.

But now it was 1917 and the country wasn't any better off. Let General John Pershing tell it in the words he confided to his war diary:

The situation ... as to aviation was such that every American ought to feel mortified to hear it mentioned. Out of sixty-five officers and about 1000 men in the Air Service Section of the Signal Corps, there were thirty-five officers who could fly. With the exception of five or six officers, none of them could have met the requirement of modern battle conditions. ...

We could boast fifty-five training planes ... all ... valueless for service at the Front. Of these fifty-five planes ... the National Advisory Committee for Aeronautics ... advised that fifty-one were obsolete and the other four obsolescent.

199

We could not have put a single squadron in the field, although it was estimated later that we should eventually need at least 300 squadrons, each to be composed on the average of some twenty-four officers, 180 men and eighteen airplanes, besides a large reserve of planes for replacements.

To paraphrase the previously quoted Benjamin Franklin on seeing his first balloon, 'America's military machine was about as useless as a new-born baby'. In time it would grow and mature into a mighty striking force, but time is always on the side of he who uses it, and the Germans were making every use of it now, hoping to achieve a decisive result before the huge giant of American production really awoke, flexed his muscles and realized the potentialities of his awesome strength.

Paradoxically, America's entrance into the war was initially a handicap rather than a help to the air strength of the Allies. It is too obvious a fact to belabour that the moral influence of her entry was incalculable, but it was a long time before she was able to offer any tangible air or military help. Previously, the British and French looked upon America as an important source of supply to which they had priority. Now that the country had to equip an army and an air force (even though both existed for the moment only on paper), she could do so only at the expense of her allies. Typical of this suddenly curtailed help to Great Britain and France was the matter of the strong, resilient silver spruce which grew so abundantly in the woods of Oregon and Washington. Experience had shown that this wood was perfectly suited for aircraft, and virtually all of it had been swallowed up by the British aircraft factories. Now America had to build aircraft herself; she needed the spruce as well as the ash and poplar produced in the Northwest, and Britain's aircraft industry suffered accordingly.

Both France and England had to accept the realistic view that it would be some time before America managed to grow wings. Premier Ribot of France sent a message to Washington immediately after the declaration of war which did at least give the American Government a well-defined goal.

His blunt message said that if America was to give effective help, she should have 4500 aircraft and personnel to man them, ready for the 1918 campaign. He added that America should produce 2000 aeroplanes and 4000 engines each month. Only by doing this could the new ally help to gain supremacy in the air.

American authorities blinked at the huge order, but decided that this voice of experience from Paris should be heeded, and an immediate appropriation of $640,000,000 was made to enable industry and the Air Force to fulfil what now amounted to a commitment. America was in the war with both feet, and if she repeated some of the mistakes made in 1914 and 1915 by France and England in attempting to rush a programme of air development completion, they were not mistakes growing out of either indifference or lack of enthusiasm; they were the inevitable result of inexperience and of amateurs trying to do the job of professionals.

The existing American aircraft industry was pathetically small in comparison with the task it faced. Many established interests, principally in the motor car manufacturing field, hastened to form aircraft and engine building plants to augment such established firms as the Curtiss Company, Boeing, Vought, L-W-F, Gallaudet, Burgess and others. Orville Wright gave his name and his talents as a consulting engineer to one new organization, the Dayton Wright Company.

One of the first big orders was placed with Curtiss for large-scale production of its JN-4D and for flying boats. The JN-4D, more familiarly known as the Jenny, was adopted as the standard pilot-training machine. The British-designed De Havilland 4 was selected as the standard front-line combat aircraft, and it, too, went into mass production. When the United States declared war on Germany, it had no aviation engines of sufficient power to propel the DH-4, and even larger engines were needed for the Curtiss flying-boats. This situation set plans in motion that would finally result in the Liberty engine, one of America's most controversial contributions to aviation during the war.

Two noted motor car engineers, who had also produced aircraft power plants, were assigned to design a suitable engine. These men, Jesse G. Vincent and J. G. Hall, went into seclusion in a hotel room which they did not leave for five days. Working alternate twenty-four-hour shifts, they turned out plans for a V-8 engine with light steel cylinders that would deliver up to 300 hp. Twenty-eight days after they started drawing, the first hand-made engines were ready for testing.

With similar speed the L-W-F Engineering Company modified one of its production models to flight-test the engine. Donald Douglas arrived from Washington at the L-W-F plant early one Saturday morning with complete details of the engine. By late the next afternoon all the engineering drawings for modifying the aircraft had been completed and the construction of modified parts was under way.

But things were changing so fast in the sky over the fighting fronts that by the time the manufacturers were tooled up for production of the engine, there was a need for greater power. So the engineers wearily set about redesigning the engine for twelve cylinders, giving it 400 hp.

Serious mistakes were made on the home front as industry tried to convert from peacetime commerce to the building, not just of aircraft, but of all the things that went into them, and of the facilities they required on the ground. One of the largest errors was that of over-optimism by motor car makers, who judged that they could speedily turn out aircraft in huge volume. Such estimates, made publicly, built up the expectations of the French and the British as well as the people at home to anticipate a miracle that did not come off. While the public reacted indignantly to the long delay in production and the sizeable cost of gearing up manufacturing facilities, the confusion did establish an irrefutable if discouraging fact : it takes time to build a little industry to a mammoth one; time that cannot be purchased with the biggest treasury in the world.

Other factors contributed greatly to the failure of the United States to field a great air force. It seems incredible now, but the one great nation in the world which had the opportunity to take advantage of the lessons learned by years of terrible trial on the part of her allies-to-be, entered the war without having any designs for up-to-date military aircraft. Research sponsored by the Government was almost non-existent. Once production got under way, the services called for model changes that hopelessly tangled the orderly output of aircraft. Manufacturing difficulties caused by such constant changes were accentuated by the lack of qualified engineers. All these matters, added to industry's inexperience in the field of aeronautics, militated against what had at first seemed like a simple job of changing over production lines from motor cars to aeroplanes.

During America's participation in the war, there were charges and countercharges over the efficiency and cost of the aircraft production programme. It was commonly believed that the Government was paying excessively for too little production, the cost figure most quoted being $1,500,000,000.

In spite of the tormented labour pains America suffered in its effort to bring forth air might, the great *accouchement* produced only a scrappy pigmy rather than the giant the public had anticipated. Few American aircraft ever got into the fight because volume production was not reached until the last months of the war, and the Liberty engine did not really mature until the war was over.

During the first weeks after the declaration of war, the Aviation Section of the Signal Corps was to the rest of the service the same annoying step-child the Royal Flying Corps had been in August, 1914. It seemed obvious that the War Department had made absolutely no plans as to what part the Aviation Section would play in case the country was called upon to become overnight a great military power. The almost unbelievable fact is that the General Staff didn't know a thing about military aeronautics. Neither then nor for several months was there a single General Staff officer in Washington who had ever attended a flying school or who through practical experience knew anything about training men to be combat pilots.

In fact, some of the regulations imposed upon the handful of men who made up the Aviation Section gave the impression that the General Staff didn't know an aeroplane from a horse. It is a matter of record that members of the Aviation Section were required to wear spurs when in uniform. The regulation was revoked—after the country had been at war for a year. It finally penetrated the military intelligence that although you might arouse a lethargic horse by the use of spurs, the same methods did not work with a weary engine. Typical of the personnel heading the Section was the officer who said frankly that he considered flying too dangerous for a married man with children and that he for one had never, and would never, go up in an aeroplane. This was a bit like appointing a man to head the cavalry who was known to be afraid of horses, but it was all merely a part of the inevitable confusion that occurs when a democracy dedicated to peace enters the unaccustomed field of war.

Now out of the confusion came the appointment of Major-General George O. Squier as Chief Signal Officer of the Army, and as such he was in charge of all Army Air Service activities. Squier was a West Pointer who had also taken a PhD at Johns Hopkins University. For the past year and a half he had served as American Military Attaché with the British Army; he had seen what amounted to miracles of production, training, and finally front-line performance, overcome the initial bungling, uncertainty and lack of faith in the usefulness of aircraft, and he insisted that the same miracles now be performed in his own country. In time, they were. He had learned one valuable lesson that many General Staff members never learned; he knew that this war, unlike any which had preceded it, could use to the fullest extent men who had succeeded in the world of civilian occupations, even though they neither knew nor cared anything about the sacred Army Regulations. He avoided the tyranny of details and commissioned outside men of known competence as his assistants (to the horror of traditionalists). He faced a harrowing job, and it wasn't solved overnight, but at least he instituted sound methods of training, eliminated red tape wherever he could, and eventually got the young Air Force off the ground.

Officers who knew anything about flying and who could be trusted to take charge of training centres were hard to find. The military mind was better adjusted to the rigid frame of tradition than it was to the flexible requirements of a war unlike any other war, and officers who transferred from the cavalry to the expanding air service in the hope of quick promotion found it almost impossible to cope with problems never envisioned by the West Point instructors. Very few of the majors and colonels who accepted posts at flying fields made any effort to qualify as pilots or observers, and they neither spoke nor understood the language of airmen or aeronautical engineers. This made it difficult for eager young student pilots to have any confidence in them or to accept their decisions ungrudgingly.

At a Texas field a newly-arrived commanding officer, a veteran of the cavalry, brought his horse along with him. The first thing he did was to order a hitching-post erected in front of his headquarters; for twenty years he had been accustomed to performing his outdoor duties on horseback and he saw no reason to change the practice. Smartly garbed in shiny leather leggings and spurs, he mounted his steed and proceeded to inspect the flying field. The horse took exception to the noise made by the engines of several aircraft being warmed up outside a hangar, snorted with fear, and began to prance nervously. The new commanding officer grew apoplectic with rage as he tried to control his jittery horse.

"Stop those damn fans," he roared, waving in the direction of the whirling propellers. "Can't you see they scare my horse?"

When the 'fans' had stopped, he resumed his tour of inspection. In one hangar he saw half a dozen relatively new aircraft smashed hopelessly. He asked if they had been properly inspected on their arrival. He was assured that they had been.

"In the cavalry," he said, "when a horse goes lame the chances are ten to one that the horse has not been shod properly. Obviously these airplanes were not made properly or not cared for properly."

"They were well made and properly cared for," his second-in-command (a flying man) said. "Trouble is, we have a new bunch of cadets and they made a lot of rough landings."

"I'll soon fix that," the CO said grimly, and immediately issued a written order that on his field as long as he was in charge there would be 'no more rough landings'.

Gradually, however, Canadian and British veterans of the air fighting were asked to help, and some Americans who had been flying with either the French or British returned. They had magnificent raw material to work with, and many of the young Americans made such startling progress in qualifying as pilots that they were impressed into duty as instructors, and often as commanding officers. Slowly the pattern of the military structure was emerging; this war would in the main be fought by civilians with Regular Army officers in command posts. There were also plenty of young Regular Army officers eager to learn this new and important phase of warfare, and the Colonel Blimps were slowly weeded out as they had eventually been weeded out in England.

The United States did have a hard core of efficient, intelligent, imaginative officers who for years had fought a hopeless battle for aviation, and eventually the ability of men like General Benjamin Foulois, Colonel Billy Mitchell, Colonel Frank Lahm and others was finally recognized and their talents utilized.

But it would not be until the middle of 1918, more than a year after America's entrance into the war, that her airmen would really make their presence felt to any important degree. While they were learning to fly on the plains of Texas, the air war reached new heights of fury in Western Europe.

The youth of America believed in this war perhaps more than did their uncertain elders; from every college campus, from every garage, office and factory they flocked to enlist. The raw material was good; as good as it had been in Kitchener's Contemptibles. One group of college students enlisted immediately for pilot training. As one of them, an irreverent, colourful Southerner named Elliott Springs, said afterwards, to keep others from directing the song at them:

Onward conscript soldiers, marching as to war,
You would not be conscripts, had you gone before.

Their preliminary training over, they were put on a transport and sent to London. They would finish their preliminary training and be commissioned as officers and then go to war. They were sent to an Air Force base near Oxford, and then these youngsters began to learn the facts of military life as expounded by the American Colonel Blimps of the day. They had trained, of course, on Jennies and now they had to master the fighting machines; they were eager and intelligent and were in a hurry to get on with the final job of polishing their flying. They were not exactly officers (their commissions had not as yet been approved); they were not exactly enlisted men —they were 'cadets'; neither fish nor fowl. They were treated as such, not by the British who received them with open arms, but by the U.S. Regular Army officers who still thought it a bit unseemly that a war had to be fought with the help of civilians. On their arrival at the Oxford base and after a few days of inactivity, except for attendance at *Fair and Warmer*, then the number one musical hit in London, an investigation of the pulchritudinous charms of co-operative London girls which they enthusiastically endorsed, and the discovery of alcoholic beverages as delightful and as potent as those they had been brought up on as undergraduates at Yale, Princeton, the University of Virginia and other centres of culture, the discovery of a restaurant called Murrays which would thereafter be London headquarters for those who survived, and the unqualified, decent and (to many of them) unexpected friendship of the people of London—well, by that time they wanted to get into action. But they found that there were certain formalities to be observed first—and certain insults to be absorbed. An American major arrived from Paris to address them. They looked at him at first in awe. His uniform was beautiful: they were clothed in issue uniforms. He was from Paris and had been a lot nearer to the war than any of them. He was a West Pointer and could undoubtedly teach them something. Some of them were puzzled, he wore only infantry insignia and they were pilots. He looked them over coldly and began to speak. To begin with, he said their uniforms just wouldn't do.

They just weren't smart enough for London or Paris, so he ordered them to go out immediately and order tailor-made uniforms at their own expense. He also added that he had heard a lot of them were complaining about the extra weeks of ground training to which they had been assigned, and he told them that if any of them complained again or failed to show up in a smart uniform, he would transfer such a malefactor to the infantry and have him in the trenches within twenty-four hours.

He went on to say that all of them had been brought up as

civilians (a word he spat out) and that thank God the remainder of their training would be in the hands of a British colonel. He turned to the colonel, who had been listening with great embarrassment, and added, "What these men need is discipline. I hope you will give it to them."

The British officer said nothing, but the next day he called them together. By that time they were knowledgeable enough to know that the small coloured ribbons he had pinned on his left breast represented the Distinguished Service Order and the Military Cross, neither of which were given for what had come to be known as 'mess-room flying'. He was about twenty-three and he obviously hated his task of addressing men of his own age as a commanding officer. He had been in this war for a long time; it was an old and tired war to him, and like the men in front of him he, too, had been a civilian before his country needed his services. He had been in combat for two years and they had sent him back for a rest and to orientate the Americans who were arriving. He made no reference to the talk made by the American officer the day before:

You men are starting on a long trip. It's a hard trip and will require a lot of courage. You'll all be frightened many times but most of you will be able to conquer your fear and carry on. But if you find that fear has got the best of you and you can't stick it and you are beyond bucking up, don't go on and cause the death of brave men through your failure. Quit where you are and try something else. Courage is needed above all else. If five of you meet five Huns and one of you is yellow and doesn't do his part and lets the others down, the four others will be killed through the failure of the one and maybe that one himself.

This individual hero stuff is all nonsense. . . . It's concerted effort and disciplined team work that will win the war.

War is cruel, war is senseless and war is a plague, but we've got to win it and there's no better use for your life than to give it to help stop this eternal slaughter. It's a war of men, strong, determined men, and weaklings have no part in it.

He looked as sincere as he talked, and it all made sense to the young Americans who had never been shot at and who had never killed a German. The brief talk gave them new enthusiasm and new respect for the British, who by now were professionals at the job.

Elliott White Springs was a temporary sergeant and he had the highest rank among them. He also had a well-off family, and he immediately cashed the letter of credit he carried with him and distributed it as far as it went so that his pals would look 'smart' in proper uniforms.

"That American major ought to have his faced shoved down his throat," Springs said thoughtfully, doling out the last of his money.

A year later, when he was Captain Elliott Springs, the number three leading American ace, outranked only by Rickenbacker and Luke, he undoubtedly would have performed the unique service with pleasure—but unhappily, he never met the major again. When the war ended, fifty-one of the 210 were dead, thirty had been wounded and twenty were prisoners of war.

Springs, a twenty-one-year-old Princeton graduate, was always ready for a fight or a frolic, and he had a rare gift for friendship, and any of his squadron mates who reached for a bill when he was throwing the party risked a broken arm. When this group of 210 was split up, half the group got together and did something unprecedented. They all contributed towards a gift to the young 'sergeant'. They wanted to give him something useful. They did—they presented him with a beautiful flask from London's excellent Fortnum & Mason's. It may surprise Elliott Springs today to know that it cost the boys seventy-five dollars. Springs wound up in the 148th Squadron, and he spent the rest of the war brilliantly in combat, happily in Paris, and comfortably with his friends, who began to include not only his flying companions, but the highest American, French and British brass. Springs was always that kind of man.

The year drew to its close, but not before the world had become conscious of the great air fighters who continued to defy all the laws of probability merely by staying alive. The fighter pilots of 1917 put their lives on the line every time they went into the air, and although most of them fell victims to the inexorable law of averages, some, incredibly, did for a time defeat the fates which govern dice, the spinning of the roulette wheel and the destinies of men. To discuss the flying careers of all of them would be impossible, but even a cursory story of aerial fighting in World War I (which is all this claims to be) would be incomplete indeed without the story of William Avery Bishop.

In 1914 Billy Bishop was a twenty-year-old second classman at the Royal Military College at Kingston, Ontario; this was the Canadian equivalent of West Point or Sandhurst. He was born in Owen Sound, Ontario, and as a child he had learned to shoot and ride a horse before he had mastered the multiplication table; as soon as the bugle sounded, he enlisted in the Canadian Mounted Rifles. He could ride any horse that could be saddled, and he could (as his countrymen said later) knock the ear off a gnat at fifty paces with a rifle.

Like young Manfred von Richthofen, he too visualized the war in terms of dashing charges by cavalry, but when he arrived in England with the 14th Battalion of the great Canadian regiment, he was sadly disillusioned. It rained steadily during the first week, there wasn't a horse in sight, and the youngster began to realize that this wasn't the kind of war he had expected. He and his battalion were living in mud up to their knees, and he hated mud. At Owen Sound at this time of the year the snow would have fallen and it would be hard under foot, and the air would be dry and clean and crisp.

One day a trim little aircraft appeared from a nearby aerodrome and circled over the mud of the camp; it swooped low and then, as though disdaining to soil itself by contact with the mud, it arose with a disapproving roar and disappeared into the distance. Bishop looked after it, entranced.

That was the place to fight this war—far above the mud. By that time he knew that war on the Western Front was as much against mud as against Germans. He decided on the spot to join the RFC, and that decision meant that one hundred additional Germans would die in the following months.

Three months later this handsome, lighthearted young Canadian who hated mud was in France as an air observer. He was there for several months, and then the RFC accepted his application as a pilot. Early in 1917, after training in England, he returned to France as Lieutenant William Bishop of No 60 Squadron. During his first two weeks of flying with the squadron, Bishop learned a great deal about what he didn't know. For one thing, he discovered that although he was a good shot with a rifle or shotgun, he wasn't at all good in the air with a machine gun.

One afternoon the squadron cook turned to the mess sergeant and said, "That new lad Bishop is a bit batty. This morning he comes into my kitchen and—so help he—he asks for all the empty tin cans I got. What's the lad goin' to do with a basket of tin cans?"

The mess sergeant, accustomed to and tolerant with the vagaries of pilots, shrugged his shoulders.

Meanwhile, Bishop had invaded the upper air, and when he reached 15,000 feet he tossed the basket of cans overboard. The wind took them and they careened crazily all over the startled sky. Bishop dived at one and let go a burst; it lived and he looped and dived at another. The can flew into a thousand pieces and he zoomed upwards to hunt another. The cans darted in and out of cloud wisps, but this relentless hunter in his Nieuport pursued them. For a week he continued his strange target-practice. Bishop didn't believe too much in luck. If you could outshoot and outfly the other fellow, you'd win—nine times out of ten.

And then came the day when his painstaking effort to master this new battlefield paid off. Bishop was one of four sent up to scare enemy observers away. Important movements were taking place on the Front, and the General Staff didn't want German aircraft to get within sight of them. The patrol moved across the lines, going well into enemy territory. Suddenly out of nowhere, three German Albatros fighters dived at the patrol. One of them got on the tail of the British machine in front of Bishop. Bishop forgetting that undoubtedly another was diving at him, went for the German.

Bishop let fifteen rounds from the Lewis go screaming into the Albatros, but the German wasn't hit badly. Panicky, he dived to get away from the stream of lead. Bishop had tasted fighting now and he liked it. He dived after the German. The two planes hurtled through the skies, only twenty yards apart. The German flattened out, hoping to zoom upwards and get away from this terrier that he couldn't shake off. Bishop flattened, too, and pressed the trigger. Tracer bullets framed the fuselage of the Albatros and then criss-crossed it. There was a startled cough from the engine of the Albatros and the machine went into a spinning nosedive. Bishop followed, his gun still spitting angrily.

The German crashed and Bishop, exulting in his first victory, levelled out. Then—a sudden silence. The dive of nearly 7000 feet had forced oil into the motor of the Nieuport, choking it, smothering it—not a healthy situation while still behind the German lines with thousands of machine guns below and only 1500 feet of altitude.

Bishop set his machine in a flat glide toward his lines two miles away. All he could do was sit there holding the useless stick, hoping that he wouldn't fall short into No-Man's-Land. He just made it.

In his official report Bishop said, 'My engine oiled up at 1500 feet and I just glided over the line.'

Only a month and a half later came the day in Billy Bishop's meteoric career which suddenly set him apart from most of his fellow pilots. It was the only day he chose to remember in later years by a memento in his study.

He was alone and flying high. He wasn't the inexperienced kid he had been six weeks before, that day he barely made it 'over the line'. He was Captain Bishop now, a tried veteran—a veteran of six weeks. It was a fairly long life on the Western Front of 1917. He'd spent those weeks shadowing death, seeing death reach out ghastly fingers, and slipping out of their clutch. In those six weeks he'd shot down twenty aircraft. He was an old hand now, a hardened ace. He was just twenty-three. He turned his head to look over the side and below, and as he turned he heard a 'ping', a sharp tingle of broken glass and a buzzing in his ears. He turned back and there in front of him was a bullethole in his windscreen. He put a hand to his helmet. The bullet had creased it alongside his left ear. There was a German on his tail. Instinctively he zoomed upwards, banking steeply to the right. The German roared past him, so near that Bishop could feel the wash from the propeller, then disappeared into a cloud.

Bishop climbed. He sensed that the German wasn't alone. Now he—Bishop—became the hunter. He roared through the skies, noting a dozen things at once. He knew his altitude, the wind drift, his speed, and he knew that he was behind the German lines just beyond Queant-Drocourt. He played tag with the clouds using them as flimsy hiding places.

Then below he sighted five enemy aircraft. They were flying at about 6000 feet—two of them flying ahead and the other three a mile or so behind. Pretty tough odds even for a Bishop. He shoved his stick forwards and the machine nosed over.

He screamed down at the rearmost of the three, and before the German knew what had happened, his aircraft crumpled up like a piece of wet cardboard—wavered for a moment as though surprised—and then fluttered to earth. Bishop straightened out, and the second German machine came at him.

The German got in the first punch. Before Bishop could turn towards him his bullets had raked Bishop's aircraft—but didn't hit a vital spot.

Bishop zoomed up at the German, aiming at the belly of his machine with the precision of a surgeon cutting into an abdomen. The German fell apart as if it were made of balsa wood—number twenty-two for Bishop.

He looked up. The three remaining Germans had gathered their wits and they were coming for him. Now, he thought, he'd better leave this party. It was getting too rough. You could only fight against such odds when you had the element of surprise on your side.

He went home and made his report. 'Three hostile aircraft being above me, I returned,' he wrote laconically. The date, by the way, was May 2nd, 1917, and it was just noon.

Two hours later he was in the air again. He bumped into two enemy craft doing artillery observation just east of Lens, and he shot twenty rounds into them. Bishop roared east with the wind in his eyes and his throttle wide open. He was hot today, and he knew it. He swung farther east and saw two more hostile aircraft. He dived at them and pumped round after round at them. They staggered back at the vicious onslaught. Now he was over Monochy, flying at 6000 feet. He dropped out of a cloud to surprise a two-seater which was returning from the lines. In his report he says plaintively, 'I fired a whole drum into him, but without apparent result.'

His ammunition and his fuel were getting low, so he turned for home. Over Peleos he sighted two more Germans. Again he swung into action, but again his report says sadly, 'No apparent result.'

He had some food while his machine was being refuelled and then he was in the air again. He was up nearly three hours this time, and he had skirmishes with three aircraft before deciding to call it a day. On his way back he sighted six hostile fighters after one British machine. At long range he fought them, annoyed them, harried them and then, when he saw his colleague scurry away to safety, he, too, turned back. It had been quite a day, and his aircraft was a sieve. At one time or another during that day he had engaged twenty-three different enemy machines.

A few days later the King was pleased to award him the Distinguished Service Order. The commendation read: 'His courage and determination have set a fine example to others.'

Now he was accepted as one of the élite. Even his fellow aviators looked at him in awe. He seemed to bear a charmed life, but actually he was alive so far because he could fly and shoot better than those he killed.

Eddie Rickenbacker thought Billy Bishop was greater than Richthofen, and once said: "Richthofen usually waited for enemies to fly into his territory. Bishop was the raider, always seeking the enemy wherever he could be found. Billy Bishop was a man absolutely without fear. I think he's the only man I ever met who was incapable of fear."

Bishop took off one morning in the grew dawn and flew into the faint crimson tinge of the east which was heralding the sunrise. It wouldn't be light for another hour, and he had conceived an amazing plan. He would surprise a German aerodrome just as the aircraft were taking off for early morning patrol. He knew they usually took off at about dawn. He'd catch them just a few minutes ahead of time.

His machine was a dark streak, its wings touched faintly

with gold, as it roared over the enemy aerodrome twelve miles behind the lines. The Germans were just coming to life. Seven aircraft were on the ground and their motors were warming up, waiting for sleepy pilots to finish breakfast. Then out of the murk came this roaring, snarling devil, spitting death and destruction. Bishop flew low—at fifty feet—and he raked the field from end to end. Pilots came running out to scramble hurriedly into cockpits. One machine taxied across the field and tried to rise, but Bishop sent it crashing with a hail of lead. Another rose to fifty feet and Bishop, 150 yards away, sent his bullets unerringly into it. It crashed drunkenly into a tree.

A third had taken the air by now, and he managed to get above Bishop. He had a clear shot at him, too, but Bishop wasn't human today. He zoomed upwards—his old trick—and his thumb pressed the trigger that sent a hundred bullets into the German. It, too, collapsed like a paper kite. A fourth arose. Bishop sent the rest of his ammunition into it—and then he waved a cheery goodbye and hurried home for breakfast.

The whole affair hadn't lasted six minutes. His aircraft was completely riddled with bullets, but he wasn't scratched. He was awarded the Victoria Cross.

Rickenbacker said that he was incapable of fear, and fear is a subject that Rickenbacker knew well, although only academically, because those who fought with him said that he too was incapable of fear. Bishop certainly wasn't afraid on that memorable day when he bid adieu to France, it was in June, 1918, that the General Staff decided that he was too valuable to be allowed to run further risks. They wanted him back in London to do administrative work and to help with recruiting. They told Bishop that he would have to leave the Front in twelve days.

Twelve days left? He'd already shot down forty-seven aircraft, but that wasn't enough. Twelve days? During those twelve days Bishop went crazy. Never since Ball had such flying or such shooting been seen on any front. In eleven days he had shot down twenty of the enemy.

Then came that final day. For the last time Bishop climbed into the cockpit of his battered Nieuport. He flew from sunrise to sunset. Again and again he returned for ammunition and fuel. When he finished the day his gun was hot, his motor was screaming its protest at the way it had been pushed, his wings and fuselage were torn and tattered—but five more Germans had been added to his list. That made twenty-five victims in twelve days. It brought his total up to seventy-two.

And so he ended his fighting career. He had the adulation of the world, more decorations than any man alive and memories such as few are fortunate enough to own. But he refused to live with them. In the study of his handsome apartment there was only one memento of World War I : it was the windscreen of the Nieuport he flew in 1917, and in the centre of it was a large hole. He became a useful peacetime citizen and he died in bed of an ordinary illness on September 11th, 1956.

Chapter Eleven

THE FINAL RENDEZVOUS

A GERMAN writer, after visiting the headquarters of what was now called Richthofen's Flying Circus, wrote :

> No weary legs hamper him; he does not have to crawl over the dead or stand up to his knees in the mire. He is the pampered aristocrat of the war, the golden youth of adventure.
>
> He leaves a comfortable bed, with bath, a good breakfast, the comradeship of a pleasant mess, the care of servants, to mount his steed. When he returns, he has only to slip out of his seat. Mechanics look after his machine, and refreshment and shade in summer and warmth in winter alike await the spoiled child of the favoured adventurous corps who has not quite the gift and never quite dares the great hazards as well as the one who dares them to his certain end.

Perhaps it was only just that the aviator should enjoy such compensations, for from his corps Death reaped the largest proportionate harvest. Whether he dared all or not quite all, the chances of his survival were remote. The brevity of his life gave him a right to its gaiety.

By 1918, Richthofen was Germany's idol. He commanded a Jagdgeschwader consisting of five Jagdstaffels (about sixty aircraft in all). He had killed more enemies of his country than any other living man in the ranks of the millions who fought for the central Powers. The veneration which France had given to Guynemer, Germany laid worshipfully at the feet of this twenty-four-year-old killer. He answered the old Teuton demand for a personal champion.

Boelcke and Immelmann, the old heroes, though not forgotten, were dead. It was the day for the live, the quick, the strong. Richthofen succeeded to the favours the old heroes had once received from the hands of fame.

From his throat she suspended the coveted gold and white enamelled cross of the order *Pour le Mérite* with a special citation from the Emperor. And on his breast she pinned the Austrian war cross from Francis Joseph.

She brought him telegrams and illuminated messages of congratulations and felicitations from notables of state, Army and Navy.

Before his eyes she unfolded the newspapers that welcomed the new d'Artagnan of the air with front-page pictures of himself and large black headlines that blazoned the name Richthofen to the world.

She decked his quarters at the Front with floral wreaths and conqueror's palms, sent from admiring organizations and individuals all over Germany, Austria-Hungary and Turkey. She filled his mail with hundreds of letters from sighing maidens, who expressed the pangs of their hero worship and adoration in passionate phrases.

Richthofen smiled as he read these letters from unknown admirers, many of whom looked up to him with soulful eyes from scented photographs. Some of them he showed to his flying mates, who clapped him on the back and told him that he was a gay young blade. Sometimes they read some of the burning epistles aloud, and discussed the writers with gales of laughter.

One series of letters he never showed. The handwriting was distinctive. One of them turned up every time the mail arrived at the Front. There was almost one for every day in the week. They were from the same girl, the one who has since remained the mystery in the haze of legend that now surrounds the life of Germany's greatest air fighter.

Her penmanship was well known to the mail orderly and to Richthofen's personal orderly. The letters were thick. They could not be mistaken. The mail orderly always removed them from the flutter of general mail, and they were turned over to Richthofen separately.

At times, returning from a raid in which he had added another victim to his string, he would be met at the hangar doors by his personal servant, who would hand him the one missive that he wanted. The Flying Uhlan, still tingling with the thrill of his latest kill, would go to his quarters alone and devour the contents of the note.

She was the one who shared his joy. She was the one he believed, among all the crowd of blind worshippers. Her words seemed to mean more to him than all the rest. Everyone in the Jagdstaffen knew about her, although none knew who the mystery girl was, and Richthofen never permitted any discussion of her.

Rumours of his love for this girl, perhaps the only warm, human emotion he had ever allowed himself, reached the Berlin newspapers, but not even the assiduous hounds of the Press could find her trail. Everything that Richthofen did was news in Germany. Berlin newspapers carried stories of the great *Kanone* (the German equivalent of 'ace') nearly every day. Feature writers were constantly on his trail, but not to this day does anyone know the name of the one girl who had penetrated the arrogant armour of the man the world now called The Red Knight of Germany.

His mother knew the girl, but she never revealed her name. So did his nurse, Katie Ottersdorf, but no one ever got a word out of her either. In July 1917, Richthofen had been most humiliatingly shot down by Lieutenant Albert Edward Woodbridge, an observer in an old FE2 pusher-type machine, completely unsuited to fighting Fokkers. Richthofen aimed his red aircraft at the FE, expecting an easy victory, but Woodbridge opened up with his Lewis at 300 yards. Shooting at that range was seldom effective, but one of the hundreds of bullets Woodbridge sent flaming out of the ugly snout of his gun creased Richthofen's skull. For a moment the German blacked out and his red machine fluttered crazily towards the earth. At 2000 feet he recovered. Blood filled his eyes, but he brushed them clear in time to get control of the aeroplane and land it in a field well behind his own lines. He was hurried to a hospital at Courtrai and the best surgeons in Germany were flown to his bedside. His wound was painful but not serious.

Within a few days he was able to receive visitors. Every day a tall, lovely-looking girl came to see him, but only the nurse, Fraulein Katie Ottersdorf, knew who she was. All of Germany held its breath until Richthofen was out of danger; a few skull-splinters were removed from his head and then he was back at the Front, pursuing the business of killing.

He had time during his convalescence to write to the little Berlin jeweller and order five additional cups which he had been too busy to send for before his wound. They brought his total to fifty-seven.

He was a great leader in the Prussian tradition; he did not nurse young pilots as did Mannock. He believed in tossing a youngster into the water with the admonition, 'Sink or swim'. Many took to swimming naturally. Some didn't. One day a new pilot was sent to his headquarters. He was assigned an aircraft and Richthofen welcomed him. At that moment a telephoned report came that a squadron of British machines was returning from a mission and would pass over Richthofen's aerodrome within a few moments.

"Get into your machine," Richthofen said curtly. "The enemy will be over soon. Go up and kill some of them or get killed yourself."

The eager young pilot obeyed orders quite literally. He went up and within ten minutes he was dead.

Never did Richthofen have any of Mannock's protective feeling towards the men he led. He could relax with them in the mess at night and drink Schaumwein or Weinbrand with them, but he was never really one of them. They felt that he was apart from them; to a man they believed that he was the greatest of all fighters, and their respect for him amounted to awe. But he didn't have the warm quality of his brother Lothar, who, with thirty Allied victims, was one of the stars of the Circus. Lothar was a happy-go-lucky, convivial soul, who was always impatient with his brother's/creed of perfection. Not for him the calculated attack with all risks minimized; he would dive headlong into a mêlée of fighting aircraft, with guns blazing, instead of depending upon the skills he had learned.

Manfred von Richthofen at twenty-four had all the traits of the Prussian. He was a strict disciplinarian and a stickler for military etiquette. He gave his friendship only to Wolff, Gussman and two or three others left of the original group trained by Boelcke. Somewhere, Richthofen had picked up a tradition of the German theatre. When one of his men took off he would never wish him the conventioned '*Gluck auf*' (Good luck); he would always toss them a '*Hals und Beinbruch*' (May you break your neck and your legs), the classic way of wishing a fellow actor all the best on the night a play opened. But beyond that, humour was a stranger to Richthofen. He wrote his mother two or three times a week and never once did he mention the light side of life at his headquarters. When his brother Lothar was brought down and wounded, he wrote his mother of her son's progress almost as though the wounded man was a stranger. His letter read:

March 23, 1918
In the Field.

Dear Mamma:

You will have received my wire advising you of Lothar's fall. I visit him daily. . . . He's really doing quite well.

His nose has already healed, only the jaw is still bad, but he will keep his teeth. Above his right eye he has a rather large hole, but the eye itself has not been damaged. Several blood vessels burst under his right knee and in the left calf.

The blood he spat out did not come from any internal injuries. He had merely swallowed some during his fall. He is in the hospital in Cambrai and hopes to be back at the Front within a fortnight. His only regret is not to be able to be with us at the present moment.

Manfred

Richthofen could never understand his laughing brother or a carefree soul like Captain Ritter von Schleich, who led one of the staffels. Schleich's twentieth victory in the air was scored over a Spad. The wounded pilot had landed it intact behind the German lines not far from his aerodrome, and the conqueror decided that this spoil of war belonged to him. He had it flown to his field and that night celebrated his twentieth win hilariously. During the height of the party he disappeared for half an hour. He returned with black paint on his hands, but he evaded questions as to what he had been doing.

The next morning, Schleich still felt like celebrating, but in his own unique way. He sent his staffel off under his second-in-command and had the Spad wheeled out. He sent word to his own anti-aircraft batteries that he would appreciate it if they did not shoot at a Spad that was due to cross the lines in a few moments. To help them identify it, he had painted black Maltese crosses on either side of the fuselage.

There was sufficient French ammunition for the Spad's machine gun to enable Schleich to protect himself if attacked in the air, so with a light heart he crossed his own lines and set off in the direction of Verdun.

The French gunners saw only a Spad, and it never occurred to them that it might bear a cross instead of a cockade. Then, over the Argonne sector, Schleich saw several French fighters in the air, but they paid as little attention to him as their brethren on the ground. Smiling to himself, he turned and made for Verdun again.

Above the famous city he saw a group of five Spads flying towards the German lines in close formation and, emboldened by the immunity accorded to him so far, he winged his way towards them. In less than a minute he had joined them and was endeavouring to follow the signals issued by their leader.

For the next five minutes he flew with the French Spads. But when they crossed the German lines, Schleich realized that something was bound to happen, for as long as he remained a member of their squadron, the German 'Archies' could not open fire on the enemy without endangering him. He therefore put his machine into a right-hand turn and spiralled down.

It was not long before the Frenchmen noticed the sudden departure of the sixth Spad and began to observe its movements. As soon as their leader caught sight of the Maltese crosses on it and divined the trick that Schleich had played, he gave the signal for attack. All five peeled off in pursuit.

The German Spad evened out, turned and started to climb again while holding a parallel course to its pursuers. When he gained sufficient height for his purpose, he circled round and dived on the hindmost of the Frenchmen. A well-directed burst sent his late colleague down out of control.

Then Schleich half rolled into a dive and dropped 6000 feet with the other Spads after him. With his wires screaming, he suddenly caught up his machine and made for his aerodrome with all the speed he could muster, as his French ammunition was exhausted.

He had secured his twenty-first victory and pulled off a joke that would keep the mess amused for a week. He was welcomed home by comrades who had given him up, for someone had seen a Spad go down, and the inference drawn was that Schleich had asked for trouble and got it. But his safe return was made the occasion for a celebration that outdid the festivities of the previous evening.

It even took the sting out of the official reproof he received the following day, when a curt communication from Richthofen warned him that hencforth it was *verboten* under severe pains and penalties to take a captured machine into action, however clearly it might be marked with the German emblem.

Richthofen couldn't understand that kind of prank. He frowned strongly on individual performances unless they were his own; he was still obsessed with increasing his own bag of victims, and there were those who whispered that he was sometimes a bit extravagant in his claims of enemy aircraft downed. But even those who were jealous of his deification by the public acknowledged that he was a genius in the matter of tactics. More than any other single individual he evolved the tactics of massed flying that became standard procedure in the last year of the war. He saw clearly that teamwork rather than individual performances would win the mastery of the air. He therefore did his best to weld his war-birds—the ones who had learned to survive—into an efficient team, the members of which could depend on themselves, one another, their machines and their leader.

He had one fundamental rule of fighting which he constantly impressed on his men. "Never shoot holes in a machine," he'd say again and again. "Aim for the man and don't miss him. If you are fighting a two-seater, get the observer first; until you have silenced the gun don't bother about the pilot."

He followed his own advice meticulously. During one thirty-day period in the spring of 1918 he shot down thirty aircraft. The French called him and his flaming red triplane '*Le diable rouge*'. He was a cold, capable, thinking, killing machine. He seemed immune from the psychological hazards that most experienced fighters came up against after long periods of combat. Most pilots constantly lived with one fear—the fear of death by fire. Towards the end of April a Berlin correspondent visited the Richthofen headquarters and his report makes one wonder whether Richthofen in his secret heart didn't share this fear. The newspaperman (Willy Lampel) arrived while the Circus was in the air. When the men returned they filed into the mess hall for lunch. Lampel introduced himself to Richthofen.

"Was it a successful flight?" Lampel asked.

"I brought down my seventy-fifth enemy today," Richthofen said, and then he turned to Weiss, Wolff and Gussmann, with whom he invariably lunched. "Queer," he said thoughtfully, "but the last ten I shot down burned. The one I got today burned, too. I saw it quite well. At the beginning, it was only quite a small flame under the pilot's seat, but when the machine dived, the tail stood up in the air and I could see that the seat had been burned through.

"The flames kept on showing as the machine dashed down. It crashed on the ground with a terrible explosion—worse than I have ever witnessed before. It was a two-seater, but its occupants defended themselves well."

"You almost touched him in the air," Gussmann interrupted, almost in a tone of reproof. "We all saw you fly so close to him that it seemed a collision was inevitable. You scared me stiff."

"Yes, it was close," Richthofen replied unsmiling. "I had to come up quite close. That observer, whoever he was, was a first-class fighting man. He was a devil for courage and energy. I flew within five yards of him until he had had enough, and in spite of the fact that I believe I had hit him before. Even to the very last moment, he kept shooting at me. The slightest mistake, and I should have rammed him in the air. It was a close call."

That afternoon he scored another kill, and when Wolff (his twelfth) and Weiss (his eighteenth) and Lowenhardt (his forty-eighth) reported victories, the men decided that this called for a party. Newspaperman Lampel noticed that at the height of the party Richthofen had slipped away. He asked why.

"He likes to be alone at night," one of the pilots said. "He reads a lot and he plans tomorrow's operations and he thinks. The rest of us," he chuckled, "feel that we're better off if we don't think."

He never confided to anyone—unless it was the unknown girl who owned his heart—what it was he thought about alone in his room at night. Had the sight of so many of his victims writhing in the agony of flames made him doubt his own infallibility? Could this happen to him too? This is nothing but conjecture and it can be dismissed as such, but his letters to his mother during this period are terse, hurried, sometimes petulant. He had received a letter from the Berlin jeweller which annoyed him. The jeweller had written apologetically that the last three cups he had made to signify Richthofen's seventy-eighth, seventy-ninth and eightieth victories had been made of lead; there wasn't a bit of silver left in Berlin. All of the emblems of his kills had been sent to his mother's home at Schweidnitz.

April 21st, 1918, a rather chilly Sunday, began like any other day. Richthofen's headquarters were at Douai, and as the sun began to stream the eastern sky, mechanics wheeled out the Fokker Triplanes. They were a gaudy-looking lot of machines.

Earlier in the war the Germans, like the Allies, had painted their aircraft with drab colours, even trying camouflage. But as the realities of aerial combat became more apparent, the pilots of the élite German squadrons took to colouring their machines with the most distinctive designs possible: from now on there would be no mistaking friend for foe in the confusion of a dogfight. Some of the triplanes were blue, others green and many used a variety of colours. Red, of course, was a favourite, for it endowed any aircraft—and especially a Fokker Triplane —with a most striking appearance in the air. But there was only one machine in the whole German Air Force which was all red—Baron von Richthofen's.

It was the British who had named the group the Richthofen Circus. It was partly due to the traditional red hue of the circus in any country, and partly because when the Richthofen group transferred from one headquarters to another it travelled much as the more affluent circuses travelled, in a private train with each car painted in the usual gay red colour, and with star performers having personal servants. It was not a derogatory term; the British had too much respect for professional competence ever to ridicule Richthofen or his men. They never felt about Richthofen as they had once felt about Oswald Boelcke or Werner Voss; these were two men who spoke their language, who were gallant opponents. By now it was plain that Richthofen was a calculating killer, not the impassioned patriot who had absolutely no regard for his own life as had Albert Ball or Guynemer, or so many others whose memory they cherished.

Richthofen and Hans Wolff walked towards their aircraft, talking about a hunting trip they were going to make in the Black Forest three days later. They were interrupted by the blare of a band. It had been sent by a nearby divisional commander to play a serenade of congratulations on Richthofen's eightieth victory. Richthofen's red 'Tripe' was waiting for him in front of its hangar. A puppy was trying to leap up on to the lower wing. Richthofen laughed and tugged at the playful dog. A mechanic asked if he could snap a picture of the pilot and the dog. Oswald Boelcke had been photographed just before taking off on his last flight, and since then no German pilot would allow himself to be pictured before going into combat.

But Richthofen, one of the few fighting pilots who had no use for superstition, nodded.

He climbed into the red triplane, looked around to see if Wolff, Karjus, Scholtz and the rest of the staffel he would lead today were ready, and then raised his right arm. Mechanics spun propellers and the Fokkers hurried down the strip, climbed into the air and headed towards the west where Richthofen had the inevitable rendezvous so many fighter pilots kept during that month which became known as Bloody April.

Twenty-five miles away at Bertangles a ground crew was readying the Sopwith Camels flown by No 209 Squadron. By now the pilots of the squadron considered the amazing little Camel the best of all fighters. A deadly weapon in the hands of a skilled pilot versed in its eccentricities which could be turned to advantage in combat, it was the despair of the novice. It was a machine with a strong, dominant personality; it spun quickly, had extremely sensitive elevator controls, and because of the great gyroscopic force produced by its rotary engine it was lightning-fast in a turn. It was remorseless with a ham-handed pilot, however, and many had lost their lives on tackling it for the first time. It would only answer properly to intelligent handling, but once a pilot made friends with the impudent-looking, snub-nosed, short-fuselaged machine he had a friend which would stand by him no matter how difficult or seemingly hopeless the situation. Along with the Fokker Triplane it was the supreme dogfighter of the war, and by the time the war was over, it would have the honour of shooting down more enemy aircraft than any other type.

The tight-flying formation introduced by Richthofen had forced the British to adopt the same tactics, and that day No 209 Squadron was going out en masse. The pilots grumbled a bit when Major Charles Butler, their commanding officer, briefed them; they were accustomed to flying in manœuvrable teams of five aircraft, but orders were orders. Today they were to patrol up and down the Front from Hangaard, north to the Amiens-Albert Road on the German side of the Somme battle lines. They were to fly in three flights of five machines each.

Each flight was to maintain a vee position with Captain Roy Brown's flight leading the formation.

Brown, a twenty-four-year-old Canadian, was finishing eighteen months of continuous combat and wasn't ashamed to say that he was dead tired and sick. He had twelve official victories to his credit, but No 209 had done a lot of fighting far beyond the German lines, and the men insisted that Brown had downed at least another dozen which could not be confirmed. But the Canadian (he was born in Edmonton) had never been one to bother about individual records. For the past month Brown had been living on bicarbonate of soda and brandy milk shakes, the only nourishment his ulcer-tortured stomach would retain. Butler had urged him to go to England for a month's rest, but Brown, knowing how desperately pilots were needed, had refused.

The arrival of a new pilot, Wilfred May, to the squadron had dramatically pointed out this shortage. 'Wop' May and Brown had grown up together in Edmonton, and Brown was delighted to see a face from the home town, until he learned that May's advanced training had been abruptly terminated because of the desperate need for men to replace those lost in action above the Somme. Brown had asked that the blond young fellow Canadian be assigned to his flight, and for two weeks he had taken May under his wing. He had put him through a course of intensive and realistic instruction. He had flown over the lines with him to accustom the fledgling to anti-aircraft fire. He had, above all, helped him to acquire what the pilots called 'sky vision', the ability to discern quickly the identity of an aircraft as soon as it was sighted. Now Brown felt that May was ready for his first try at combat.

"I'm taking you up today, Wop," he said slowly, a worried look on his fatigue-drenched face. "I want you to get the feel of things. But I don't want you to take any chances. If we tangle with the Huns, you keep clear; if you happen to get above a straggler, all right, dive on him, give him a burst, but if you miss him keep right on going. If there's a general engagement, you keep out of it."

"Okay, Roy," the twenty-two-year-old May responded.

Ten minutes later they were in the air. They spied fat white

227

puffs in the air over Cerisy and they knew that there were Huns about (British anti-aircraft shells burst into white blossoms, while German 'Archie' was black). Roy Brown, leading the patrol, headed towards the area where there might be hunting; he saw two British two-seaters, harried by four Fokkers, coming home from observation. His flight was far above them and he waggled his wings, the signal to dive and attack. The whole squadron of fifteen Camels swooped down joyously, but then Brown saw something else. To the right he spotted what appeared to be a sky full of triplanes coming fast. Now the engagement broke into a wild mêlée, but Brown's three flights tried to hold some sort of formation.

Brown recognized the gaily painted triplanes for what they were, and he knew that this was going to be a tough fight. To make things worse, he suddenly noticed twelve Albatroses also heading for the mêlée. There was no question of heading for home; the Fokkers were between his men and the British lines.

As leader of the patrol, Brown did not permit himself the luxury of engaging in any single combat. His job was to go to the aid of any of his men who were in trouble. A frantic five minutes followed. Brown saw MacKenzie knock a triplane out of control; he saw Mellersh send a Fokker with a blue tail into a death-dive towards earth; he saw Taylor send an Albatros down in flames. And then he saw May on the outside of this swarm of twisting planes and he saw the youngster make his first kill.

May, exultant that he had tasted blood on his first combat mission, turned, looking for a second victim. For a moment he had an all-red triplane in his sights and he opened up with both guns. But in his excitement he forgot one of the fundamentals of gunnery; he held the guns open too long and both jammed. For a frantic few seconds he hammered at the breechblocks but he failed to clear either gun. There was only one thing for him to do now—try to get home. He zoomed upwards to gain some altitude before passing over the lines and the German barrage of shells, and then he levelled off.

Suddenly he heard machine gun fire, and he remembered something Brown had told him only the day before. 'If you can hear the sound of a machine-gun, the chances are fifty-to one it is a gun being aimed at you.' Now he heard the deliberate *tack-tack-tack* and he saw slender tendrils of smoke trails spearing past his cockpit. Someone was shooting at him.

He was a good pilot, and he automatically threw the stick over, kicked the rudder hard and the Camel lurched to the left. One quick look behind him showed him the blood-red Fokker which he had missed. Flame was jumping from its twin Spandaus. He didn't know that the black-helmeted, goggled figure hunched in the cockpit of the Fokker was Richthofen. The German had often boasted that any flier who got below and in front of him had to die. Death's most able ambassador should have killed the neophyte with his next burst. May was unarmed; the only defensive weapon he had was the skill he had acquired from Roy Brown during the past week.

One bullet creased his right arm, but he never even felt the pain as he nosed his Camel downwards, slipping, banking, doing everything possible to shake off the red machine. Finally, May ran out of sky. He picked up the River Somme and fled up its valley, only fifty feet from the water, and waited for the death that was inevitable. The Fokker was only a hundred yards behind him and the persistent chatter of those guns grew louder, and then suddenly stopped altogether.

Roy Brown had seen the Fokker go after May and he had nosed his Camel down, hurling it towards the one-sided duel that was taking place below. He had only one drum of ammunition left, but he began firing as soon as he was within range. His tracers tucked a seam along the body of the Fokker and then the red triplane faltered, its nose rose slightly and it glided earthwards. There was no hand on the throttle except the lifeless hand of the Red Knight of Germany. And yet the machine landed just beyond the trench positions and gun pits of the 53rd Australian Field Battery of the 5th Division. It did not crash, but bumped along the uneven ground and came to a stop.

The Australians rushed to the aircraft to prevent the pilot from setting fire to it. One of them leaped up on the lower wing, peered into the cockpit and cried out unbelievingly, 'He's dead.' Richthofen was sitting strapped into his seat, the control stick between his knees with his right hand still clutching it. He had been hit with just one bullet, but it had penetrated his chest and traversed it from right to left. The bullet may well have come from one of Brown's machine guns.

Meanwhile, both May and Brown had reached the airfield at Bertangles. May landed first. When Brown climbed out of his Camel, May threw his arms around him. "Thanks, Brownie," he said simply. "You saved my life. That fellow was awfully hard to shake off."

"Do you know who that fellow was, Wop?" Brown asked. May shook his head.

"I'm not sure," Brown said slowly, "but I think it was Richthofen."

May's face blanched. "I think," he said shakily, "I need a drink. Come on, Brownie."

They walked into the mess hall. Each man had a double. May drank a double brandy, Brown drank a double bicarbonate of soda.

The day after his death, Richthofen was buried with full military honours. Six members of No 209 carried a plain black-stained wooden coffin containing the body from the tent hangar where it had reposed all night, to an open Army gun carriage. The word of Richthofen's death had spread all over the front, and every nearby British air squadron sent floral tributes to their late enemy. The flowers covered the black box on the army gun-carriage. Preceded by a guard of Australian infantry who carried their rifles reversed, and followed by more than a hundred pilots, the funeral cortège proceeded slowly down the road beside the aerodrome to the cemetery on the outskirts of the town. The casket was lowered gently into a grave while an English chaplain in white surplice repeated the words of the burial service of the Church of England. There was no music except for the rumble of the guns four miles to the east.

And then, for a moment the sound of the guns died. An officer gave a sharp command and the double rank of Australians lining one side of the grave came to attention. Another order and they raised their rifles. Three volleys rang out over the remains of a respected foe. The grave was filled.

The following day, one of the pilots of No 209 flew low over the aerodrome at Douai. He dropped a metal container which fell just in front of the hangar where Richthofen had allowed his picture to be taken three days before. It contained a photograph of the firing party firing its parting salute over the grave, and a message which merely read:

To the German Flying Corps
Rittmeister Baron Manfred von Richthofen was killed in combat on April 21st, 1918. He was buried with full military honours.   From the British Royal Air Force

If 1917 was the year of heroes, 1918 was the year in which many of them died. James McCudden, who had shot down fifty-seven Germans, was killed when his machine stalled and crashed just after a routine take off, and the British public mourned. Now Mick Mannock was acknowledged as Britain's number one air fighter. Mannock was not only a great fighter —he was a great leader. Guynemer, Ball, Bishop, Lufbery were loners, brilliant individualists.

Mannock was sent to one squadron after another to teach young pilots his fighting methods. He knew the strength and the weakness of every German aircraft; he knew just what a Spad, a Nieuport or a Camel could do and how far you could push it. He would talk to his pilots and instruct them collectively, and then he would take one of them on a patrol with him. He would nurse the young pilot in combat, keeping a watchful eye on him, and his guardianship gave the youngster the confidence that all young pilots needed.

One of Mannock's men kept a diary which perhaps better than anything reveals what manner of man this leader was. The day after joining the squadron as a raw, inexperienced recruit he wrote:

I arrived at the Squadron late at night, rather shy and frightened. Mannock was in the Mess, and he looked after me just like a big brother. I was posted to his Flight, and he did not allow me cross the lines for over a week; during this time he took me up twice on a line patrol and we had several practice flights. His advice to me was to always follow my leader, keep my eyes and ears open and keep a silent tongue.

It was wonderful to be in his Flight; to him his Flight was everything and he lived for it. Every member had his special thought and care.

It wasn't merely the inexperienced newcomers who felt this way about Mick Mannock. Lieutenant Ira 'Taffy' Jones of No 74 Squadron, to which Mannock had been transferred, was one of the finest of fighters, who compiled a remarkable record in a relatively brief period. He wrote in his diary:

28.5.18—The CO saved Giles's skin today. Giles very carelessly allowed a black Albatros to pounce on him while he was concentrating on the destruction of a silver-grey two-seater. Giles has had his leg pulled unmercifully; we declare he was decoyed. Pilots hate admitting that they have been taken in as a sucker! Clements tells me that Mick saved his life tonight, too. Mick and Clements went up for a bit of fun after tea. They each got what they wanted. . . . Clements spotted a large formation of Huns obviously making a beeline for them. Clements put on full throttle . . . to catch up to Mick, who as usual was wasting no time in getting at his enemy. Mick had seen the Hun formation all the time . . . he turned west quickly and dived, the Huns following and firing. Mick saved Clements by losing height directly beneath them and so drawing them on to him, while Clements got clear. Clements says it was a rotten sight to see one SE being attacked by such a bunch, and that had it been anyone except Mick, he would have been anxious about his safety. (We all believe that no Hun will ever shoot down Mick.) One Pfalz followed him very closely, and suddenly Mick went down apparently out of control; on his back—spinning—and doing everything imaginable from 8000 to 4000 feet. At 5000 feet, the Hun, completely fooled, flattened out to watch the crash. Mick then decided he had had enough, and flattened out too and made for our lines—diving hard. . . .

29.5.18—. . . Mick took Clements and me up at 7 pm . . . Mick spotted about a dozen Huns coming from the direction of Roubaix; we were then over Lille. As we had not too much time for a fight, having already been up for over an hour, he decided to go straight at them, as we had a slight advantage of height. The Huns, who were Albatros Scouts, were of the stout variety, and they accepted our head-on challenge. Both Mick and the Hun leader opened fire at one another as they approached from about

232

300 yards' range, but nothing happened. This burst of fire was the signal for a glorious dogfight—as fine and as frightening a dogfight as I've ever been in. Friend and foe fired at and whistled past one another at a tornado pace. . . . I have never been so frightened in my life. Of late I have been able to keep very cool during the actual flight, but tonight I became so flustered that occasionally I fired at my own pals in an effort not to miss a chance—thank God, my shooting was erratic. How terrible it would have been if I had, say, shot Mick down! The thought gives me the very creeps. . . . Mick sent two slate-blue Albatroses down out of control, and Clements crashed his first Hun. He is very bucked about it. It is wonderful how cheered a pilot becomes after he shoots down his first machine; his moral[e] increases by at least 100 per cent. This is why Mick gives Huns away—to raise the moral[e] of the beginner. . . .

But even the incomparable fighter who had just downed his seventy-fourth German was not immune from depression or from edgy nerves. In July he wrote his sister:

RAF
16.6.18

Dear Jess,

Your letter dated 15th May to hand a few days ago. How careless of you to have wrongly addressed it. Your fault. . . . It is a pity you did not write sooner. You knew my address quite well, and you also knew I was out here. Perhaps you did not feel like writing after a heavy day at the factory. Well, we will let the matter drop. . . .

I suppose you are still on the munitions job. It must be pretty hard work, but not quite so hard as the war out here. Things are getting a bit intense just lately and I don't quite know how long my nerves will last out. I am rather old now, as airmen go, for fighting. Still, one hopes for the best. I hope mother and Nora are getting along OK. These times are so horrible that occasionally I feel that life is not worth hanging on to myself, but 'hope springs eternal in the human breast'. I had thoughts of getting married, but . . . ?

I am supposed to be going on leave on the 19th of this month (if I live long enough), and I shall call at Birmingham to see you all.

Cheerio,
Yours,
EDWARD

Two weeks later he was killed. But no German pilot could claim credit this time. He had hit a German aircraft and he followed it down to be sure of the kill; he flew too low and death came from a bullet fired by a German infantryman.

Not long afterwards, His Majesty the King was pleased to award Mick Mannock the Victoria Cross. Corporal Edward Mannock received the decoration on his son's behalf.

Men fought and men died and at home designers and engineers worked feverishly, trying to produce aircraft that would give them a better chance of survival. By now both French and British knew that the United States could not be counted on; she was sending pilots and mechanics on every boat, but there were no machines for the pilots to fly except those the French could spare. Aircraft production was stepped up to the limit, but you couldn't produce aeroplanes the way you could produce bars of soap. But occasionally you could produce a new one in limited quantities that did excite the pilots. Such a plane was the Sopwith Snipe the British sent to the Western Front in the summer of 1918. This little snub-nosed speedster which could do 121 miles an hour at 10,000 feet was the ultimate development of the rotary-powered fighter peculiar to World War I; it was the culmination of all previous experience, and although only ninety-seven of them reached the Front, the machine brought fame to three British squadrons and immortality to one man—Major William G. Barker. Billy Barker's career had many points in common with that of Billy Bishop. Both were Canadians who began their military careers in the cavalry. Barker joined the Canadian Mounted Rifles as a private, transferred finally to the RFC, serving first as an observer and becoming a pilot in 1917. It is a matter of incredible history that he flew solo after one hour of dual instruction. Modern Air Force instructors say that such a feat is unknown to them—Barker must have been either crazy or a flying genius. Those who flew with him say he was the latter, and without exception they verify the story that he flew after one lesson on a dual trainer. (So does the official Air Force report.) He began by flying two-seaters, and his coolness, calmness and fearlessness won him the MC, but instructors were badly needed in England, and to his immense disgust he was made a captain and sent to England. This husky, vivacious, gay Canadian disliked teaching when there were Germans to be killed, and he made immediate if unorthodox plans to get back to combat. When he wasn't teaching he was defying the rules by stunting, and when he flew low over the Air Ministry in London (at long last a fact), irate Air Force brass hurried the grinning Canadian back to France as a flight commander piloting a Camel.

His fearless tactics soon resulted in another decoration—a Bar to his MC. His squadron was moved to the Italian front, and over the Alps the ace soon became the terror of the Austrian pilots. About this time he had an experience which made a lasting impression on him. He shot down an Austrian observation balloon. The two observers leaped for safety with their parachutes and were already half way to the ground when the blazing wreck of the falling balloon enveloped them in its folds and bore them down in a sheet of flame. Barker was so upset at this ghastly spectacle that he never attacked another balloon. "I do not fight men who cannot fight back," was his terse comment. (He ignored the fact that when he returned there were forty holes in his machine from ground fire.)

His hair-raising exploits did much to raise the drooping morale of the Italians. He once attacked a group of six huge Gothas, broke up the formation and sent one down in flames. For this feat he was personally presented with the Italian Silver Medal for Valour by the King of Italy; he was also awarded the DSC.

During the early months of 1918, back in France, he played havoc with the enemy forces in the air and on the ground. Victory after victory fell to his all-conquering guns. On one occasion he attacked eight enemy fighters and shot two of them down, receiving a second Bar to his MC in recognition. He had risen to the rank of major and commanded No 201 Squadron, equipped with the brand-new Sopwith Snipes.

It was in October, 1918, that he fought an engagement that compared with the great battle Werner Voss had waged nearly a year before—but Billy Barker lived to laugh about it. The war was nearly over, but the German Air Force never collapsed; it was strong, still hopeful, and as competent as ever on October 27th, the day Barker earned his Victoria Cross. He shot down a two-seater at 21,000 feet over the Marmal Forest, and saw one of its occupants take to his parachute—a life-saving instrument still denied to the Allies.

Almost immediately he was engaged by a Fokker and wounded in the right thigh. He lost control, went into a spin, and pulled out of it to find himself surrounded by fifteen Fokkers, two of which he hit and drove off. A third was shot down in flames from a range of ten yards, and then Barker was wounded once more, this time in the left thigh. Once more he went into a spin, during which he lost consciousness. On regaining it he again found himself in the midst of twelve to fifteen enemy machines. He shot the tail off one of them from a range of less than five yards, and as he did so a bullet shattered his left elbow. For a second time he fainted, and on coming to found himself for a third time surrounded by German machines. By then heavy smoke was pouring from his aircraft and he thought it to be on fire. Determined to bring one of the enemy to earth with him, he sought to ram the nearest Fokker but, changing his mind as the two machines were about to collide, opened fire and sent it in flames to the earth. It was his fifty-second victory. Barker then dived away and eventually reached the lines, where he crashed near a kite balloon. He recovered from his wounds and made the Snipe the most talked-about aeroplane at the Front.

Chapter Twelve

THE LOOK OF EAGLES

WHEN THE United States declared war, Dr Gros, who had fathered the Lafayette Flying Corps so efficiently, was commissioned a lieutenant-colonel in the United States Air Service and made head of a liaison group between the American and French Air Forces. He knew that in the corps he helped organize there existed a nucleus of trained and seasoned pilots about which could be built the fighter branch of the American Air Service, and he knew too that most of the men would like to wear the uniform of their own country. Only two things were necessary: to persuade the French to release the men and to convince the American authorities of the wisdom of accepting them. But during the first months of a nation's entrance into a war, undue haste seems to be traditionally indecent.

Two hundred and sixty-seven men had enlisted in the Lafayette Corps and 180 of them had served at the Front in fighter, observation or bombing squadrons. Their collective and individual records were distinguished. Fifty-one of them had been killed while serving with the French, nineteen had been wounded, fifteen captured, and eleven had died from flying accidents or illness. Members of the corps had shot down 199 enemy machines. It wasn't until February, 1918, that ninety-three of them transferred to the American Air Service, while twenty-six, tired of waiting for Army commissions, joined the US Naval Aviation. About twenty remained with French escadrilles.

American Air Service requirements were in some ways much higher than those of the French and British; America had young, fresh and unlimited manpower, and the physical qualifications for pilots were such that some veterans of years of actual combat flying did not measure up to them. Many pilots like Raoul Lufbery, John Huffer, Charles J. Biddle, Phelps Collins, Kenneth P. Littauer, David McK. Peterson, Robert Soubiran, Robert L. Rockwell and Kenneth Marr were over the age limit set by the General Staff. It took a special order by Pershing to waive the requirements in the case of these doddering oldsters, some of whom had reached the hoary age of thirty-two. William Thaw could never have entered any branch of the American Army. He had defective vision in his left eye which 'showed atrophy, plus pigmentation in local area'. His hearing was defective and a 'recurrent knee injury limited his ambulatory activities. But he had had three years of actual fighting experience at the Front, and once in a single air battle he had destroyed three German aircraft. Pershing again waived the physical imperfections which apparently hadn't prevented him from being one of the finest fliers and best leaders among the Lafayette men. Walter Lovell learned for the first time after examination by American Army doctors that not only was he colour-blind but that he had been listening to the roar of engines for so long that his hearing had been impaired. Pershing looked at his record and wrote out a waiver, as he did for Dudley L. Hill, Charles H. Dolan and a dozen others.

These men became invaluable adjuncts to the American Air Service. Some, like Lufbery, achieved spectacular fame; others, like Littauer, who specialized in the dangerous drudgery of observation work, won whole-hearted respect from the men with whom they flew and the high Air Force command.

Airmen used standards of their own to measure the stature of a fellow fighting man. Occasionally they felt that some publicized hero had achieved success by a combination of luck and fortuitous circumstances. In their letters home, in the diaries which so many of them kept and in their official reports (if they were commanding officers) they gave honest estimates of the men with whom they fought, and it is almost impossible to read the faded letters, the published and unpublished diaries, without coming again and again across the name of the man they called 'Kepi' Littauer. His calm courage, his superlative skill and his gentle humour shine through these records, most of which were never intended to be read by outsiders.

Littauer began his fighting early in 1916 when casualties among observers on photographic missions had been high, and he was assigned to flying observation machines. He flew the Caudron two-seater, a temperamental machine which all pilots hated and few outlived. Littauer, a cool and skilful pilot, seemed to have a special affinity for the aeroplane, however, and in two years of continuous flying before being attached to the American service he always managed to bring both machine and observer back. James Norman Hall, in writing at that time about Littauer, said, 'By some miracle he manages to survive. As flight commander of the 88th Observation Squadron he invariably flies at low altitudes; he is always being pounced on by enemy pursuit ships, and one day a bullet punctured his windshield right in the middle, the bullet missing his head by the thickness of a cigarette paper.'

Colonel Harold E. Hartney, himself an outstanding fighting pilot, who eventually became commanding officer of the First Pursuit Group, the greatest of all American fighting units, wrote of him:

It was in 1918 that I met Captain Kenneth Littauer, one of the really great officers of the American Air Service and one of the few actual flyers given high command. Commanding officer of the 88th Observation Squadron at that time, he had trained his boys into a highly efficient and valuable adjunct of the American effort in France. Shot down with his observer, Lieutenant T. E. Boyd, severely wounded, Littauer brought his plane down safely and successfully completed his important mission. He was always a source of encouragement and enthusiasm to his men. It was inevitable that he should go higher, and on September 19th, 1918, he was put in command of the Observation Group of the 3rd Army Corps, and about October 25th was raised to Chief of Air Service of the entire 3rd Corps.

He was awarded nearly every French decoration, given the coveted Belgian *Chevalier de l'Ordre de Leopold* and the American Distinguished Service Cross; but once, when asked by a correspondent which of his many awards he coveted most, he answered with a straight face, "Windshield with hole attached."

No aircraft, of course, had as yet arrived from the United States, and the growing First Pursuit Group, of which the 94th and 95th Squadrons were the first to see action, still used machines borrowed from the French. The French, understandably enough, gave their new machines to their own fliers; the Americans had to take what was left over. This was another reason why so many of the original Lafayette boys remained in French escadrilles. One of them, Charles Veil, dropping in to see his old friend Colonel Gros in Paris, was introduced to a newly arrived Air Service colonel.

"Why aren't you in the American Army?" the colonel demanded sharply. "Most of the Lafayette Flying Corps have shown their patriotism by transferring. You should be in an American uniform."

"There are two reasons why I'm not in an American uniform," Veil said calmly. "One is, I can't get in; the other, I don't want to commit suicide."

"What do you mean?" The colonel was aghast.

"I was examined by the American doctors," Veil explained. "They said I wasn't physically fit to fight in any army, and that in my condition I couldn't even fly an aeroplane. They told me I had a game leg, a stiff neck, a hole in my groin, and a blood disease among other things. Since that examination I've brought down a few Germans, but my medical report is even worse."

"In view of your record, we might get a waiver on your physical condition," the colonel suggested.

"Not a chance," the pilot said with determination. "The planes the Americans are using are second-rate, most of them French rejects; the American mechanics are badly trained. An American pilot can't live long flying those crates."

Colonel Billy Mitchell was one officer who did his best to get first-rate aircraft for the use of the young American pilots. Mitchell, a flamboyant, irreverent, dedicated airman, had studied the theories of Giulio Douhet thoroughly, and when he had arrived early in 1917 as an official military observer representing the American General Staff, he had listened long and hard to 'Boom' Trenchard and had profited much by the latter's experience and wisdom. He liked Trenchard's philosophy of aerial war; Trenchard thought of the aeroplane only as an offensive weapon, and although he had been harshly criticized for the high RFC casualties, he justified them by showing Mitchell that the Germans had accomplished only about four per cent of the damage done by the British. Trenchard thought in terms not of dogfights but of air armadas engaged in strategic bombing, and he crystallized much of Mitchell's early thinking. Now Mitchell realized that this calm, hard-headed British officer, who thought only in practical terms, had the same thoughts that he himself had been criticized as a visionary for voicing. It renewed his determination for fighting not only for a separate air force but for large concentrations of aircraft that could penetrate enemy territory and destroy the arteries of supply and communication and production. But for the moment, the young American colonel's activities were limited by the number of machines he could cajole from the French and British, and—even though he had the title 'Chief of Air Service'—by the attitude of the American Staff. Mitchell indiscreetly and angrily confided in his diary:

The General Staff is now trying to run the Air Service with just as much knowledge of it as a hog knows about skating. It is terrible to have to fight with an organization of this kind, instead of devoting all our attention to the powerful enemy on our front.

I have had many talks with General Pershing . . . some of them very heated, with much pounding on the table on both sides. One time he told me that if I kept insisting that the organization of the Air Service be changed he would send me home. I answered that if he did he would soon come after me. This made him laugh and our talk ended admirably.

To make 'Black Jack' Pershing laugh when he was in one of his table-pounding moods was something few of his subordinates were able to do. Apparently, however, after Mitchell left, taking his peculiar charm with him, Pershing did not go on laughing. The more he thought about the Air Service, the more convinced he became that it should be run, like any other branch of the Army, by a West Point general who had proved himself efficient in other fields. It didn't matter in the least whether he knew how to fly or had the faintest understanding of aircraft.

He put General Mason Patrick, an engineer, in charge of the entire Air Service, despite the protests of the West Pointer, who confessed his ignorance of the subject. Patrick pleaded that at least he have charge only of administration, leaving the actual air command to someone who at least knew a fuselage from a carburettor. But Pershing was adamant: he wanted one man on whom he could pin the whole responsibility. Mitchell was demoted to Chief of Air Service, 1st Army Corps, and General Benjamin Foulois given his post. Mitchell, accustomed to disappointment, swallowed his bitterness and went to work. Happily, the 1st Army Corps was commanded by General Hunter Liggett, a man who shared Mitchell's views on the importance of air power. The war had dragged on for nearly three years and had developed into a static, stagnant conflict, with ground won at huge cost and then subsequently lost. Mitchell saw aviation as co-operating with the Army—not subservient to it, and Liggett, the ground commander, agreed with him. They made a wonderful team, their ability to work together based first on mutual respect and second on mutual affection.

Mitchell himself did a great deal of flying alone in his Spad, and before he accepted aircraft from either British or French he tried them out himself. The British offered him the earlier version of the Camel; he cracked up in one and then tried another. He felt that its one vicious characteristic (the pilot had to fight continuously to keep it from whipping into a right-hand spin) could only be mastered by the most experienced pilots, and he rejected the Camel. His boys, trained on the slow, relatively honest Jennies, didn't have the experience or time to master the delicate intricacies of the Camel. He had to settle for the Nieuport, and eventually he managed to get his men some Spads. If Mitchell, in speech and, for that matter, uniform, was flamboyant, he also had the knack of dramatizing the needs of the Air Service and the deeds it (and he himself) performed. It was a calculated manœuvre on his part; he knew that the high brass had to be jolted out of the archaic mental process of thinking of this war in terms of the last war. And when Mitchell made a statement which seemed extravagant, he could usually back it up.

In July, 1918, for instance, he put on a one-man act that endeared him to the French and highlighted the vital importance of aerial observation. One day, flying across the lines, he noticed that the roads which three days before had been merely white streaks, were now greyish-green lines. He flew low to investigate and saw that masses of German troops were moving steadily towards five bridges across the Marne. Mitchell hurried back, reported the intelligence to General Liggett and to French GHQ, and Foch moved quickly to defend the vital bridges. This one report saved a great many French lives, the story circulated quickly and the name of Billy Mitchell blazoned across the Allied front and permeated the Allied high command. He was still a colonel, but now even Pershing listened to him with more attention, and General Foulois took the unprecedented step of not only praising Mitchell's activities but of actually suggesting that Mitchell replace him. The suggestion was not carried out, and it would not be until October 1st, 1918, that Mitchell would be made a brigadier-general and put in charge of the American Air Service. But meanwhile, his influence was great on the relatively few squadrons made up exclusively of Americans, some of whom began to emerge from the anonymity of the herd who survived to perform active duty in World War II.

Not all of the heroes were fighter pilots, but Raoul Lufbery, Frank Luke and Eddie Rickenbacker captured the imagination of the American public to a far greater degree than did many of them, and there is no doubt that in skill and courage they deserve to rank with Mannock, Bishop, Guynemer, Fonck, Richthofen and Udet. Lufbery was America's first air hero even before the country joined the war. He was well known and popular in France, for he was a Parisian at heart.

In January, 1918, he received his commission as major in the American Air Service. He already had seventeen victories to his credit and expected, of course, to start fighting immediately in his new major's uniform. But the brass had other plans for him. For some strange reason they sent him to Issoudun, a training centre for newly arrived American pilots, gave him a rolltop desk, a writing pad, a pencil and absolutely nothing to do. Lufbery knew nothing and cared less about the routine of making reports. He would leave Issoudun as often as possible and go searching for old friends in Paris. He usually ran into Fonck, Nungesser or some other French fighters, and a glad cry would go up, *"Tiens, Luf! Comment ça va, mon vieux?"*

Sometimes he would find Bert Hall or Bill Thaw at the New York Bar and he'd have a few nightcaps with them, and the old cronies (as time was measured in those days) would re-fight air battles; and if anyone in the place was so inclined, would joyously oblige with a fight. Luf would sing some of the songs the arrival of the Americans had inspired:

The trip was long, the boys arrived
They ripped off shirts and collars,
The pretty maid who welcomed them
Made thirty thousand dollars.

Luf said that the young Americans were good fliers, but occasionally the Army produced strange characters who seemed a bit out of place in the Air Service. He explained that two squadrons, the 94th and the 95th, had finally been formed and that the day they were to be sent to front-line bases one of the commanding officers had them all lined up on the parade ground.

"Men," he said, "I am about to address you for the last time. I want you to promise me—in fact, I am putting you on your honour—you will keep your teeth clean. Now, I have here a tooth brush, issue, just the same as you will find in your kit. You are to brush your teeth, night and morning, like this, up and down—not sideways."

And he proceeded to give an exhibition of how this miracle was accomplished.

"I wonder if he thinks the boys are going to bite the Germans," Lufbery said gloomily.

Finally, Lufbery was posted to the 94th Squadron, stationed in the Champagne sector, as an instructor. For one month he worked with the new men, teaching them combat tactics, flying with them as far as the lines and then reluctantly leading them home. He couldn't cross the lines because as yet the aircraft were not equipped with guns, a state of affairs which made Lufbery furious.

"We've been in the war now for a year," he'd storm, "and they appropriated $600,000,000 for the Air Service and we haven't got enough guns to equip a dozen aircraft."

But he was enthusiastic about the American pilots. "Three of them look exceptionally good to me," he told Bert Hall on one of their nocturnal prowls in Paris. "Eddie Rickenbacker, who used to be a racing driver, a boy named Douglas Campbell, and Reed Chambers."

The guns arrived two weeks later, and Major Raoul Lufbery was made commanding officer of the squadron. Now he could test these young Americans of whom he had grown so fond. One night he looked around at the men and said casually, "I'll take a couple of you across the lines tomorrow so you can see what the war is like. Rick," he added, "you and Campbell be ready at eight-fifteen."

Neither Rickenbacker nor Campbell slept much that night. They had come to fight, and at long last they were going to have a chance. Both were ready long before the appointed hour, inspecting their Nieuports on which had been painted an emblem that would soon be famous, the hat-in-the-ring, suggested by the squadron doctor. Lufbery appeared and gave his two fledglings a few words of advice.

"Stick close to me," he said, "and if we get into any trouble, just stay in formation."

They took off under the envious eyes of the others and flew through the German 'Archie' (always a frightening experience for the neophyte). The shells from ground batteries burst close to them and the concussion tossed their slim machines about the sky as a ping-pong ball would be tossed by rough water. But Luf led them right through it and gradually Rick and Campbell realized that these shells weren't bursting as uncomfortably close to them as it had at first appeared.

The two young pilots stayed close to their leader; they followed his manœuvres faithfully. Occasionally they wondered why he took what appeared to be evasive action, but they kept near him. Afterwards, Rickenbacker, in discussing his first flight, told his squadron mates: "Sometimes I fell behind—my machine isn't as fast as the major's—and then he'd make a virage and come within a hundred feet of me as though to say, 'Don't worry, kid, I've got my eye on you.'"

Then Lufbery led them home. The whole squadron was waiting as they landed and the two new men were plied with questions. Campbell and Rickenbacker donned what they hoped to be satisfactory looks of bored indifference. The anti-aircraft fire? It was nothing, they said casually, but the Germans must have spent a million dollars throwing stuff at them. Enemy aircraft? No, they hadn't seen any aircraft at all.

"You didn't see any aircraft?" Luf chuckled.

They shook their heads.

"As we crossed the lines," Lufbery said dryly, "one formation of five Spads crossed below us. Ten minutes later a flight of five Spads passed within five hundred yards of us. Luckily they weren't Huns. Just before we turned back, four German Albatroses appeared two miles ahead of us. Crossing the lines towards home there was a German two-seater looking us over, a thousand feet above us."

A few days later, Luf decided that his boys were ready to fight on their own, and on April 18th, 1918, history was made. Late the night before, an order had been posted that Captain Peterson, Lieutenant Reed Chambers and Lieutenant Edward Rickenbacker were to take off at 6 am and patrol the lines from Pont-a-Mousson to Saint Mihiel at 16,000 feet, returning at 8 am. Everyone in the squadron envied the lucky three in charge of Captain Peterson, who were to have the honour of being the first to carry the 94th Squadron in all-American combat. There was a postscript to the order: Lieutenants Alan Winslow and Douglas Campbell were to stand by during the period of this patrol, just in case the original three were chased home by Germans and needed help. Right after the three exuberant pilots left the field a fog began to creep over the district. The first American patrol proved ineffectual and Peterson and Rickenbacker, defeated by the heavy weather, returned to the field, while Chambers became lost but made a safe landing at a nearby airfield. A few moments after Peterson and Rickenbacker had landed, their fuel exhausted, two German aircraft were reported to be in the vicinity. Campbell and Winslow immediately took off, and then the fog began to clear.

Three minutes later a German aircraft fell on the outskirts of the field—Winslow had shot it down. A moment later a second machine crashed less than 500 yards from the aerodrome—Campbell had scored this point for his side, and the people of Toul had seen it all. Both German pilots were alive, and they said that they had been sent up after the three patrolling American machines but had lost them in the fog. Trying to find their way home they had mistaken the Toul field for their own and had come down to 500 feet. Winslow and Campbell had managed to climb above them and had no difficulty in winning the first air victories officially credited to an American squadron. The remains of the two German aircraft were hauled to the public square in Toul, and the joyous French celebrated in the Gallic manner. They had heard a great deal about how the Americans would end the war—now in their own backyard they had seen tangible evidence of it. And best of all, the two American fliers had been piloting the Nieuport, a product of their own country. Treasured bottles of old Moselle wine were dragged from cellars; champagne and brandy waiting for weddings were requisitioned and forced upon the equally happy members of the 94th Squadron.

Billy Mitchell, informed immediately, lost no time in sending the news back home. Mitchell, the brilliant student of air strategy, never deserted Mitchell the showman. The next day all America knew that there was an American Air Force in combat composed of men good enough to beat experienced German fliers. The psychological effect was great, not only at home but among all Allied airmen. Until now they had received only promises; now two youngsters trained in America had in four and a half minutes demonstrated that they and their flying mates were ready.

During the following weeks Luf taught them all a great deal. So did Captain James Norman Hall, and Major John Huffer, and Captain David McK. Peterson, all Lafayette veterans. Lufbery flew nearly every day, helping new pilots to acquire 'sky vision', and at night they'd sit and listen to the man they now idolized not only as a great pilot but as a warm, sympathetic friend. They would throw hundreds of questions at him and out of the vast fund of his fighting experience he'd answer them in practical terms. There was one question new pilots often asked with hesitation. 'What can you do if your plane starts to burn?' Lufbery explained that often you could put the flames out by sideslipping steeply, by using the wind as fire extinguisher to fan the flames away from yourself. "But above all," he'd emphasize, "never grow panicky and leap out. A lot of pilots have died that way when, if they'd stuck to their ship, they might well have made it to the ground."

Members of the 94th felt about Luf much as the British had thought of Mannock; death might come to others but not to this one. Yet Lufbery himself knew that he would get it sooner or later. How could he survive when Guynemer, Richthofen, Ball, Mannock and McCudden had died? Once someone asked him what he intended to do after the war, and Luf laughed, "There won't be any after the war for a fighter pilot." But he never allowed what he felt to be inevitable to dim the jauntiness of his spirit; it was as though he felt that the personal doom fate had ordained was a good friend whom he intended to greet gaily. Luf belonged to the balladiers and the boulevards—he was out of another age, and he would face death as he had faced life.

It was on May 19th, 1918, that he forgot to follow his own advice to stay with a burning aircraft. He was fighting a two-seater Albatros which should have been easy for him. The battle took place almost over the field. Luf fired two short bursts which staggered the Albatros, and then the men of the squadron were horrified to see bright flames bursting from the Nieuport. The machine began to dive towards the earth, and now the flames had enveloped it. Two hundred feet from the ground Lufbery jumped. It might have been that he was aiming for a nearby stream, but he missed and fell into a garden just outside Nancy.

Two members of the First Pursuit Group now began the winning of the only two Congressional Medals of Honor given to American airmen during the war; they were Frank Luke and Eddie Rickenbacker. Luke was an undisciplined, carefree maverick out of Arizona, who, without too much technical skill, managed to accomplish one of the fighting miracles of the war—he destroyed fifteen enemy balloons and three German aircraft within the space of seventeen days. Most pilots felt that getting a 'sausage' was a great deal more difficult and far more dangerous than engaging even the best of the German fighters. So valuable were the reports of observers perched in baskets 1000 feet in the sky with high-powered telescopes, that the Germans took every means to insure their protection. They usually had an umbrella of Fokkers above the balloons. As soon as there were reports that an Allied aeroplane was en route, the sausage would be hauled down and if the Allied pilot managed to evade the dive of the enemy interceptors, he then had to contend with the fire from twenty to fifty machine guns which were waiting and the fire from hundreds of rifles handled by the balloon ground-crews. He seldom had the element of surprise in his favour; usually by the time he arrived the balloon would be pulled down. If he tried to evade the aircraft diving from above, or zig-zagged to get away from the barrage of lead coming up from the ground, it was impossible to hit the sausage. He could only be successful by making a steady run at the balloon just above treetop height and aiming point-blank—and then he had to avoid the flames of the balloon and get away at treetop height.

When Frank Luke reported for duty with the 27th Squadron in August, 1918, his squadron colleagues were not impressed. He was cocksure, high-tempered, vociferously talkative and highly disdainful of the views of the more experienced pilots. He was mischievous, irresponsible and absolutely impervious to any squadron regulations. His confidence was such that they soon named him The Arizona Boaster. Major Hartney, the group commander, took Luke up to try him in a mock dogfight, but the tow-headed kid from Arizona couldn't evade even the more elementary attacking tactics of his CO. But Hartney was stuck with him, and he did his best to teach him some of the rudiments of self-protection in the air. There was one thing the boy could do—he could shoot.

One day Hartney led a flight of twelve aircraft across the lines to protect Major Littauer and six of his photographic machines from the 88th. Some Spads had arrived and the men had been having a great deal of trouble with them: a poorly housed reduction-gear which would get out of line with the slightest nick in the propeller was causing severe mechanical difficulties. When the engine began to miss, pilots had orders to hurry home before it quit altogether. On this afteroon one engine after another showed signs of packing up, and machine after machine headed for home. Finally, Hartney was at 18,000 feet with only one other Spad following him. It was a grim, heat-hazy day, and it was difficult to spot an enemy. When tracer bullets began to streak by, Hartney himself decided it was time to return and headed for his field at Coincy. The other pilots had returned and were swearing loudly at the French who had wished these broken-down crocks on them. Hartney joined wholeheartedly and then a single aircraft came in to land.

"That's your friend Luke," one of the men said to the CO. "He said he was going to get his first Boche today or not come back. Let's see what the blowhard has to say for himself; I bet he claims one."

Sure enough, he did. He said excitedly that he had shot a machine down that was on Hartney's tail. "I never opened up until I had my gun right in that baby's cockpit," he said. "And I didn't leave him until he hit the ground with me not more than two hundred feet behind him."

No one believed him—except Harold Hartney, and Hartney did everything possible to get Luke's kill confirmed. But no one had seen an enemy aircraft dive to earth, and the men in his squadron ignored the pilot they were sure had been lying. For a time Luke was a lonely, despised man with only one friend—Lieutenant Joseph Wehner, son of a poor German cobbler from Everett, Massachusetts. Twice during his training period in Texas he had been picked up and accused of being an enemy agent (merely because of his name). Wehner was a placid, easy going, quiet man who was a good listener. Despite their completely diverse personalities, the two became firm friends and flying partners. Luke decided that he'd do something to dispel the unhappy climate of distrust and suspicion in which he existed, and late one afternoon he and Wehner took off to hunt for balloons.

They headed towards the German lines, where two balloons hung on the horizon. Luke flew directly towards the bags, while Wehner climbed high above Luke to protect him against enemy air attack.

It was well towards dusk when they returned, but long before the pair landed the squadron received word that two balloons had gone down in flames. Wehner reluctantly reported that while protecting Luke from an overhead attack he had shot down an enemy aircraft. Within a week nine more balloons and four more enemy machines had been shot down by the firm of Luke and Wehner. Then they seemed to run out of targets. The Germans were loath to sacrifice their expensive

Drachen. They sent them up later in the morning and hauled them down earlier in the afternoon so as not to be caught unawares by incendiary bullets fired from an aeroplane shooting down upon them in the dim light of dawn or in the dusk of early evening.

Luke performed one of his most brilliant deeds on September 17th, when he set out on a mission to destroy three German *Drachen* that kept altogether too vigilant a watch upon American operations. Wehner and Luke were tearing towards their objective when a formation of Fokkers attempted to intercept them. Wehner engaged in combat while Luke continued towards the first balloon. Incendiary shells known as 'flaming onions' flashed around him. He flew through this barrage, penetrated the ring of Archie shells, aimed, fired—and the balloon went down in flames. He headed towards the second bag. It met the same fate as the first, but not before Wehner had successful frustrated a fresh German fighter attack. But while Luke had downed the second balloon, Wehner had also fought his last fight. He was hit and crashed. Luke, infuriated over the fate of his friend, tore into the fray. He downed two of the Germans. The rest retreated. As Luke neared friendly territory, he saw four French machines circling a German observation aircraft. He dived on the German, firing as he came on. The German went down.

It was a different Luke who landed on the aerodrome that night. There was no glee in his voice, no vivid account of what he had accomplished. He had downed two balloons and three aircraft within ten minutes, but he did not care. Wehner had paid with his life for the victory, and Luke was silent.

He had performed all this before the eyes of the famous Rainbow Division (42nd). No need to seek confirmation: the squadron telephone kept ringing with messages from officers who had seen the fight and who wanted to know the name of the incredibly courageous pilot who had performed so brilliantly. They never again called him The Arizona Boaster.

Older pilots like Rickenbacker tried hard to persuade him to a more disciplined method of fighting. Luke admired Rick tremendously, but he just couldn't do things any way but his own. He counted on his luck and the suddenness of his attack against the balloons. He was the despair of Captain Alfred (Ack) Grant, CO of the 27th Squadron, and of Hartney. As often as not he'd fly off into the dusk, fire one or two balloons and then find refuge for the night at some French aerodrome or with an American balloon company. He had the same disdain for the orders of his superior officers that he had for enemy bullets. By September 27th, 1918, the boy had a record of having shot down a total of eighteen sausages and aircraft, and he was now known to everyone in the group as The Balloon Buster. His mates did everything possible to make up for their previous distrust; they realized that they'd been wrong about Luke from the beginning. But Frank Luke went his lone way, obsessed with destroying balloons.

Death? It was the last thing he ever thought of. Death was for suckers, not for a man who had the guns ready to flame into action at the touch of his thumb. If he ever had the slightest doubt of his own infallibility, he kept it to himself. There was one man he may have confided in—the priest in the village near the base, but his lips were sealed by the oath of the confessional.

Luke was a fabulously successful crapshooter, and he usually made a shambles out of the Saturday night games in the mess hall of the 27th. "All or nothing," he'd chant, leaving his original stake for five rolls of the dice. When another man rolled, he'd cover all bets. "Two to one on the ten . . . even money you can't make it six . . . for anything you've got."

Every Sunday morning he'd go to Mass in the village and dump his winnings on the collection plate, and often after the services he'd stop and chat with the friendly little priest, but what they talked about no one ever knew.

By now Luke seemed imbued with the idea that he could take on the whole German fighter and balloon services single-handed without any support of any kind. His continued success strengthened his belief in his own invulnerability; he'd come home, the fabric of his fuselage and wings shredded with hundreds of bullets, but he'd only shrug his shoulders and sneer at the bad shooting of the Germans. By now he had the reputation of being the most reckless, unafraid and confident flier in the American Air Service.

After the death of Joe Wehner, he teamed up with Lieutenant Ivan Roberts, another lad from Massachusetts. Roberts was a fine pilot, far more skilful than Luke, and the men of the group hoped that he would be able to protect Luke when trouble came. He did his best, but one afternoon the two, flying low, were attacked by five Fokkers and Roberts was killed. It was after this that Luke developed a habit of flying alone. One day Grant, badly upset, complained to Hartney.

"Major, Luke is going hog wild," he said. "I can't handle him unless you'll back me up. He thinks he's the whole Air Service. Rumours are about that he no longer intends to go out with the squadron on patrol. Says he is going on a balloon strafe alone and claims you'll okay it. What about it?"

"Yes, Luke is going up to the Verdun field for a balloon strafe tonight, but I have issued absolute orders that his plane is not to stir off the ground until five-fifty-six pm," the group leader said. "That will bring him over the balloon after dark when all the Boche planes have gone home to roost."

Grant perhaps understood something which the group commander had left unsaid. Hartney knew that Luke was too undisciplined to be of much use in formation flying; he also knew that two fine men and fine pilots had been killed trying to keep up with Luke. Perhaps it would be better for everyone concerned if Frank Luke did fly alone.

That evening Hartney was surprised to hear the engine of an aircraft roaring into action at five-thirty. He rushed out of his office to see Luke sitting in his machine with the engine going, all set to take off.

"Stop that damn engine," he roared, "and get out of that ship. If you take off a second before five-fifty-six, I'll ground you and send you to the rear."

Luke smiled sheepishly and climbed out of the cockpit. Hartney shook his fist at the youngster in mock anger. Luke waited until the appointed time and then zoomed into the air. Fifteen minutes later a Spad flew over an American balloon group composed of Luke's pals. It dropped a note, 'Watch out for those three nearest balloons at D1 and D4 positions—Luke.' Obviously he wanted to be sure of eye-witnesses if he managed to get any of them. The men watched and then there was a flash of flame, in a moment there was another and then a third. Luke had done it again.

He made his usual getaway, streaking across the treetops, but, contrary to custom, the Germans had fighters sitting above that night. He sent two of them down in flames—and then there was silence. Hartney and Grant received telephoned reports of Luke's exploits, but there was no word from him. Rickenbacker joined the two men on the field and the three stood there peering into the dusk, waiting to hear the unmistakable roar of the Gnome-Rhône Hispano engine which powered Luke's Spad. Hartney ordered the dummy airfield four miles down the road to be lighted. He and Grant had worked this decoy airfield out themselves. The real field had a system of indirect lighting, used only when the pilot was ready to come in and when he had identified himself with a blinker recognition signal. As soon as he landed the dim lights were turned off. Meanwhile, the Germans were bombing the dummy airfield once or twice every week. If Luke was on his way home with German aircraft after him, they might make for the lighted decoy while Luke slipped in unobserved. Other pilots joined the three tense men. Now it was two hours since he had taken off and his fuel would be just about exhausted.

"Maybe he dropped in to spend the night with his pals in one of the balloon companies," Rick suggested.

"If he did, I'll court-martial him," Grant snapped, and then added slowly, "But if he comes back I'll recommend him for the Medal of Honor."

He didn't come back, and it wasn't until after the war that the story of Luke's last fight was told. It was told in a sworn document signed by Auguste Garre, Mayor of Murvaux, and thirteen of his townsmen. It read:

AFFIDAVIT

The undersigned, living in Murveaux, Department of the Meuse, certify to have seen on 19th September, 1918, towards evening an American aviator followed by an escadrille of Germans in the direction of Liny, descend suddenly and vertically towards the earth, then straighten out close to the ground and fly in the direction of Briers Farm, where he found a German captive balloon which he burned. Then he flew towards Milly where he found another balloon which he also burned in spite of incessant fire directed towards his machine. He shot down a third balloon and two aeroplanes. Then he apparently was wounded by a shot from rapid-fire cannon. From there he came back over Murvaux and still with his guns he killed six German soldiers and wounded as many more.

Following this he landed and got out of his machine, undoubtedly to quench his thirst at the stream. He had gone fifty yards when, seeing the Germans come towards him, he still had the strength to draw his revolver to defend himself. A moment after he fell dead following a serious wound he received in the chest.

The undersigned themselves placed the body of the aviator on the wagon and conducted it to the cemetery:

CORTINE DELBART
VOLINER NICHOLAS

Seen for legalization of signatures placed above, Murvaux, 15th January, 1919.

THE MAYOR
AUGUSTE GARRE

(Seal of Murvaux)

Now Eddie Rickenbacker began to show the stuff that would not only make him America's foremost ace but also a leader whose qualities were in many ways much more important than his individual victories. The war produced only a few Mannocks, Richthofens and Rickenbackers, who combined the impulsive personality of the fighter with the more exhausting demands of a commanding officer.

When his country entered the war, Rick did two things: first he changed the spelling of his name from the Teutonic-sounding Richenbacher to the Americanized version with two 'k's'. Then he gave up his annual earnings of $40,000 a year as the country's foremost driver of racing cars to enlist. Rickenbacker was much more than a successful racing driver; he knew as much about engines and about the engineering of a motor car as any man alive, and the Army, wishing to utilize these talents to their fullest, allowed him to take primary flying training, then immediately shipped him to Issoudun to deal with engineering problems in connection with the aircraft being used to give arriving Americans advanced training. The day he arrived he made an official application for transfer to a flying combat unit. But the officers of Issoudun knew they had struck oil in this brilliant twenty-eight-year-old racing driver, who could listen to a motor with one ear and tell you what was wrong with it. They told him he was too old to fly; they gave him all sorts of excuses, but meanwhile Rickenbacker learned the techniques of advanced flying by himself without the benefit of much instruction. Flying presented no problem at all to a man with his amazing reflexes and his eye. He had driven in one of the world's most important races of all, the 500-mile Indianapolis classic, and the sports writers and his opponents had agreed that he had two superlative qualities: patience and a marvellous judgment of speeds and distances. But the Army kept him so busy with engineering problems that there was little time left for advanced instruction.

Accidents were frequent at Issoudun, and each week there were more white crosses in the little cemetery they called Field Nine. There was a great deal of rain and lots of mud at Issoudun, and the mud was a contributing cause to fatal accidents. Often on the dash down the field preliminary to takeoff, the churning wheels of the aircraft threw up clods of earth, mud, stones, and occasionally a propeller would be nicked. A few moments later, at 15,000 feet, the propeller might give way—and there was the chance of another white cross at Field Nine. Rickenbacker designed a mudguard arrangement for the wheels which cut down the possibility of damage to the propeller. Meanwhile, on his own, he was perfecting the aerobatic manœuvres essential to surviving in aerial fighting. His calm, calculating, mature mind and his perfectly attuned reflexes helped him to master the intricacies of combat tactics, but he was as far away as ever from joining a combat unit.

General Pershing, who knew Rickenbacker, transferred him to his Paris headquarters so he could have the services of the finest driver in the Army. One day he was assigned to drive Major Townsend Dodd, Pershing's Aviation Officer, who with Colonel Billy Mitchell was to inspect a French squadron. Mitchell had a powerful Mercedes. Dodd, driven by Rick, was behind him when Mitchell's car broke down. Neither Mitchell

256

nor his driver could do anything constructive about it, and then Dodd asked Rickenbacker to help out. In a few moments he had located the trouble and had the car running smoothly. He then went back to the wheel of Dodd's car.

"Who is that?" Mitchell asked.

"Eddie Rickenbacker, the great racing driver," Dodd replied.

"He'd make a fine pilot," Mitchell said thoughtfully, and the next time Rick applied for a transfer it was granted. He began his career with the 94th Squadron of the First Pursuit Group and his first flying partner was James Norman Hall, the man who had once told Colonel Gros that he couldn't even drive a car. But he could handle an aeroplane, and day after day one of the finest car drivers of the world and the man who didn't know a carburettor from a connecting rod went hunting Germans. Rickenbacker scored his first victory while flying with Hall. They made a fine team—in the air and on the ground—and Rick was heartsick the day his partner was forced down. Hall's experience was one of the most hair-raising any pilot had to endure during the war. Hall, Rickenbacker and Edward Greene had just finished an inconclusive air battle with four enemy aircraft when Greene and Rick were horrified to see Hall's machine go into a spin and land behind the German lines. An anti-aircraft shell had struck his engine, but instead of exploding had smashed a cylinder head and lodged itself where the cylinder normally fitted. The impact of the shell had thrown the machine into a spin; somehow Hall had managed to get control and make a landing of sorts in a clear field. He broke an ankle and his nose, but when he saw the live, unexploded shell he felt that two broken bones were a reasonable price to pay for his life, even though he had to finish the war in a German prison camp.

Rickenbacker was made a flight commander, which meant that he led a flexible patrol of from three to six aircraft. For some weeks he had been bothered with an earache, but hadn't paid too much attention to it. But one day he showed a high fever and he was grounded in bed. That night Captain Kenneth Marr, commander of the 94th, visited the ailing pilot to give him the news of the day. None of it was good. Lieutenant

Walter W. Smythe and Lieutenant Alexander B. Bruce of the 94th had collided in the air that afternoon and both had been killed. Smythe had been a special friend of Rick's. He had begun the war with the French ambulance service and had then transferred to flying duties. A week before his fatal accident his father had died, and he had received a notice that his mother was seriously ill. He had asked for leave to go home for a brief period to see his mother, but the 'compassionate leave' of World War II was unknown in 1918, and his request was refused. Rickenbacker and his squadron mates were highly indignant. And now the boy was dead.

"We did our best, Rick, to get him permission," Marr said.

"I know," the fever-ridden Rickenbacker said sadly. And then he added, "I hope you have no more bad news."

"No," Marr said casually, "except that you're going to Paris tomorrow to have that ear looked after."

Rickenbacker was too sick to protest. Three days later he had a mastoid operation, a critical ordeal before the days of penicillin. He spent two months in the hospital, and it is likely that to this day Rickenbacker regrets what he always felt to be two months lifted out of his life.

But then he returned, as healthy as ever. By that time the news had arrived that Jimmy Hall was not killed but was a prisoner of war. Rick teamed up with quiet, twenty-two-year-old Douglas Campbell.

And then Campbell was wounded badly enough to end what in a few brief months had amounted to a spectacular flying career. Alan Winslow too had been shot down, and was a prisoner of war, and eight other men had been killed. In retrospect, one can only wonder why the whole First Pursuit Group wasn't wiped out, because the French machines they were using were in every way inferior to the new Fokker D-VII which had replaced the triplane fighter in the German Fokker squadrons. The success of the triplane had of course brought Tony Fokker back into favour, especially with the front-line pilots. A group of them, feeling that something better than the triplane might emerge, petitioned German Air Force headquarters asking that a competition be held, open to all German aircraft manufacturers, and that the leading staffel commanders be permitted to judge which new aircraft to accept. The influence of pilots like Ernst Udet, Hermann Goering, Bruno Loerzer and other aces who had signed the petition was enormous, and the competition was announced. Open competition was what Fokker had been campaigning for all during the war. When the terms of the free-for-all stipulated that the Mercedes 160-horse-power engine would be available to every designer, Fokker was overjoyed. He designed a biplane, and after testing it himself, decided that, although it gave a great all-round performance in his hands, it was too sensitive for the ordinary pilot: it had a tendency to spin under the slightest provocation and was too eagerly responsive to controls, especially on turns. Two days before the competition was to be held at Johannisthal, Fokker decided on a radical change— he would lengthen the fuselage. He and a group of his men worked forty-eight hours without rest, and then the trim little machine was ready. It had to prove itself against the Albatros, Pfalz, Dornier, Rumpler, Aviatik and other designs, and it did. The D-VII was one of the best single-seater fighter aircraft produced during the war.

The pilots liked it because its thick wings gave it the quality of sensitive control at high altitudes where even the best of the French and British planes became sluggish in the thin air. On the fourth day of the competition, General von Hoeppner, who had watched the tests, asked Fokker, "How many aircraft can you build at once?"

"If I was sure I could have the Mercedes engine . . ." Fokker began.

"We want 400 of these immediately," the chief of the Air Force said curtly.

"You'll have them," the exuberant Fokker said.

By the summer of 1918, Rickenbacker and the whole First Pursuit Group (consisting now of the 94th, 95th, 27th and 147th Squadrons and the 185th (night fighter) Squadron was fighting against this superb machine. Loerzer, Bolle, Goering, Bongartz and Udet were given the D-VII for their staffels, and in one month (August, 1918) they brought down 565 Allied aircraft.

Rickenbacker had mastered his trade by trial and error. He

realized that you couldn't make a single mistake in combat, any more than you could in a motor race. Nor would you live long if you underestimated your opponent. One day he and five of the squadron were ordered to protect several two-seaters out to photograph enemy installations or movements between the Vesle and Aisne rivers. The pictures taken, the aircraft made off for home when Rick, flying high himself as cover, saw five Fokkers diving from a great height. He made for them, firing at long range, feeling reasonably secure that they would probably ignore him to get to their primary targets, the two-seaters, and the precious pictures they carried. They did just that. They shot by him and he zoomed upwards. To his amazement he wandered into a dogfight between a French squadron and a formation of Fokkers. It was like walking innocently into an alley and suddenly finding yourself in the midst of a free-for-all. Rick saw a Spad miss a Fokker and keep going; the Fokker swerved to the right, almost in Rickenbacker's sights. He gave it a burst and the Fokker turned over and began to fall crazily earthwards. Rick watched him fall and then, unexpectedly, flaming bullets began to streak past his face. Almost instinctively he dropped over on to one wing, kicked his rudder crosswise and fell 300 feet in a spin. Then, low in fuel, thoroughly disgusted with himself, he hurried for home. When he landed, he found three large bullet-holes in his fuselage close to the cockpit. He asked his mechanics to bring him some paint and a brush. He drew circles around each of the three holes.

"Cover the holes," he said grimly, "and paint a small Maltese cross over each one. I learned a lesson today, and every time I see them it will remind me of that lesson."

"What did you learn?" one asked curiously.

"I learned that whenever you're over the lines you have to keep twisting your neck in all directions every minute, or you're sure to be surprised. I was surprised today because I forgot to look behind me."

He never forgot again. Rickenbacker thought a great deal about combat tactics: Why was it that some pilots were able to amass such a fabulous total of victories? Was Fonck a superman? Was Ernst Udet so much more skilful than the men he brought down? He decided that the great pilots had learned the limits of what an aeroplane could do; they had fully and intelligently plumbed its potential and never asked the impossible of it. Many Allied pilots had died diving their Nieuports which, as Rick said, 'had a grim tendency to shed their wings in a dive'. It was impossible to strengthen the wings; one could only remember the limitations of the Nieuport and never get in a position where the only chance of survival was a steep dive. He knew that he had missed scoring four or five victories when his guns had jammed. Why didn't the guns of the great aces jam? For that matter, why did a gun jam? He gave some thought to this and discovered that as often as not it was a defective cartridge that stuck; after that he examined every single bullet that went into an ammunition drum and rejected any that seemed oversize. Gradually he learned to minimize the chances of failure. This was a game of skill, he decided, and if you insisted upon throwing yourself into combat with headlong impetuosity or with blind rage, you were blunting your talents. Mannock and McCudden were absolutely right: you couldn't allow hatred, anger or a desire to revenge dead comrades interfere with the cold, calculating precision of your tactics.

At last the Spads arrived and Rick no longer had to worry about fabric-shedding wings. He liked the fast-climbing machine enormously, and he learned its strength and its limitations, and with his knowledge came a new confidence. He had learned to forget everything but the job in hand, once he strapped himself into his Spad and cried 'Contact'. It was hard to put the death of gallant Quentin Roosevelt out of your mind; it was difficult to ignore the fact that Charles Chapman and Frank Luke had been killed, that Alan Winslow had been shot down—that nearly every night there were empty seats in the mess and new faces of replacements to be seen each morning. But he (a warm and friendly man) steeled himself to be a machine and thus he discovered the secret not only of survival but of phenomenal success, just as Mannock and McCudden and a few others had discovered before him.

In September, Major Hartney was faced with the task of naming a new commander of his 94th Squadron. It wasn't an easy decision. Major Kenneth Marr, to his dismay, had been ordered back to the States to help with the training programme. The men who had started with the squadron were tried pilots now, the Lafayette fliers who had survived were old hands, but to the consternation of Billy Mitchell, Hartney proposed Rickenbacker as the CO for the 94th. Mitchell's faith in Rick and in Hartney was profound, but to promote the newest-appointed flight commander over the heads of a dozen men who had higher rank and more seniority could conceivably cause dissension. Hartney had an answer for this. He had discussed the whole matter with Jimmy Meissner, David Peterson, Bill Thaw, Reed Chambers and other leading members of the group and they agreed with him that Rick was the man to head the outfit. Why? There were many reasons. One was the rather unorthodox one that the mechanics worshipped the tall, quiet, thoughtful flier. He was a better mechanic than any one of them; he talked their language, and if they reported 'six machines unavailable', he'd diagnose the ailments of each to find out just why the aeroplane had to sit in the hangar and the pilot sit in the fine bar across the field set up by the neighbouring 95th Squadron. Rickenbacker had already established his reputation as a great aerial fighter; he was older, more mature than most of the men, and the younger pilots instinctively looked to him for leadership. Like Mannock, he always took the newcomers assigned to his flight out a few times before allowing them in actual combat. Rick had adopted another of Mannock's habits. Often while he was chaperoning a neophyte over the lines a combat would ensue, and more than once Rick allowed the new man first crack at an enemy aircraft. If the youngster missed, Rick would finish him off and then on returning to the base would loudly congratulate the pilot on his kill, and it would be recorded to the youngster's credit. (This is mentioned more than once in diaries kept by members of the 94th and in reports made by Harold Hartney.)

It was enough for Billy Mitchell, who wasn't one to interfere with his group commanders anyway, and especially an able, experienced one like Harry Hartney. Hartney as usual had picked the right man. The first thing Rickenbacker did was to hold a meeting of the mechanics. He told them coldly that the

27th Squadron had (chiefly because of Frank Luke's victories) got ahead of the 94th, a condition which he, Rickenbacker, damn well wouldn't tolerate. Part of the success of the 27th Squadron, Rick told them bluntly, came from the fact that its machines were always flyable. Henceforth he never wanted to see any numbers on the bulletin board under the heading, 'Machines Unavailable'. He talked to them as he had once talked to his mechanics in the pit at Indianapolis, and they took it and liked it because they respected him. Then he called the pilots together and mentioned that only he, Reed Chambers and Thorn Taylor were alive or available of the original squadron and that they were pretty annoyed that a relatively new unit in the group, the 27th, had surpassed them in victories.

On the morning of September 15th, he went up alone and before breakfast had downed two German aircraft. It was as good a way as any for the new boss to start work, and the effect on the squadron was electrifying. He wasn't going to be snowed under by the paper and administrative work which was part of his responsibility. He was going to keep on fighting, and this heartened them all. Within a week, the 94th had overtaken and passed the 27th Squadron, and it was never thereafter surpassed. Rick gave his pilots a feeling of pride in belonging to the hat-in-the-ring gang; perhaps without knowing it he was a master of practical psychology. And Rickenbacker did continue to fight with cool, calm, intelligent calculation. He downed twelve of the new Fokkers and he fired Albatroses and Rumplers and he sent five balloons up (or down) in flames. He had mastered aerial tactics just as he had once mastered the dangerous technique of dirt-track racing before he graduated to Indianapolis. By October he was far out in front of every other American flier, with twenty-six confirmed victories, a total which brings chuckles from his old flying mates and commanding officer. For there is no doubt that he sent down at least a dozen others too far beyond the German lines to receive confirmation. A confidential report which came to the desk of General Billy Mitchell had this to say about the First Pursuit Group in general and about Rickenbacker in particular:

Captain Rickenbacker furnished, by his example, an ideal squadron leader. He and the three other squadron commanders in the group were the type of squadron commanders it was absolutely necessary to have in pursuit aviation. It is useless to send out from the rear officers to command squadrons who have not had experience at the front. It is absolutely essential that squadron commanders be experienced and daring pilots. It is their duty to lead their squadrons into battle and to furnish them always a most glorious and enviable example. Captain Rickenbacker obtained results himself and his pilots could not help but emulate him and do likewise. A squadron commander who sits in his tent and gives orders and does not fly, though he may have the brains of Solomon, will never get the results that a man will, who, day in and day out, leads his patrols over the line and infuses into his pilots the esprit de corps, whch is so necessary in aviation and which, so far, has been so lightly considered by the military authorities.

Had he not been a squadron commander, charged with the direction and administration of a large group of pilots, mechanics and administration officers, and had he instead been given the kind of roving assignment Billy Bishop and Albert Ball were given, his total (my authority is Billy Bishop himself) might well have been twice the twenty-six aircraft for which he received credit. But, except for a brief time, he was never allowed to free-lance. His record is the more incredible when it is considered that Rickenbacker had only seven months in which to compile it—and that he spent a little over two months of this recuperating from his mastoid operation.

To pay so much attention to the First Pursuit Group is perhaps to do an injustice to other fine fighting units. But it was the first American group on the scene, and before the war ended its four squadrons brought down 285 enemy aircraft, far more than any other group. One does not have to apologize for spotlighting the spectacular careers of Frank Luke and Eddie Rickenbacker; they were the only two airmen to win the Medal of Honor. There were others equally courageous and colourful. George Vaughn of the 17th, Field Kindley and

Elliott Springs of the 148th Squadron—each of these three
downed twelve Germans, and David Putnam and Jacques
Swaab were just behind them.

Chapter Thirteen

THE END OF THE BEGINNING

IT WAS on September 13th, 1918, that America began her
most important offensive by sending 500,000 troops into
battle at St Mihiel, twenty-three miles south-east of Verdun.
So vital was the engagement considered that 2,900 cannon and
400 tanks were allotted to the fifteen AEF divisions (and four
French divisions) which launched the attack. The ground
troops were under the command of Marshal Foch. In addition
to the enormous concentration of artillery and tanks, 1481 aircraft took part in the battle, and these were under the command of Billy Mitchell.

It had taken Mitchell a long time to sell his idea of a combined strategic and tactical air attack to Pershing, but he had
done it and at last an air force engaged in battle, not merely as
an unimportant arm of the army, but virtually as an independent power co-operating with the army. The theories of Giulio
Douhet and 'Boom' Trenchard were finally put into practice
by a vigorous American showman who was also a meticulous
planner, and the result was so successful during the four days
of the battle that the pattern of air attack was established once
and for all time.

Mitchell had in his command 701 fighters, 366 observation
machines, 323 day bombers and ninety-one night bombers
from all air forces. Included were units of Trenchards Independent Bombing Force, now a separate command. The
weather was bad during the first two days, but Mitchell got
his machines into the air. The St Mihiel salient was shaped
like a pointed horseshoe or a rather uneven vee.

Great bodies of Allied troops were drawn up along the sides,
hemming in the Germans so that their only movement could

be to the rear unless they broke through the flanking forces. But Mitchell knew that if the enemy's Air Force could cross these flanks and break out of the horseshoe, it could do serious damage to the rear of the troops, cutting off their supplies. His great preoccupation was to keep every German aircraft inside the horseshoe, always over their own armies, never over the Allies.

He formed two attack brigades of some 400 machines each. One of them attacked the right side of the vee, drawing all the German aviation there to defend the flank. This left the rear—the open part of the vee—defenceless, and to it Mitchell sent bombers to cut off the communications of the enemy troops in the salient. He then sent his second attack brigade to the left side of the salient while the first refuelled, so that the enemy Air Force had to rush to that side. In this way he gave the German aviators no rest, no respite: he kept them constantly within the salient with their rear for ever open to the terrorizing bombing. This manoeuvre, coming as a total surprise and operating with clockwork precision backed by unprecedented strength, delivered a crushing blow from which even a determined enemy could never recover.

It was not a physical blow as such things are reckoned in war. Casualties on both sides were surprisingly low. But morally it was a catastrophe. An army without a rear, cut off from its homeland, thwarted in both advance and retreat, and covered from above, is an army lost.

In two days, 16,000 Germans surrendered. In two more days the entire St Mihiel salient was destroyed as an enemy strongpoint. Afterwards, the Germans found it impossible to rally their Army for further attack. From then on they were continuously on the defensive, grimly struggling to hold what they had against 1,000,000 fresh American soldiers. That they kept their resistance tough to the end, no one who witnessed the slow sweep through the Argonne Forest will ever forget. But new confidence had come to the tired British, the exhausted French *poilus* and to the vigorous but bewildered Americans, and much of it, in those dark, wet autumn days, came out of the sky. On the first day of October, Mitchell was promoted to brigadier-general and put in command of the air service of the group of armies.

During the four short days of the battle he had proved that an intelligently directed air force could not only destroy enemy trains, depots, ammunition dumps, railway stations, lines of communication, aircraft, hangars and ground troops, but could destroy the morale of the enemy as well. Day and night his machines had penetrated twenty miles behind the lines, shooting at anything that moved, spreading not only destruction but terror with the 127 tons of explosives they dropped. He used his 1481 aircraft as cavalry had once been used, as an active arm in itself. The aeroplane as a weapon was reaching maturity. It was the biggest air operation in history, and it made Billy Mitchell an international hero.

Flushed by his victory at St Mihiel, Mitchell launched a similar aerial offensive against the Germans in the Meuse-Argonne sector; he was convinced that concentration in the air was the answer to success. He sent out his bombers at night to rip up the enemy's communications and military strongpoints, and the next day additional fighters and bombers began a vicious attack aimed directly at the German troops. For a time it looked as though the brilliant and bold thinking of Billy Mitchell might pay off again—but then the truth of the foremost axiom of the air asserted itself: you cannot attack the ground with consistent effectiveness without first having control of the air. The Germans immediately sent hundreds of fighters against Mitchell's forces and cleared them from the sky before the attack had any chance of fulfilling its mission.

Undaunted, Mitchell once more sent his collected forces against the Hun in the Meuse-Argonne. Reconnaissance had reported that the enemy was grouping his reserves out of range of artillery-fire for a counter-attack on American ground positions. On October 9th, more than 350 fighters and bombers under the command of Billy Mitchell fought off a determined aerial defence and proceeded to strafe and bomb the German formations in what was to be the heaviest single air bombardment of the war. Over thirty tons of bombs—actually less than can be carried in one of today's giant bombers—were dropped on the utterly surprised and confused reserves, and the attack was completely successful. It so disrupted and demoralized the gathering German forces that the counter-offensive was called off. For Mitchell it was a dream come true. 'It was indeed,' he announced, 'the dawn of the day when great air forces will be capable of definitely affecting a ground decision on the field of battle.'

But if these attacks made effective contributions to the war below, they didn't win the air war for the Allies. There were still three great German 'Circuses', or *Jagdgeschwader*, operating skilfully under the command of three remarkable personalities: Captain Ernst Udet, who had sixty-three victories to his credit, Captain Bruno Loerzer with forty-two, and Captain Hermann Goering with twenty-six.

Udet had sensitive hands; they could cajole either aeroplane or pencil. He was one of the finest caricaturists in Germany, and many examples of his biting wit and technical excellence survive him. His hands were never idle; no matter where he was dining, he would have a pencil in his hands, busily sketching on the tablecloth the faces of people around him. American and British correspondents who knew Udet during the 1930s and who lunched with him at their headquarters, the Adlon Hotel, used to hear Fred Schultz, the veteran bartender who presided over the little room, say unhappily after Udet had left, '*Er ist ein Zerstöhrer von Tischteuchern.*' He was indeed a destroyer of tablecloths; in World War I he was also a destroyer of men but, like Oswald Boelcke before him, he killed without heat or hatred: he was a German and it was his duty to give his talents to his fatherland.

Bruno Loerzer was as well known in the cafés on the Unter den Linden as he was at the Front. He, too, was in love with life; not for him the aestheticism of a Richthofen. Goering had originally been his observer and then he encouraged him to become a pilot. Goering never quite achieved the superb flying quality of either Udet or Loerzer, but what he lacked in sheer technical skill he made up for in courage and aggressiveness. Goering had Richthofen's old Circus, and although, like all German airmen, he worshipped the memory of the Red Knight, he was the direct antithesis of the Prussian in personality and in his outlook towards war. This was not the gross Goering the world would learn to hate twenty-five years later; this was a slim man of charm and humour, a friendly, convivial leader, respected and liked by the men who flew under his command.

During the last month of the war the Richthofen Circus under Goering fought with desperate courage. Never in his writings or in his authorized biography (*Hermann Goering, Ein Lebensbild*) did he state that he had absorbed the British doctrine of aerial warfare as expounded since the beginning by 'Boom' Trenchard, but it is certain that he adopted the very same tactics.

Boelcke had always told his eager young fliers, 'It is better to have the customers come to your shop than for the shopkeeper to go out looking for customers', and Richthofen had acted upon that principle. Goering went out looking for customers. All three circuses in general and Goering's in particular fought without calculation. They roamed far and wide in the new aircraft Fokker had given them. His last production of the war was the revolutionary Fokker D-VIII. Loerzer was one of the first to use the slim little monoplane, called The Flying Razor by the British. When it flew out of the sun, its frontal area was so small that it was almost impossible to see. It could fly at 125 miles an hour, and probably would have boosted Allied losses considerably had not official meddling prevented this excellent machine from going into full production.

Despite their truly heroic efforts in the air, the German pilots couldn't do much to help their exhausted ground troops. During the last days of September the Allies launched an all-out four-pronged attack. The Americans pushed west of the Meuse towards Mezières; the French attacked west of the Argonne; the massed British force aimed for Maubeuge, and the Belgians with the British Second Army advanced through Flanders towards Ghent. The Hindenburg Line crumbled, and now every flyable aircraft in the Allied command was out dropping bombs, giving accurate reports to Allied artillery commanders and strafing the retreating German troops. The retreat became a rout and low-flying aircraft brought terror and panic to the ordinarily well-disciplined German troops who jammed the roads leading away from the front.

Finally, Nature, as though weary of watching four years of slaughter, sent low-hanging clouds, fog, chill rains and clinging, ankle-deep mud to the battle front. Darkness came unseasonably early during November and aircraft could go up only during intermittent periods of flyable weather. The war did not end in any crescendo of battle sounds; it ended almost in an exhausted whimper. It was November 11th, 1918. Officially the war was to end at eleven am and that morning every commander issued orders that no Allied machines was to cross the lines. They went on routine patrols and when they returned at the magic hour of eleven the pilots stunted madly over the aerodromes, knowing that, for the first time, possible death was neither above them nor behind them. That night there was wild jubilation among British, French and American squadrons, and almost as though by prearrangement hundreds of pilots sent star shells and Very lights into the suddenly clearing skies, and mechanics rolled barrels of petrol on to the airfields and set fire to fuel which would never again be used to send fighting aircraft into battle.

The German pilots, bewildered, resentful, sat in their mess halls in gloomy and sullen silence. The war was lost, but they knew it had not been lost by them but by someone else. The Army? The High Command? The Government? They only knew that they had fought the good fight and were still ready to fight on. The men of the Richthofen Circus were especially resentful; they had ignored the horrible weather of the past week and had searched through the gloomy murk for enemy aircraft and had, in fact, downed twenty-five of them during those final seven days. And they had flown low, harrying the British and French tanks and occasionally finding vital chinks in the armour of the iron monsters. That night they talked in low tones about the thousand aerial battles they had won, about the eighteen pilots among them who had won the *Pour le Mérite*. Word came during the night that they were to fly their machines to Darmstadt, where they were to be turned over to the victors. The German Air Force was to be wiped out. One pilot walked to the blackboard where orders for the day had so often been chalked, and wrote bitterly, '*Im Krieg geboren, im Krieg gestorben*'. Born in the war—died in the war; such was the epitaph of the Richthofen Circus and the rest of the German Air Force.

France was frankly relieved when the Cease Fire order came. For a year she had been scraping the bottom of the personnel barrel, and her pilots had been less than adequate. During the four years her Air Force had lost 3500 men in combat; 3000 had been wounded or injured in flying accidents, while another 2000 had been killed at training centres. (Some of these were killed by bombs, but most in accidents.) During the final weeks, France had an Air Force of but 13,000 pilots, observers, and ground crew, but France had the incredible René Fonck running his total of victories up to seventy-five. He had never suffered even a scratch, and after two years of almost constant fighting only one bullet had ever hit his aircraft.

There was wild rejoicing in every RAF mess that night. From the beginning they had born the brunt of the fighting. The little Royal Flying Corps was now the mighty Royal Air Force; the handful of pilots, mechanics and observers of 1914 had grown to a strength of 291,175 men. During the four terrible years, 6166 of their number had found honoured graves in the soil of Flanders, France, Italy, Macedonia, Syria, Palestine, Arabia, Africa, Germany, or in the waters of the North Sea, Mediterranean or English Channel. The 6166 had in four short years built a magnificent tradition which would endure for all time and be enhanced in another war. They had proved that air power was as vital to the safety of their country as sea power, and that, possessing both, Britain could never be conquered. But they weren't concerned with statistics on that glorious night when the war ended. They had lived— that was the miracle they celebrated—and if many offered prayers of thanksgiving they were offered silently, and then their voices were raised in the songs which had grown to be part of the tradition they had built:

'The young aviator went stunting,
And as 'neath the wreckage he lay—he lay,
To the mechanics assembled around him,
These parting words did he say—did say:

CHORUS

'Take the cylinders out of my kidneys,
The connecting rod out of my brain—my brain
From the small of my back take the crankshaft,
And assemble the engine again.'

They talked that night of the great ones who had gone, and
toasted them far into the night. One hundred British pilots
had been acclaimed as aces who had brought down ten or more
enemy aircraft. Twelve of them had brought down fifty or
more. Most had enjoyed short lives, but a few of the great
ones had survived.

The men of the Tiger Squadron (No 74) paused in their
celebration at Clamarais to drink a toast to their late beloved
Mick Mannock. Mick was dead, but Ira 'Taffy' Jones had survived and he felt that by shooting down forty Germans he had
in some small way avenged his friend's death. It was he who
offered the toast to the man he called that night 'King of Air
Fighters', a title Mannock richly deserved, for there is little
doubt that he was the greatest.

No 74 was a young but remarkable squadron; most of its
men had been lucky enough to have had McCudden as an
instructor. It also had a great leader in the New Zealander,
big, dark-haired Keith Caldwell, always called 'Grid' because
he never referred to an aeroplane as anything except a 'grid'.
The squadron had not been formed until the spring of 1918,
yet it destroyed 225 German machines with the loss of only
fifteen of its own pilots. No 74 had a right to celebrate that
night. It would celebrate again on the night of May 8th, 1945,
for No 74 Squadron never died; it kept embellishing its history, and if it didn't have Mick Mannock in World War II, it
still had Taffy Jones and it had Adolph 'Sailor' Malan, without question the outstanding British ace of that war.

In 1914 the young British airmen had been at best objects
of curiosity; now the world was acclaiming them as sublime

and gallant heroes. In 1914 their 'bird cages' had been ridiculed; now they had the finest aircraft in the world. And Britain, which had started so slowly, had produced 50,000 of them; 36,000 of these had been destroyed. Nearly a generation had been wiped out by casualties, but they had contributed something to their country and quite incidentally to the progress of aviation that can never be evaluated.

America finally had an air force in action, and though small compared to either the French or British, it had made its presence felt. On November 11th only 650 American pilots had seen combat, and 110 of these were former. Lafayette Corps men. But they had made outstanding individual records, eighty of them accounted for five or more enemy aircraft or balloons. Rickenbacker, Luke, Springs, Vaughn, Kindley, Hartney and several others had demonstrated flying ability and courage comparable with that of even the experienced British fighters. In all, American pilots had downed 927 enemy aircraft and balloons. But the young American air force was distinguished more for its potential than for its real accomplishments. Had the war lasted another six months, it would have reached full maturity. Actually, American units on Armistice Day were in possession of only 740 aircraft, of which 196 had been made in America. For all practical purposes the American aviation production programme had been a ghastly failure. The grandiose boasting by irresponsible officials as to the American aircraft which would soon darken the skies of Western Europe had been taken seriously by no one except the Germans. Believing the absurd estimates of what America would produce, they had stepped up their production to the point where they had produced 10,000 aircraft between America's entry into the war and Armistice Day. The famed Liberty engine was still having bugs taken out of it; within another year it would in fact be a truly great engine, but on Armistice Day it was still an unruly, under-developed adolescent.

It was all over now, and it was time to evaluate the mistakes and the accomplishments of aerial warfare. It had been a strange war, this first war in the air. In the beginning it was no war at all; four years later each side had brought to terrible perfection its ability to kill and destroy in the lonely battlefield of the sky—and neither side, amazingly enough, was anywhere near defeat. Air power itself had been born, though very few realized it, and even fewer remembered it as the war became history. Only the memory of heroes remained, for never, in any other war past or present, had so many individuals become public figures and household names. The pilots of that first war are still better known today than the equally great—and more numerous—aces of World War II. And no higher tribute could be paid to those fledgling fliers than to say that they mastered their trade so well that the air fighters of future generations have gone back to the old diaries and memoirs to learn their secrets; the basic tactics created then are as valid today as they were forty years ago. But the unique development, and one which will probably never be repeated again, was the fact that the first war in the air unexpectedly returned the ancient concept of the duel to modern warfare, and along with it a code of conduct which had been considered obsolete for centuries. There was no more ghastly death than to be caught in a flaming machine of wires, wood and fabric at 10,000 feet, and each side respected the other because each faced the same destruction. But, in spite of these horrors, the early pilots will still laugh when they tell of putting a stove lid under their cockpit seat for makeshift armour, or of the primitive little hammer they were issued with to smash the tubes of their mysterious radio sets if they were forced down, so that they Germans could not reproduce them. Nor would there ever be another war in which a hero like Richthofen could name his successor in his will and have that wish respected by the High Command. It was a war which was never won and never lost, yet it shaped the future, for it marked the beginning of the most powerful military weapon now on earth.

Giulio Douhet and Ferdinand Ferber had been proved to be accurate prophets. Without any question, 'Boom' Trenchard had emerged as the war's foremost architect of aerial activity. From the very beginning he saw with clear vision that the aeroplane was essentially an offensive weapon; his attitude was reflected in the offensive spirit of the British pilots. He saw too that an air force, to be fully effective, had to be an independent service, not merely an adjunct of army or navy. He fought constantly for a force devoted entirely to strategic and tactical operations—as did his disciple, Billy Mitchell—and the thousand-bomber raids into the industrial heart of Germany in the 1940s were merely extensions of his vision. The great military experts paid tribute to Trenchard by adopting all of his theories in World War II.

But aerial combat in World War I produced more than a new pattern of warfare and improved aircraft: a race of gallant men emerged from the conflict. Archidamus was wrong when he moaned, "Oh Hercules, the valour of man is at an end." Never was the valour of men so evident as it was during the four years when they first fought for the sky.

BIBLIOGRAPHY

Anonymous, *Death in the Air*, London, Heinemann

Archibald, Norman, *Heaven High, Hell Deep, 1917–1918*, London, Heinemann

Arnold, Major-General H. H., and Eaker, Colonel Ira C., *Winged Warfare*, New York and London, Harper Bros.

Ashmore, Major-General E. H., *Air Defence*, London, Longmans, Green

Barnett, Lieutenant Gilbert, *VCs of the Air*, London, edited by J. Burrow & Co. Ltd.

Biddle, Major Charles J., The *Way of the Eagle*, New York, Scribner's Sons

Bingham, Hiram, *An Explorer in the Air Service*, London, OUP

Bishop, Major William A., *Winged Warfare*, London, Hodder & Stoughton

Black, Archibald, *The Story of Flying*, New York and London, Whittlesey House, McGraw-Hill

Bond, A. Russell, *Inventions of the Great War*, London, Appleton

Bordeaux, Henry, *Georges Guynemer, Knight of the Air*, translated by Louise Morgan Sill, London, Chatto & Windus

Burlingame, Roger, *General Billy Mitchell*, New York, McGraw-Hill

Capart, Captain G. P., *A Blue Devil of France*, translated by J. C. Drouillard, New York, W. J. Wyatt

Chapman, Victor, *Victor Chapman's Letters from France*, a memoir by John Jay Chapman, New York, Macmillan

Cleveland, Reginald M., *America Fledges Wings*, New York, Pitman

Codman, Charles, *Contact*, Boston, Little, Brown

Coleman, Frederic, *From Mons to Ypres with General French*, New York, Dodd, Mead

Coppens, Willy, *Days on the Wing*, translated by A. J. Insall, London, John Hamilton

Cuneo, John R., *The Air Weapon, 1914–1916*, Harrisburg, Pennsylvania, Military Service Publishing Company

Drake, Vivian, *Above the Battle*, London, Appleton

Fokker, Anthony H. G., and Gould, Bruce, *Flying Dutchman, the Life of Anthony Fokker*, London, Routledge

Freudenthal, Elsbeth E., *Flight into History—the Wright Brothers and the Air Age*, Norman, Oklahoma, University of Oklahoma Press

Gibbons, Floyd, *The Red Knight of Germany*, London, Cassell

Gowans, Adam L. (editor and translator), *A Month's German Newspapers*, London, Gowans & Gray

Grey, C. G., *The Luftwaffe*, London, Faber

Grinnel-Milne, Duncan, *Wind in the Wires*, London, Hurst & Blackett

Hale, Richard W. (editor), *Letters of Warwick Greene, 1915–1928*, Boston and New York, Houghton Mifflin

Hall, Lieutenant Bert, *En l'Air!*, London, Hurst & Blackett

Hall, Lieutenant Bert and Niles, Lieutenant John J., *One Man's War*, London, John Hamilton

Hall, James Norman, *High Adventure*, London, Constable

Hall, James Norman, and Nordhoff, Charles Bernard (editors), *The Lafayette Flying Corps*, Volumes I and II, Boston and New York, Houghton Mifflin.

Hall, James Norman, *My Island Home*, Boston, Little, Brown

Harrison, John B., *This Age of Global Strife*, Chicago, Philadelphia and New York, J. B. Lippincott

Hart, B. H. Liddell, *Strategy, the Indirect Approach*, London, Faber

Hartney, Lieutenant-Colonel Harold E., *Up and At 'em*, London, Cassell

Heinkel, Ernst, *He1000, Memoirs of a Pioneer of the Air Age*, Jurgen Thorward (editor), London, Hutchinson

Hemingway, Ernest, *Men at War*, New York, Crown Publishers

Heydemarck, Hauptmann, *Double-Decker C666*, translated by Claud W. Sykes, London, John Hamilton

Holland, Maurice (with a preface by Jimmy Doolittle), *Architects of Aviation*, New York, Duell, Sloan & Pearce

Johns, W. E., *Fighting Planes and Aces*, London, John Hamilton

Johnson, Owen, *The Spirit of France*, Boston, Little, Brown

Jones, H. A., *The War in the Air*, in twelve volumes, London, OUP

Jones, Wing-Commander Ira, *King of the Air Fighters*, London, Nicholson & Watson

Prince, Norman, *A Volunteer who Died for the Cause He Loved*, a Memoir by George F. Babbitt, Boston and New York, Houghton Mifflin

Raleigh, Walter, *The War in the Air*, Oxford, Clarendon Press

Reynolds, Quentin, *The Amazing Mr Doolittle*, London, Cassell

Richthofen, Captain Manfred Freiherr von, An Autobiography, translated by T. Ellis Barker, New York, Robert M. McBride & Company

Rickenbacker, Captain Edward V., *Fighting the Flying Circus*, New York, Frederick A. Stokes

Roberts, Lieutenant E. M., *A Flying Fighter*, New York and London, Harper Brothers

Saunders, Hiliary St George, *Per Ardua*, London, OUP

Schröder, Hans, *An Airman Remembers*, translated by Claud W. Sykes, London, Aviation Book Club

Sigaud, Louis A., *Douhet and Aerial Warfare*, New York, Putnam

Strange, Lieutenant-Colonel L. A., *Recollections of an Airman*, London, John Hamilton

'Theta' ('A Pilot'), *War Flying*, Boston and New York, Houghton Mifflin

Thetford, O. G., and Riding, E. J. *Aircraft of the 1914–1918 War*, Marlow, Bucks, Harleyford Publications

Throm, Edward L., and Crenshaw, James S., *Popular Mechanics Aviation Album*, New York, Popular Mechanics

Toulmin, H. A., Jr, *Air Service, AEF, 1918*, New York, D. Van Nostrand

Unknown, *War Birds, Diary of an Unknown Aviator*, London, John Hamilton

Veil, Charles (as told to Howard Marsh), *Adventure's a Wench*, London, Bles

'Vigilant', *French War Birds*, London, John Hamilton

'Vigilant', *German War Birds*, London, John Hamilton

'Vigilant', *Richthofen, the Knight of the Air*

Winslow, Carroll Dana, *With the French Flying Corps*, London, Constable

Wintringham, Tom, *The Story of Weapons and Tactics*, London, Faber

INDEX

Aerial Operations Committee
  See War Priorities Committee
Aeronautical Battalion, Italian,
  36
Aeroplane, The, 35, 61
Air Ministry, 163, 235
Aisne, Battle of the, 73
Althaus, von (German pilot), 80
Ansaldo (manufacturer), 95
Antwerp, evacuation of, 66, 72
Archdeacon, Ernest, 41
Arnold, Major Henry H., 95, 199
Ashmore, Brigadier-General E.
  B., 159, 160
Atkinson, Lieutenant K., 56
Atlantic Monthly, 147
Awcock, Lieutenant, 77

Babington, Flight-Commander
  John T., 68, 69
Bach, James (US pilot), 88, 134
Ball, Albert, VC, 79, 167–177,
  183–4, 192, 215, 225, 231, 248,
  264
Balloons, observation, 149, 235,
  248–9, 251
Balsley, Clyde (US pilot), 136,
  139
Bares, Colonel, 120, 161
Barker, Major William G., VC,
  167, 234–6
Barlow (British pilot), 183
Becherau (manufacturer), 95
Belgian Army, 55
Bernard-Thierry, Captain, 84
Berry, Captain, 79
Biddle, Charles J. (US pilot),
  237
Bigelow, Stephen (US pilot), 148
Billings, Lieutenant Pemberton,
  68, 69
Bishop, William Avery ('Billy'),
  VC, 79, 167, 170, 210–16, 231,
  243, 264
Blanchard, J. P., 79
Blériot, Louis, 31, 38, 41, 42, 45,
  61, 84

Bliss, Robert W., 134
Bloomfield, Major, 172–3
Boelcke, Captain Oswald, 27, 80,
  82, 83, 85, 96, 98, 100–104,
  110–14, 124–8, 145, 168, 177,
  217, 220, 225, 268, 269
Bohme, Erwin, 125, 128
Bolle (German pilot), 259
Bombing, early methods of, 63,
  67, 68, 72, 75
Bond (pilot in No 40 Squadron),
  185
Bongartz (German pilot), 259
Bordeaux, Jules, 84
Borton, Lieutenant A. E., 56
Bowman (pilot in No 56 Squad-
  ron), 168
Boyd, Lieutenant T. E., 239
Brandenburg, Captain (Gotha
  bomber commander), 159
Brandon, Lieutenant A. de B.,
  154
Brandt, Deck-Officer Paul, 159
Bridgemen, Ray C. (US pilot),
  148
Briggs, Commander E. F., 67, 68
Brown, Captain Roy, 227–30
Browning synchronizing system,
  24
Bruce, Lieutenant Alexander B.,
  258
Buckler (German pilot), 80
Burke, Major Charles James, 40,
  59
Butler, Major Charles, 226

Caldwell, Keith ('Grid'), 272
Campbell, Lieutenant C. D. M.,
  73
Campbell, Courtney, Jr (US
  pilot), 148
Campbell, Douglas (US pilot),
  244–6, 258
Cannon, Sub-Lieutenant R. P.,
  68
Caproni (manufacturer), 95

280

281

Derek Robinson

GOSHAWK SQUADRON   35p

'A brilliant first novel . . . savage, funny and heartbreaking' – *Sunday Telegraph*

'The most readable novel of the year . . . totally authentic' – *Daily Telegraph*

'Uproarious, fast-moving and relentlessly cynical' – *The Times*

'If only World War One aces could read this story. They would stand up and cheer'
     – *Western Daily Press*

'You wouldn't know an enemy if he bit you in the arse'

Flying with Woolley is like living with a maniac. Brutal, callous and obscene, he moulds green young pilots into red-eyed, ruthless killers.

For the coming bloodbath, Goshawk Squadron with their patched-up planes must first learn to shoot the Boche in the back . . .

By 1918, chivalry had been a long time dead . . .

Frederick E. Smith

A KILLING FOR THE HAWKS   35p
By the author of 633 Squadron

ROYAL FLYING CORPS
The Western Front, Spring, 1917

To survive you thought of your enemies as vermin, your friends as expendable, and kept all your sympathy for yourself . . .

When a young Norman McConnell first joined 55a Squadron his commanding officer, the aristocratic John Seymour, seemed one hell of a man . . .

Then he fell in love with Helen, Seymour's wife, and knew the truth – his hero was a man who gloried in killing . . . a sadist . . . a man who wanted women to cry out in pain as he made love to them . . .

Now as McConnell manoeuvres his SE5 Scout against the murderous Albatross of Richthofen's circus he waits for death . . . But Seymour takes revenge in his own way . . .

'The actual descriptions of dog-fighting over the Western Front are as good as any of their kind' – *Daily Telegraph*

'Brilliantly told . . . will be thoroughly enjoyed'
    – *The Aeroplane*

B. H. Liddell Hart

HISTORY OF THE FIRST WORLD WAR 75p

'The outstanding military historian'
— *Sunday Express*

'The most influential British military writer of his time' — *The Spectator*

'Scrupulously accurate, brilliantly lucid'
— *British Army Review*

'Brilliant . . . the best one-volume history of the First World War ever likely to be written'
— *Naval Review*

HISTORY OF THE SECOND WORLD WAR 95p

'The greatest British military thinker of this century' — *Soldier*

'This most civilised and compassionate military historian' — *The Times*

'Unlikely to be surpassed' — *Sunday Telegraph*

'The book has the mark of the author's genius — a lucidity and insight such as no other military writer can match . . . it will long be read with profit and enjoyment by all interested in the military art' — *The Army Quarterly*

These and other PAN Books are obtainable from all booksellers and newsagents. If you have any difficulty please send purchase price plus 7p postage to PO Box 11, Falmouth, Cornwall.
While every effort is made to keep prices low, it is sometimes necessary to increase prices at short notice. PAN Books reserve the right to show new retail prices on covers which may differ from those advertised in the text or elsewhere.